"What a wonderful book! I thoro~~~'~ ... 's book embraces an attachment-focuse ... ntities, and uniquely combines both pr ... ctives. The diverse chapters richly exp ... sonal and professional experiences of t~ ... (planation of clinical process. This inc ... ~~~~ical and teaching literature, such as clients ...~~ and ongoing abuse. The final two chapters, which co ...~~ections from those with lived experience, complete the book beautifully".

Kate McMaugh, *Psychologist, Sydney, Australia*

"*Dissociative Identities: Attachment-based Approaches to Psychotherapy* is worth reading for clinicians, family members, those with dissociated selves, and anyone interested in the effects of trauma. The chapters by individuals with dissociative identity disorder are particularly compelling, well written, and illuminating. Overall, the book provides the best available explanation of the attachment-based treatment of dissociated identities. The chapters are readable, nuanced, and detailed. I highly recommend the book".

Dr Colin Ross, *MD, President of The Ross Institute for Psychological Trauma; Past and President of The International Society for the Study of Trauma and Dissociation*

"Since Janet's pioneering descriptions, dissociative identity difficulties remain one of mental health's many orphans. In this rich and multifaceted collection, attachment-oriented therapists and those with dissociative identity collaborate to paint a vivid account of the family origins, current experiences, and therapeutic possibilities offered by an attachment approach to psychotherapy with this condition. Compassion, hope, and understanding shine throughout the text. A must-read for therapists at all levels!"

Professor Jeremy Holmes, *MD FRCPsych, University of Exeter, UK*

"Attachment traumas and post-traumatic dissociation are widespread, impacting a significant portion of the population. *Dissociative Identities: Attachment-based Approaches to Therapy* is a must-read for any mental health professional looking to deepen their understanding and treatment of trauma survivors through attachment-informed techniques. The editors have curated a rich tapestry of practical knowledge, clinical insights, and therapeutic approaches applicable to any trauma-informed practice. Offering a unique perspective, this book explores the lived experience of dissociation through the combined wisdom of expert practitioners and empowered survivors of relational trauma. I highly recommend this book to all mental health practitioners regardless of theoretical orientation!"

Dissociative Identities

Dissociative Identities draws on expertise from practitioners and survivors to explore therapeutic approaches to dissociation resulting from complex trauma. The contributors provide a vivid insight into what it is like for therapist and survivor to be alongside one another in the therapy room. They highlight the challenges of work with the fragmented internal worlds of those who have survived attachment trauma and explore together what approaches can promote healing and repair.

Dissociative identity is reframed from being a disorder to an essential survival skill, and the book includes an open recognition from the perspectives of both therapist and survivor of relational challenges, pitfalls, and their impact on the healing process.

Dissociative Identities will be invaluable for all professionals working with survivors of complex trauma, including psychotherapists, nurses, social workers, clinical psychologists, and counsellors. It will also be of interest to survivors and their networks.

Sue Richardson is a member of The Bowlby Centre and a UKCP-registered attachment-based psychotherapist and supervisor.

Melanie Goodwin is an expert by experience and co-founder of First Person Plural, an organisation which raised awareness and provided training and support for people with dissociative conditions and their allies from 1997 until its closure in 2023.

Emma Jack is a Minster Centre-trained relational psychotherapist. She is Clinical Director for The Clinic for Dissociative Studies.

Michele Jowett is an expert by experience as a person living with a formal diagnosis of dissociative identity disorder. Committed to sharing her experiences of dissociation and informing professionals through writing for the ESTD, ISSTD, and FPP newsletters, she was instrumental in producing The Survivors Trust resources website.

The Bowlby Centre Monograph Series

A series of books taken from the Annual John Bowlby Memorial Conference, produced in association with The Bowlby Centre, London.

For further information about this series please visit https://www.routledge.com/The-Bowlby-Centre-Monograph-Series/book-series/KARNBCM

Dissociative Identities

Attachment-based Approaches to
Psychotherapy

Edited by
Sue Richardson, Melanie Goodwin,
Emma Jack, and Michele Jowett

Routledge
Taylor & Francis Group

LONDON AND NEW YORK

Designed cover image: © Kim Noble/Ken, Within/June 2018/Acrylic on Canvas

First published 2025
by Routledge
4 Park Square, Milton Park, Abingdon, Oxon OX14 4RN

and by Routledge
605 Third Avenue, New York, NY 10158

Routledge is an imprint of the Taylor & Francis Group, an informa business

British Library Cataloguing-in-Publication Data
A catalogue record for this book is available from the British Library

ISBN: 978-1-032-69670-6 (hbk)
ISBN: 978-1-032-69665-2 (pbk)
ISBN: 978-1-032-69672-0 (ebk)

DOI: 10.4324/9781032696720

Typeset in Times New Roman
by Taylor & Francis Books

In memory of Elizabeth Balgobin

Contents

Illustrations

Figures

Table

Contributors

Orit Badouk Epstein is a UKCP-registered attachment-based psychoanalytic psychotherapist, a training supervisor, and a training therapist. She trained at The Bowlby Centre, London where she is an editor emerita of the journal *Attachment: New Directions in Psychotherapy and Relational Psychoanalysis*. She specialises in attachment theory and trauma and regularly lectures, teaches, writes, and presents papers on these topics and consults worldwide on attachment theory. She runs a private practice and works relationally with individuals, couples, and parents. Orit has a particular interest in working with individuals who have experienced extreme abuse and trauma and have symptoms of dissociation. She is the co-author of *Ritual Abuse and Mind Control: The Manipulation of Attachment Needs* (Badouk Epstein, Wingfield and Schwartz, 2011, Routledge), and *Terror Within & Without* (Yellin and Badouk Epstein, 2013, Routledge) and editor of *Shame Matters* (2022, Routledge; Gradiva Award 2023). She was the co-editor of the European Society for Trauma and Dissociation (ESTD) newsletter for ten years as well as being a regular contributor of articles and film reviews. In her spare time Orit enjoys the cinema, reading philosophy, and writing poetry.

Melanie Goodwin is an expert by experience who lives with dissociative identities and has experienced life-changing dissociation-focused therapy. She co-founded First Person Plural, a survivor-led organisation, in 1997 initially to help address the isolation that she was experiencing. Over the next 26 years Melanie wrote many articles, chapters for books, and resources for those working and living with dissociative identities. She led on establishing support groups and is continuing to share her expertise widely. With her colleague, Kathryn Livingston, she used many forums to help raise awareness of the needs of those experiencing dissociative identities. The training DVDs produced by First Person Plural continue to be used worldwide. Melanie ran her local playgroup for many years. Her paid employment was in libraries where she led on developing their work with children and mental health, recognising the need for them to diversify and become genuinely fully inclusive. Melanie owes her husband and grown-up children so much in helping her to reach the place she is at today and her grandchildren for allowing her to witness the truly wonderful outcomes of good-enough attachments as they are growing up.

Catherine Holland has worked in health and social care as a practitioner, commissioner, policy-maker, trauma interventionist, and organisational consultant for over 40 years. She trained at The Bowlby Centre and is a UKCP-registered attachment-based psychotherapist, a clinical and training supervisor, and an organisational consultant. Catherine currently works in private practice and is a Trustee of The Bowlby Centre and the Organisation Promoting Understanding of Society (OPUS).

Emma Jack is Clinical Director at The Clinic for Dissociative Studies. She is a Minster Centre-trained relational psychodynamic psychotherapist and has specialised in working with severe clinical presentations for the past 15 years. Emma has worked for Bexley Psychotherapy Service in the personality disorder service, The London Ambulance Service, and in private practice. She was the joint Head of Foundation Year and clinical supervisor at the Minster Centre until 2022.

Michele Jowett is an expert by experience as a person living with dissociative identity. She uses her passion for writing as a platform to share her experiences of dissociative identity and inform others through writing for the ESTD, ISSTD, and First Person Plural newsletters. She has presented at the ESTD-UK conference in York and was instrumental in producing the Survivors Trust Resources website. Michele has studied dissociation and complex trauma exhaustively but her passion to become a therapist in the field of complex trauma and dissociation has been thwarted by a lack of understanding surrounding her formal diagnosis of dissociative identity disorder. This has fuelled her resolve to educate others about the condition and advocate for it. Michele currently supports survivors of sexual violence in whom she frequently encounters dissociation and dissociated identities. Her work provides an opportunity for her to apply her knowledge of complex trauma and dissociation and to achieve her goal of giving survivors a voice and making a difference. Michele is a published children's author, but her greatest achievement is her three adult children.

Mark Linington is an attachment-based psychoanalytic psychotherapist with The Bowlby Centre and the Clinic for Dissociative Studies in London, UK. From 2013 to 2018 he was chair of the executive committee at The Bowlby Centre, where he continues to work as a training therapist, clinical supervisor, and teacher. He worked for 12 years in the NHS as a psychotherapist with children and adults with intellectual disabilities who have experienced complex trauma and abuse, including those with dissociative identity. He also worked as a psychotherapist for several years at a secondary school in London for young people with special needs, including autism, ADHD, and dissociative disorders. He has written a number of papers and book chapters about his clinical work and presented papers on attachment theory in clinical practice at a number of conferences. He is currently CEO at the Clinic for Dissociative Studies, where he is also a specialist consultant psychotherapist working with people with dissociative identities, and a clinical supervisor. He works in private practice offering therapy to children, adults, and families, providing supervision to individuals and groups and training to organisations.

Sue Richardson is a member of The Bowlby Centre and a UKCP-registered attachment-based psychotherapist and supervisor. She has over 40 years of experience in the helping professions and has integrated her extensive knowledge of child abuse and child protection into her work with adults who have survived complex trauma. A founder member of the UK network of the European Society for Trauma and Dissociation, Sue has been instrumental in raising awareness of dissociation and developing face-to-face and online training modules. She is committed to working in partnership with experts by experience with whom she has collaborated in making two educational DVDs and an online training package addressing disscociation. The co-editor and co-author of two books and several published papers, her publications include *Child Sexual Abuse: Whose Problem?* (revised 2nd edition, 2018) and "Reaching for relationship: Exploring the use of an attachment paradigm in the assessment and repair of the dissociative internal world" *Attachment: New Directions in Psychotherapy and Relational Psychoanalysis*, 4: 7–25, 2010. Sue's personal attachment networks are in the north of England where she has been in independent practice for many years and where she is planning her forthcoming retirement.

Adah Sachs PhD is an attachment-based psychoanalytic psychotherapist and a member of The Bowlby Centre. She has worked for decades with adults and adolescents in psychiatric care, was a consultant psychotherapist at the Clinic for Dissociative Studies, and an NHS consultant and a London borough psychotherapy lead (now retired). Her main theoretical contribution is outlining subcategories of disorganised attachment, with links to trauma-based mental health disorders. Adah lectures, assesses, and supervises worldwide on attachment and dissociation. She is the author of over 200 training day materials, conference papers, book chapters, and journal articles, including three co-edited books. She is a fellow of the International Society for the Study of Trauma and Dissociation (ISSTD).

Valerie Sinason is a poet, prolific writer, child and adolescent psychoanalytic psychotherapist (retired), Bowlby Centre attachment-based psychotherapist (retired), and adult psychoanalyst. She has specialised in trauma and disability for over 40 years within the public sector at the Tavistock Clinic, St George's Hospital Medical School, and schools for disturbed children, and has edited, co-edited, or written 25 books, several hundred papers, reviews, and chapters, and lectures nationally and internationally. Founder and now Patron of the Clinic for Dissociative Studies UK, President of the Institute for Psychotherapy and Disability, she is a Fellow and current board member of the International Society for the Study of Trauma and Dissociation (ISSTD). She has received the ISSTD 2017 Lifetime Achievement Award, the British Psychoanalytic Council's Innovation Excellence Award, 2022, and life membership of the Swedish Organisation for Psychologists Working with Intellectual Disability (POMS). She is an honorary consultant psychotherapist at the Cape Town Child Guidance Clinic. Her first novel was *The Orpheus Project* (2022). She has just completed her second novel, *Hotel Mirabelle and the Wonderful Wheelchair Company*.

Foreword

Mark Linington

For people who experience dissociative identities, establishing connection, communication, and collaboration internally between different identities and externally between these identities and another person helping them is crucial to the achievement of good mental health. It establishes more secure and enjoyable relationships, and a better quality of functional life. This establishment of increased connectedness between identities can be facilitated through a secure trauma and dissociation-informed attachment-based psychotherapeutic relationship.

This monograph of the Annual Bowlby Centre Conference in February 2023 is the result of a partnership with the Clinic for Dissociative Studies, providing an important space to explore theory, clinical practice and the reflections of two experts by experience.

The renaming of multiple personality disorder as dissociative identity disorder was perhaps in part a recognition that the multiplicity of selves is not in itself problematic, but rather that the poor quality of (dissociated) relationships between these different identities is the difficulty. Hence, an aim in therapeutic work with someone with dissociative identities is not to work with them to reduce themselves to a singularity. Rather, the aim is to help them find a way to develop more secure internal attachment-based relationships, with a consequential impact on the quality of their external life.

Research by Daniel Stern shows that the quality of attachment relationships in any psychotherapeutic relationship is fundamental to good outcomes (Stern, 1995). A key feature of a good clinical attachment relationship includes consistent attention to the five therapeutic tasks outlined by Bowlby (1988) with regard to psychotherapeutic work generally. Firstly, the provision of a secure relational base, from which the person can explore their traumatic and post traumatic experiences. Secondly, a further exploration of how aspects of these early models of relationships, conscious and unconscious, including expectations, feelings, and behaviour, are active in current relationships. Thirdly, to examine how such internal working models are imported into the relationship with the psychotherapist and are thus an active part including "all those perceptions, constructions and expectations of how an attachment figure is likely to feel and behave towards them" (Bowlby, 1988, p. 178). Fourthly, to support the person to reflect on how their "current perceptions and expectations and the feelings to which they give rise" may have been produced by relational experiences during childhood and adolescence, especially those with parents, and other caregiving figures. The therapist's fifth task is to enable the person to recognise that such models of themselves with others, derived often from past relationally abusive experiences, may not serve them well in the present and future. The task is then to begin to help the person, where they so wish or need, to develop new ways of being, that better support them in their current life. This has sometimes been referred to as the "restorative process" (Heard, Lake and McCluskey, 2009; McCluskey and O'Toole, 2020).

For most people with dissociative identities, and the psychotherapists who work with them, a significant difficulty inherent in engaging in these tasks can be the high degree of understandable fear that is still experienced by some or all of the identities which form their fragmented or disconnected self. Such fear, often evoked powerfully in the present by certain responses from other people, or "lookalikes" who remind them of their past (McCluskey, personal communication), is a feature of disorganised attachment (Main and Solomon, 1986). For people with dissociative identities, an especially complex form of disorganised attachment, the development and maintenance of relational and emotional security within and across their multiple identities can be especially challenging. Different identities, each with a potentially different knowledge of their total relational history, may present with a variety of different attachment patterns. Together they have different ways of communicating, and a variety of adaptive functions in relation to the maintenance of well-being in their original traumatic relational or attachment experiences. Functions which, whilst adaptive in the past to ensure survival, in the current day may undermine the person's ability to live their life in a way which supports their well-being.

An additional specific challenge for psychotherapist in work with people with dissociative identities can be the range of developmental ages of the different self-states of the person which present in the therapy. Often people can present as identities who seem, and experience themselves as, chronologically young, sometimes adolescent, sometimes toddlers and sometimes an even earlier age. The developmental ages of these identities often seem related to the ages at which abusive trauma has occurred. Psychotherapists also work in the societal context of women's experience of misogyny and domestic and sexual abuse. Presentations of opposite gender identities, as children or adults, may also come into the room. The capacity in the psychotherapist, and in other professionals who have contact with people with dissociative identities, to be able to be empathically attuned to and "meet" (McCluskey, 2005) these identities at their different developmental stages or with their different gender identities requires a profound flexibility and wide range of abilities. These include an ability to move between and understand the needs of different relational configurations, an ability to adapt the language and mode of responsiveness as part of the therapeutic process, an ability to play with, listen to and reflect upon the meanings of interactions, as well as a capacity to contain and understand their own emotional, often counter-transferential, experiences as psychotherapists.

Since the late 1980s, The Bowlby Centre (under its different names of The Institute of Self-Analysis and the Centre for Attachment-based Psychoanalytic Psychotherapy) has been training psychotherapists in the application of attachment theory in psychotherapy. In addition, The Bowlby Centre was one of the few and earliest psychotherapeutic training institutes to include a significant amount of teaching about working with structural dissociation and dissociative identity, as a standard topic within its curriculum. As a result, over the years, the understanding and skills needed to work with people with dissociative identities has developed significantly, and the number of attachment-based psychoanalytic psychotherapists who themselves identify as being dissociative has grown.

Since its foundation by Valerie Sinason in 1998, the Clinic for Dissociative Studies, an organisation dedicated to the NHS-funded provision of psychotherapy for people with dissociative identities and other dissociative disorders, has also applied attachment theory as one of the essential pillars of its work (Sinason, 2002).

There is a growing community of people with dissociative identities, which has led the developing recognition of the expertise and significant knowledge of people who live with dissociative conditions. For people who have experienced awful early ongoing abuse from caregivers and who have lived with its emotional and relational consequences, the significance of developing a strong voice that promotes the understanding of what helps in a restorative process is in itself a support in the recovery from such trauma. Their voice also ensures that there are a growing number of psychotherapists, psychiatrists, mental health workers, social workers and other professionals who have a deeper understanding of this way of being in the world.

What does a restorative process look like for a person with dissociative identities? To an important extent, it is something that is defined subjectively, particularly about the issue of multiple identities. Each person may have a different view of what restoration regarding issues of their identities' relationships, quality of daily life, and experience of well-being will involve for them. Many people with dissociative identities do not lose their multiplicity as part of this recovery process. Rather, it is the increased connection, communication, and co-operation between their identities which is a key part of the recovery process. Achieving this takes significant care and understanding. This is also an understanding that has been achieved by an increasing number of practitioners themselves, connecting, communicating, and co-operating about their understanding of the complex and often challenging work they are doing. This monograph, and the conference from which it originates, are two important examples of thinking and work by the broader professional system of those trying to help people with dissociative identities and are significant indicators of the importance of such ongoing connections.

References

Bowlby, J. (1988). *A Secure Base: Clinical Applications of Attachment Theory.* London: Routledge.

Heard, D., Lake, B., and McCluskey, U. (2009). *Attachment Therapy with Adolescents and Adults: Theory and Practice Post Bowlby.* London: Karnac.

Main, M., and Solomon, J. (1986). "Discovery of an Insecure-Disorganized/Disoriented Attachment Pattern", in Yogman, M. and Brazelton, T.B. (eds), *Affective Development in Infancy.* Norwood, NJ: Ablex, pp. 95–124.

McCluskey, U. (2005). *To Be Met as a Person: The Dynamics of Attachment in Professional Encounters.* London: Karnac.

McCluskey, U., and O'Toole, M. (2020). *Transference and Countertransference from an Attachment Perspective: A Guide for Professional Caregivers.* London: Routledge.

Sinason, V. (2002). *Attachment, Trauma and Multiplicity: Working with Dissociative Identity Disorder.* London: Routledge.

Stern, D. (1995). *The Motherhood Constellation.* New York: Basic Books.

Acknowledgements

The conference on which this publication is based was the result of a collaboration between the conference organiser Tori Settle, Elizabeth Balgobin, former CEO of The Bowlby Centre, and Mark Linington, CEO of the Centre for Dissociative Studies. We appreciate their organisation of a successful online event and the contribution of the authors to the arrangement of the programme. Sadly, we acknowledge the loss of Elizabeth Balgobin who died in March 2024, to whom this book is dedicated.

A big thank to all the people with dissociative identities under the pseudonyms of Bridget, Lilly, Nevar, Odette, and Sky who have so generously given their permission for parts of their story to be included. Their brave and moving work has an essential and powerful role in what the book wishes to convey. They help to make this publication unique as it captures the individuality of each and every person living with dissociative identities and provides an invaluable resource for therapists and others through allowing many voices to be heard. We also thank Sia for permission to use her poem.

We are very grateful to Kim Noble, an accomplished artist with dissociative identities, for permission to use the artwork on the cover, painted by one of her personalities, Ken. We welcome the comment provided by another of Kim's personalities, Patricia:

> I am unable to fully comment on Ken's painting because I do not know what he was thinking nor feeling while painting this piece of artwork. However, from an observer's point of view the painting is quietly chaotic. Underneath the sea of blue, it seems there is a sense of rigidness that has been overcome by something disruptive. What I see in the middle of the painting is three people in a circle, perhaps Ken is depicting the mental struggle within himself. The depth of using the colour blue has an awakening feeling for the viewer and creates a sense of turmoil.

We thank Kate White, the series editor, for her continued enabling commitment and her constructive help and suggestions.

Our thanks are also due to the commissioning editor at Routledge, Susannah Frearson, and to all the staff at Routledge involved in the production of this book.

Introduction

Sue Richardson

This collection of papers presented at the 26th John Bowlby Memorial Conference shares developments in the application of an attachment framework to work with dissociation. For the first time, this annual event was held in partnership between The Bowlby Centre and the Clinic for Dissociative Studies and presented uniquely in collaboration with experts by experience, Melanie Goodwin and Michele Jowett.

This introduction provides a brief background to some of the theoretical concepts informing the chapters and highlights their application to practice. Despite Bowlby's awareness of dissociation and the work of forbears such as Pierre Janet, the history of its study and recognition has been beset by controversy, myths and misinformation (van der Hart and Dorahy, 2009; Reinders and Veltman, 2021; Salter, 2023). The clinical and research base in this field has increased exponentially, supported by advances in neuroscience. Brand et al. (2014) draw on four decades of research to dispel common myths which have been behind much controversy and under-diagnosis, such as the belief that dissociative identity is rare and its recognition primarily attributable to over-zealous professionals. This establishes a sound context for the chapters which follow.

In founding what became The Bowlby Centre, the late John Southgate pioneered the inclusion in psychotherapy training of work with trauma and dissociation, an approach which this volume continues. The chapters illustrate the strengths and challenges of attachment-based therapy and its potential for healing via relationship even in the absence of justice. They shine a light on how to co-create the interpersonal conditions which allow for the exploration and processing of trauma and interactive repair. The contributors show how this can be achieved via an attuned relationship between therapist and client and within the client themselves which is strong enough to tackle the paradox of dissociation as both problem and solution.

The integral role of experts by experience is in keeping with Bowlby's exploratory spirit. The inclusion of reflective comment by experts by experience extends the relational conversation which is so crucial to effective therapy. This coming together of psychotherapists and experts by experience provides an insight into what it is like both to have dissociative identities and what it is like

DOI: 10.4324/9781032696720-1

to work with dissociative identities in the therapy room. In combination, these contributions change the map of relating between professionals and survivors of complex trauma.

As part of this equal, respectful alliance and sensitivity to the significance of language, the term 'dissociative identities' is used throughout this volume in preference to the term 'dissociative identity disorder'. This is consistent with the commitment of The Bowlby Centre to a non-pathologising approach to mental distress which is seen as arising from failed attachment relationships. As one client affirmed at the same time as acknowledging the inevitable impact of her trauma: 'There is not something wrong with us. We are not broken'.

Foundations of Attachment Theory

Bowlby's seminal work on attachment has been endorsed by all subsequent research. It has been greatly extended over time (Mikulincer and Shaver, 2007; Dushinsky, 2020) and shown to apply across cultural dimensions (Mesman et al., 2008). Bowlby described attachment as a biologically based instinctive organised behavioural system. It is wired in from birth and characterises human behaviour 'from the cradle to the grave' (Bowlby, 1979, p. 129). Attachment behaviour is activated whenever there is a threat to wellbeing, prompting a careseeker to seek proximity to a caregiver. Attuned, sensitive, empathic caregiving deactivates the attachment system via a felt sense of safety and security and the restoration of wellbeing. Repeated interactions between the careseeker and caregiver result in the formation of relatively stable dynamic internal working models which reflect a sense of self as acceptable and worthy of care and protection along with the caregiver's availability and desire to give care and protection. Unempathic, mis-attuned, unresponsive, unreliable caregiving leaves the careseeker in a state of distress and the formation of insecure attachment patterns. These can be hyper-activating of attachment behaviour in an anxious, preoccupied pattern or de-activating in a dismissive, avoidant pattern.

Attachment trauma in childhood by one or more physically, emotionally, or sexually abusive caregivers has major adverse effects (Bacon and Richardson, 2001). It leaves the careseeker with 'fright without solution' (Main and Hesse, 1990) marked by a chronic approach-avoidance conflict as seen in unresolved and dis-organised attachment. Interpersonal trauma disrupts the dynamic interaction of the attachment system resulting in a person's interpersonal and intrapersonal relating being profoundly and adversely affected by fear and self-defence. Depend-ing on the attachment pattern and relational context, some responses to adverse experiences are down-regulated while others can be up-regulated. Common to all insecure patterns is that the careseeker has to change their affective responses in order to maintain a relationship with a frightening caregiver and minimise harm. Liotti (1999, 2004, 2006) proposes that the absence of a coherent strategy to obtain proximity to caregiver resulting in disorganised attachment is itself a dissociative process and acts as the precursor of dissociation induced by trauma.

Attachment and Dissociation

Bowlby vividly understood the dilemma of the abused child whereby the child must disconnect from what they know and feel (Bowlby, 1988). He identified dissociation as the defensive exclusion of information too painful to bear and the partial or complete de-activation of the behavioural systems involved in attachment (Bowlby, 1980).

An attachment-informed definition of dissociation is of:

> early, multiple, incoherent, reciprocally incompatible and dramatic representations of the self, mediated by interpersonal relationships with a frightened or frightening caregiver, and based on the inborn human need for protective proximity to another human being when one is in danger of suffering.
>
> (Liotti, 1999, p. 309)

Experts by experience have called dissociation 'A logical way of being' (Learning Resource, www.firstpersonplural.co.uk). Melanie Goodwin in chapter seven and Michele Jowett in chapter eight share their lived experience of just how much dissociation is a logical response to complex trauma. A roundtable discussion of leading professionals agreed that:

> Dissociation is a paradoxically resilient response to the disconfirmation and invalidation of insecure attachment situations that allows the child to maintain proximity to the parent.
>
> (Chefetz in Itzkowitz et al., 2015, p. 46)

Dissociative identity is frequently accompanied by a sense of shame, often reinforced by being met with stigma (Gleaves and Bennett, 2023). The shame and fear of stigma borne by those with dissociative identity can be colossal and severely wounding (Badouk Epstein, 2022). The lived experiences shared in chapters seven and eight underline the personal impact of this dimension.

The need to attach and defend simultaneously against abusive caregivers fragments the personality into differing internal representations of the self, such as child and adult parts, some of whom may be internal representations of the perpetrator. Catherine Holland (chapter two), Emma Jack (chapter three) and Orit Badouk Epstein (chapter four) all comment on the different experiences, feeling states, values and attitudes held by different parts which can emerge, and which influence attitudes towards therapy.

Finding an Interface Between Attachment Theory and Clinical Work with Dissociation

The interface of attachment theory and work with complex trauma and dissociation involves the adaptation of existing theory and the evolution of new approaches. The approaches to clinical practice shared in this volume reflect work in progress. In chapter one, Mark Linington applies an extension of attachment theory and its perspective on the systems involved in the dynamics of attachment, especially the way in which careseeking and caregiving can be either effective or ineffective in reaching the goal of wellbeing.[1]

Attachment research relevant to working with trauma developed since Bowlby includes the identification of the Hostile-Helpless category by Lyons-Ruth and her team (Lyons-Ruth et al., 2005). This category acknowledges that the coding of the Adult Attachment Interview was not designed with traumatised populations in mind. Six frequency codes explore the extent of co-existing states of mind which devalue a hostile caregiver at the same time as a confused identification with them. This leads to the development of a sense of self as bad, given to denying vulnerability, with consequent ruptured attachments. This profile has been identified in parents who themselves have a history of unresolved loss or trauma and who can subsequently become frightened or frightening caregivers, promoting fearful arousal in their children. Catherine Holland in chapter two and Emma Jack in chapter three give a flavour of clinical encounters with these conflicting states of mind in individual clients. In chapter four, Orit Badouk Epstein explores the dynamics of frightening caregiving, conceptualised as 'scare-giving', and considers the consequences and clinical implications.

The concept of infanticidal attachment, symbolic and concrete has been put forward by Adah Sachs (2007) to explore the consequences of the child as the object of caregiver's covert or actual threats, hate and wish to do them harm. Symbolic infanticidal attachment concerns the caregiver's harmful state of mind. In its concrete form, the child is exposed to 'parental concrete acts of murder or torture, which the infant endures, witnesses or is forced to commit' (Sachs, 2007). Bearing witness to the traumatic impact of infanticidal impulses demands courage and resilience of the practitioner, demonstrated in the work of the contributors to this volume. In a lively and thought-provoking conversation with Emma Jack, in chapter six Adah Sachs develops her thinking about the nature of this encounter and what it means for our engagement with and understanding of the dissociative self.

The Absence of Attachment Representations (AAR) (Koren-Karie et al., 2003) can aid an understanding of parts of the personality who have deactivated their attachment system in response to being overwhelmed by extreme fear. The authors used the Adult Attachment Interview with a group who had lost both parents in the Holocaust. The group appeared to have erased from their internal representations the prior existence of attachment relationships. The authors raise the possibility that:

> some devastating experiences in childhood might cause an unrecoverable crash in already established patterns of attachment to an extent that

adulthood will be characterized by a state of mind that bears no emotional tie to even a single attachment figure.

(Koren-Karie et al., 2003, p. 381)

In response to other kinds of extreme experiences, some dissociative parts of the personality may correspond to this category. Such parts can present as devoid of any feelings and emotion. They may identify as robots or other non-human entities or even as parts who are believed by other parts of the client to be dead. Their existence emphasises the extent of the therapeutic challenge, especially in work with those who have suffered organised and extreme abuse. Examples of therapeutic work with clients with this history can be found in chapters two, three and four.

Phobia of attachment and attachment loss featured in the structural model of dissociation (van der Hart et al., 2006). Amos et al. (2011) explore this further proposing the term 'attachment-related dissociative part of the personality' (ARDP) to explain the experiential avoidance of relationship and complex psychological processes involved in structural dissociation following relational trauma. Ways of overcoming the paradox of the client simultaneously engaging in and avoiding the therapeutic relationship are illustrated in chapters one, two, three and four.

Multiple Attachment Patterns

Attachment patterns in dissociative persons are multiple (Liotti, 1999; Steele, 2002). This explains contrasting behaviour in relationships and presentations in therapy. Steele administered the Adult Attachment Interview to adult women with a formal diagnosis of dissociative identity disorder. Differing attachment styles in different parts of the personality were clearly observed. Experience in clinical practice notes similar patterns (Richardson, 2010). Young parts of the personality with an anxious preoccupied attachment pattern can desperately, often indiscriminately, seek attachment and their needs can be hard to assuage. Older, more avoidant, dismissive parts can be phobic of relationship and of the younger parts who seek it. Contradictory states of mind concerning attachment reflect a fragmented self, with different goals, defences and internal working models, marked by fluctuating shifts towards and away from relationship. A vivid illustration is given in Table 1.1 in chapter one. Dissociation provides a way of preventing the disorganisation which would otherwise result.

Multiple attachment patterns tend to be fixed, hard to change and embedded in the structural dissociation of the personality. They pose a challenge to the therapist of providing a secure enough base and a relational bridge to the whole system to promote more effective internal careseeking and caregiving in a more supportive internal environment. The therapist's task entails a roving process of 'dissociative attunement' (Hopenwasser, 2008) to all parts of the personality with its inherent pitfalls: attunement to one part of the personality can mean misattunement to another. The clinical work described in this collection illustrates the sensitive and demanding navigation of this process.

Clinical experience is that survivors may also speak of an imaginary attachment to self-created internal parts such as maternal figures, partners and other caring beings. These internal relational figures provide a feeling of comfort and security in place of relationships in the external world. As one client put it when describing her preference for internal rather than external relating 'Out there is painful. In here is comfort. Leave me out of it'.

The Impact of Fear

In chapter four, Orit Badouk Epstein emphasises the impact of fear on attachment in the context of a frightening caregiver. Her evocative term 'scaregiver' emphasises how a caregiver who arouses chronic fear in the careseeker results in dissociation as a means of surviving in the relationship. Mark Linington in chapter one describes the role of this fearful arousal on the systems involved in attachment in preventing the restorative process.

Guilding (2020) argues that the chronic failure to de-activate the fear system is the source of complex trauma. The fear and attachment systems are activated simultaneously by threat. The fear system has its own neural circuitry and neurobiology (Bell, 2009). It subsides if a good enough attachment figure is available. If fear is persistent, overwhelming and protection absent, the attachment system shuts down and the brain reverts to primitive responses of flight, fight or freeze/collapse. Middleton's (2013) study of ongoing abuse in adult women emphasises the role of high levels of fear resulting from perpetrator's extreme sadistic violence and threats of violence. Fear leads to rapid conditioning which is hard to extinguish. Fear-based learning can result in stimuli bypassing the higher but slower cortical structures which evaluate threat, and the brain reacts to alarm signals even when no actual danger is present (LeDoux, 2015). This lies behind the prevalence of traumatic triggers which commonly trouble and destabilise survivors and can be very hard to manage.

Faced with the impossibility of the restoration of wellbeing via attaining proximity to a caregiver who is also the source of fear, the systems involved in the attachment dynamic described in chapter one become segregated. The traumatic responses of fight, flight, freeze, submit or attach become held by separate parts of the personality along with multiple and incompatible perceptions of attachment figures. A range of outcomes affecting attachment behaviour can follow. In response to the impossibility of tolerating its unassuaged hyperarousal, some parts of the personality may deactivate their attachment system and avoid relationship altogether. A client speaks of equating safety with being alone and how she decided:

It was just not worth risking the pain and humiliation of being rejected over again or bothering to try. I will never get it right and getting it wrong hurts too much.

(Carol, B., 2010, p. 32)

Other parts may adopt the kind of strategies which have been observed in abused children, such as compulsive caregiving or controlling and/or controlling-punitive behaviour (Moss et al., 1999). Yet others may disconnect from the memory of the trauma. Those parts which continue to show attachment behaviour towards the perpetrator are often amnesic for the trauma (Liotti, 2004). This enables them to approach a frightening caregiver with only the awareness of non-abusive aspects of the relationship. An expert by experience has described this as 'pseudo-attachment', necessary for survival but coming from a dissociated part of the self (Melanie Goodwin, personal communication).

The Victim–Perpetrator Dynamic

The dynamics of the victim–perpetrator relationship are complex and can be hard to understand for survivors themselves, their therapists and others who are aware of this issue. Chapters two, three and four give clinical examples of the considerable challenges to the therapist of relating to perpetrator identified parts of the personality and its crucial role in therapy. As many survivors and their therapists know only too well when addressing the need to separate from a traumatic attachment to the perpetrator:

Disentangling their relationship from the harm which is done in the relationship is as painful as the harm itself, and very hard to reach.

(Middleton et al., 2017, p. 250)

A model of trauma-coerced attachment explains affiliation to the perpetrator as resulting from 'myriad and micro forms of aggression, degradation, intimidation and manipulation' (Doychak and Raghavan, 2023) along with dependency and alternating punishment and rewards. Sinason (2017) gives examples of chilling narratives held by some parts of the personality who are identified with the perpetrator and for whom sado-masochistic behaviour has acquired an addictive quality. Adah Sachs (2007 and chapter six) opens up an additional area for debate by hypothesising that those exposed to infanticidal attachment can experience some form of felt security via engaging with a sadistic caregiver.

Schwartz (2013) is of the opinion that it is too simplistic to see survivors as basically wounded children. He holds that an inherent victim–perpetrator dichotomy means that it is essential to dialogue with unfeeling, apparently malign parts to help them find a sense of agency which is not based on the perpetrator's world view.

Schimmenti (2017) views the behaviour of perpetrator-identified parts of the personality as arising from fear rather than any category of attachment. He describes traumatic identification as a complex psychological process to ensure survival in response to unregulated fear. Three types of traumatic identification are described: with the victimised self; with the perpetrator's self and with a 'ghostly other' (the internalisation of an absent or neglectful parental state of mind). In chapter four, Orit Badouk Epstein describes creative therapeutic ways of navigating this kind of internal world.

Organised and Extreme Abuse

The term 'dissociative identity' does not fully describe those whose personalities have been purposefully manipulated via torture and severe attachment trauma in order to install parts of the personality subject to control by the perpetrator. The abuse can be ongoing into adult life (Sachs, 2013; Middleton, 2013; Salter, 2017). Training and practice need to be inclusive of survivors of barely imaginable horrors of the kind described by Hoffman (2014, 2016), Lacter (2011) and Miller (2012). In many forms of organised abuse and ritual violence the dynamics of attachment, especially careseeking and caregiving, are deliberately targeted and manipulated. Anecdotal, clinical and criminal evidence speaks of torture and other methods designed to disrupt attachment behaviour. Examples of this include being told one's biological parents are not one's parents, encouraging attachment to perpetrators or their associates by the provision of intermittent soothing care and the installation of fears and beliefs designed to undermine any genuinely benign relationship. For those born into intergenerational networks of torture-based mind control, pre-natal stress due to abusive practices inflicted on the expectant mother of the kind described by Hoffman (2014) are another source of heightened vulnerability.

The nature of organised, extreme abuse means that there are two kinds of dissociation to address. First, what can be termed organic dissociation as the sequelae of interpersonal trauma. In this case, any sense of self and self-agency is fragmented and held by different self-created parts of the personality. The second, deliberately induced installed dissociation is the sequelae of the use of terror designed to maintain the perpetrator's power and control and undermine any sense of self. The deliberate manipulation of the biological system of attachment produces a paradox in which wellbeing is governed by fear and experienced by the victim as maintained via loyalty to the perpetrators. In this scenario, what governs behaviour is reversed. For example, keeping safe might mean returning to perpetrators when instructed and doing what they demand. There can be installed barriers to relationship with anyone outside the perpetrating group, preventing any other experience of relationship and impeding therapy.

It is not unusual to come across poly-fragmentation and unusual internal representations, such as internal beings whose identity is non-human, like animals and mythical creatures as the product of the deliberate creation of multiple states of mind. By virtue of their origin, parts of the personality created by the perpetrators may suffer from the absence of attachment representations with a profound loss of agency.

The task of repair involves dealing with extreme fear states and is complex. The clinical examples in chapters two, three and four illustrate the exploration of this frontier. Included in chapter three are essential considerations for therapeutic work with this client group.

The Nature of the Dissociative Self

The developmental legacy of trauma is highlighted throughout this volume along with its inherent implications for the sense of self. Chapter six opens a discussion about how we might consider the nature of the self in a person with dissociative identities. In conversation with Emma Jack, Adah Sachs puts forward the view that, despite their apparent differences, all parts of the personality share a common purpose in self-protection and survival. This denotes an intentional stance, consistent with the goal-directed nature of the systems involved in attachment described in chapter one. Like Michele Jowett in chapter eight, some survivors may have a core sense of self. Others may be more like someone who has described her sense of self as constantly changing:

> We are just a motley crew: that is what we are. I am not the same person for any length of time at all. I am always a conglomeration of several & even they swim in & out of consciousness and come and go, being sometimes more than the majority of us, and sometimes fading away and even going and hiding somewhere or just watching from the shadows.
> (Motley Crew, 2011, p. 12)

The reflections in chapter six, with their empathic approach to the selves of a dissociative person, resonate with the experts by experience, Melanie Goodwin and Michele Jowett (chapters seven and eight). Much is likely to depend on the nature and severity of the trauma and the quality of attachment experiences. The existence of a core self, as hypothesised in chapter six, is endorsed by lived experience in chapter eight. A different view is taken in international guidelines which note that developmental models:

> posit that DID does not arise from a previously mature, unified mind or 'core personality' that becomes shattered or fractured. Rather, DID results from a failure of normal developmental integration caused by overwhelming experiences and disturbed caregiver–child interactions (including neglect and the failure to respond) during critical early

developmental periods. This, in turn, leads some traumatized children to develop relatively discrete, personified behavioral states that ultimately evolve into the DID alternate identities.

(Chu et al., 2011)

The existence of a core pre-trauma self may be in particular question for survivors whose parts of the personality are installed via torture-based mind control. The narrative of survivors of this kind of trauma bears witness to 'the foundational destruction' (Hoffman, 2014, p. 55) of the self from pre-birth onwards. For those trapped in this horrific context, rather than a pre-trauma self, there exist only parts which have been constructed to serve the perpetrators. Any sense of self has to be built from new relationships, free from ongoing trauma and mind control, often in therapy. The therapeutic work described in chapters two, three and four illustrates this endeavour.

While there is a wider discussion to be had about the nature of the dissociative self put forward in chapter six, the chapter underlines three important themes of this collection. First and foremost, the importance of a genuine encounter with the client based on empathic attunement. Second, how an attachment-based therapeutic response goes beyond diagnostic labels to a meeting with the individual nature of the person's identities. Third, the exploration of new frontiers in work with complex trauma and the creative development of hypotheses. Whatever the nature of the dissociative self, all the contributors underline the survival of the attachment system and its hope for a restorative, healing process.

Wider Context

The creation of a supportive therapeutic environment for traumatised individuals needs a supportive societal and political one. The societal and institutional denial of the prevalence of trauma and dissociation is highlighted by Sinason (2020 and chapter five). This context persists despite advances in individual therapy. Wider societal responses are not only fear-driven but can also be institutional. In response to government mandated institutional betrayal in the US, Freyd calls for institutional courage versus institutional betrayal in response to trauma (www.institutionalcourage.org/).

Practitioners who have exposed the endemic nature of abuse have been subject to vicious attacks accompanied by denial of its widespread existence. Campbell (2023) focuses on institutional betrayal in the UK following the emergence of child sexual abuse into the public domain in Cleveland in 1987. Here the medical diagnosis of sexual abuse in 127 children led to a public outcry of disbelief, vilification of the professionals and a major public inquiry without a brief to establish the facts of the medical findings. Campbell's meticulous research details the consequences of subsequent decades of failure to investigate the abuse of children and young people. This includes the enormous difficulty of the investigation of suspects with links to the establishment. Campbell quotes a director of social services being told that he was 'probably wasting his time' raising these links as 'there were too many of them over there' in Whitehall and Westminster (Winning, 2014 quoted in Campbell, 2023, p. 142). In chapter five, Valerie Sinason discusses the implications of perpetration by persons of public prominence and the impact of high-profile cases on our own sense of attachment security.

Trajectories of Repair

Attachment-based therapy is underpinned by advances in neurobiological research which shows the impact of childhood trauma on the developing brain (Schore, 2003). Trauma-informed work is increasingly informed by a focus on the dysregulation of the sympathetic nervous system responsible for self-defence and the need to reset the autonomic nervous system responsible for safety, regulation and connection (Brand et al., 2022; Schore, 2012). Lack of neural integration impedes the capacity to use relationships as a secure base. Instead, patterns of response are fearful, inflexible and deeply entrenched.

The spontaneous creation of a dissociative self can be a truly life-saving solution to the contradiction of trauma caused by an attachment figure. This presents a challenge to healing and repair. Research on clinical outcomes (Brand et al., 2013; Keating et al., 2018) underlines the role of a reparative relationship both with and between parts of the self. This volume explores the practice of achieving this and provides an insight into realistic aims of therapy. Essentially, the authors show that a secure enough base in therapy can increase reflective functioning, enhance emotional regulation, provide a more coherent narrative of experience, and overcome deep divisions in the personality. These changes are accompanied by neurophysiological shifts which reduce over- and under-reactivity in the brain and changed working models of relationship.

The vignettes in this volume show how a safe relational connection can replace the internal conflict inherent in dissociation and disconnection with the foundational concept of the '4 C's' of comfort, communication, co-operation and connection (Steinberg and Schnall, 2001, pp. 253–274) in a more supportive environment, both internal and external. A useful reflection on the task of repair is that even the children deemed to suffer from the Absence of Attachment Representations are viewed as not necessarily lacking in the capacity for attachment but rather as having de-activated their attachment systems in response to catastrophic experience (Koren-Karie et al., 2003).

In chapter two, Catherine Holland acknowledges the time it takes to feel confident and competent in negotiating the complex therapeutic task. Along with Emma Jack in chapter three, she brings an awareness of the complexity of what is deeply split off in the client and the impact of such profound disconnection on the therapist. Orit Badouk Epstein in chapter four adds to an understanding of how the relational connection of the therapist with the segregated internal world is the vehicle of change. She emphasises how a healthy attachment via engagement with the therapist is a core component of reorganisation and the alternative to living in fear. Mark Linington in chapter one describes how more effective external caregiving can help to rewire the structure of the personality and restore wellbeing. In chapter six Adah Sachs poses the question of whether or not this constitutes the restoration of an essential self which existed pre-trauma.

The reflections of experts by experience in chapters seven and eight provide a unique perspective on how the therapeutic approaches outlined in this collection resonate with their lived experience. Their lived experience of therapy which is not attuned to their needs, in contrast to appropriate trauma-focused therapy when it can be found, is a powerful message to practitioners in many settings.

Conclusion: Moving Forward

Expanding relational capacity and promoting the formation of more secure attachment, not only with the therapist but also between parts of the personality, is a key aim of therapy. The transformation of established internal working models means working with the whole person, not just with their trauma and dissociative symptoms. It means both client and therapist surviving cycles of disruption and repair and involves nothing less than changing the neuronal structure of the brain. There are no quick fixes and the road to the repair of trauma is usually long. It demands much of the survivor in terms of trust and of the therapist's resilience. The journey is not possible for everyone. Fear, societal and individual denial can stand in the way. Therapeutic and investigative resources are always not commensurate with the need. Practice development, training and awareness raising have come from the grass roots by the kind of committed practitioners and experts by experience contributing to this collection. What remains is a need for systemic change via a major collaborative educational, public health and training initiative to ensure an end to the long years of disbelief, silence and avoidance. Honouring the testimony of survivors, and actively seeking alliances across domains can provide a healing integration. Individually and socially integrated, we can maintain awareness of the unspeakable truth of childhood trauma, can combat its violations and seek to heal the legacy of its wounds.

Note

1   The goal of wellbeing is usually described by writers and researchers in the attachment field as felt security, gained though regular proximity to a secure base provided by an attuned and responsive caregiver. The term 'wellbeing' used here and in chapter one is taken from the work of the late Dorothy Heard and Brian Lake. These two clinicians point out how, in response to Ainsworth's work, Bowlby put less emphasis on instinctive goal-directed behaviour and more on felt security (Heard and Lake, 1997). Research carried out by Una McCluskey affirms their additions to Bowlby's model of complementary goal-corrected systems and their

reconceptualisation of felt security (Heard, Lake and McCluskey, 2009). The authors propose a restorative process involving the dynamic interaction of seven systems involved in attachment which restores wellbeing after it has been threatened. These systems and their interaction are described in chapter one.

References

Amos, J., Furber, G., and Segal, L. (2011). 'Understanding Maltreating Mothers: A Synthesis of Relational Trauma, Attachment Disorganisation, Structural Dissociation of the Personality, and Experiential Avoidance'. *Journal of Trauma and Dissociation*, 12, 5, pp. 495–509.

Bacon, H., and Richardson, S. (2001). 'Attachment Theory and Child Abuse: An Overview of the Literature for Practitioners'. *Child Abuse Review-Special Issue: Attachment and Child Protection*, 10, pp. 377–397.

Badouk Epstein, O. (ed.) (2022). *Shame Matters: Attachment and Relational Perspectives for Psychotherapists*. London: Routledge.

Bell, D. (2009). 'Attachment Without Fear'. *Journal of Family Theory and Review*, 1, 4, pp. 177–197. doi:10.1111/j.1756–2589.2009.00025.x.

Bowlby, J. (1979). *The Making and Breaking of Affectional Bonds*. London: Tavistock.

Bowlby, J. (1980). *Attachment and Loss*. Vol. 3, *Loss: Sadness and Depression*. London: Penguin.

Bowlby, J. (1988). 'On Knowing What You Are Not Supposed to Know and Feeling What You Are Not Supposed to Feel', in Bowlby, J. (ed.), *A Secure Base*. London: Routledge, pp. 99–118.

Brand, B.L., McNary, S.W., Myrick, A.C., Loewenstein, R.J., Classen, C.C., Lanius, R. A., Pain, C., and Putnam, F.W. (2013). 'A Longitudinal, Naturalistic Study of Dissociative Disorder Patients Treated by Community Clinicians'. *Psychological Trauma: Theory, Research, Practice, & Policy*, 5, 4, pp. 301–308. doi:10.1037/a0027654.

Brand, B.L., Loewenstein, R.J., and Spiegel, D. (2014). 'Dispelling Myths About Dissociative Identity Disorder Treatment: An Empirically Based Approach'. *Psychiatry: Interpersonal and Biological Processes*, 77, 2, pp. 169–189.

Brand, B.L., Schielke, H., Schiavone, F., and Lanius, R. (2022). 'The Neurobiology of Trauma-Related Disorders: What Patients and Therapists Need to Know', in Brand, B., Schielke, H., Schiavone, F., and Lanius, R. (eds), *Finding Solid Ground: Overcoming Obstacles in Trauma Treatment*. Oxford: Oxford University Press, pp. 39–61. doi:10.1093/med-psych/9780190636081.003.0003.

Campbell, B. (2023). *Secrets and Silence: Uncovering the Legacy of the Cleveland Child Sexual Abuse Case*. Bristol: Policy Press.

Carol, B. (2010). 'Reflections on an Ongoing Therapeutic "Relationship"'. *Interact, Journal of the Trama and Abuse Group*, 10, 1, pp. 31–34.

Chu, J.A., Dell, P.F., Van der Hart, O., Cardeña, E., *et al.* (2011). 'International Society for the Study of Trauma and Dissociation Guidelines for Treating Dissociative Identity Disorder in Adults, Third Revision'. *Journal of Trauma & Dissociation*, 12, 2, pp. 115–187.

Doychak, K., and Raghavan, C. (2023). 'Trauma-Coerced Attachment: Developing DSM-5's Dissociative Disorder "Identity Disturbance Due to Prolonged and Intense Coercive Persuasion"'. *European Journal of Trauma and Dissociation*, 7, 2. https://doi.org/10.1016/j.ejtd.2023.100323.

Dushinsky, R. (2020). *Cornerstones of Attachment Theory.* Oxford: Oxford University Press. doi:10.1093/med-psych/9780198842064.001.0001.

Gleaves, D.H., and Bennett, A.A. (2023). 'Stigma Regarding Dissociative Disorders'. *Journal of Trauma and Dissociation*, 24, 3, pp. 317–320. doi:10.1080/15299732.2023.2191240.

Guilding, M. (2020). 'What Is Complex Trauma? Perspectives On Complex Trauma'. *Journal of the Complex Trauma Institute*, 1, 1, pp. 3–17.

Heard, D., and Lake, B. (1997). *The Challenge of Attachment for Caregiving.* London: Routledge.

Heard, D., Lake, B., and McCluskey, U. (2009). *Attachment Therapy with Adolescents and Adults: Theory and Practice Post Bowlby.* London: Karnac.

Hoffman, W. (2014). *The Enslaved Queen: A Memoir About Electricity and Mind Control.* London: Karnac.

Hoffman, W. (2016). *White Witch in a Black Robe: A True Story About Criminal Mind Control.* London: Karnac.

Hopenwasser, K. (2008). 'Being in Rhythm: Dissociative Attunement in Therapeutic Process'. *Journal of Trauma and Dissociation*, 9, 3, pp. 349–369.

Itzkowitz, S., Chefetz, R., Hainer, M., Hopenwasser, K., and Howell, E.F. (2015). 'Exploring Dissociation and Dissociative Identity Disorder: A Roundtable Discussion'. *Psychoanalytic Perspectives*, 12, 1, pp. 39–79.

Keating, L., Muller, R.T., and Classon, C.C. (2018). 'Changes in Attachment Organisation, Emotion, Dysregulation and Interpersonal Problems Among Women in Women in Treatment for Abuse'. *Journal of Trauma and Dissociation*, 19, 2, pp. 247–266.

Koren-Karie, N., Sagi-Schwartz, A., and Joels, T. (2003). 'Absence of Attachment Representations (AAR) in the Adult Years: The Emergence of a New AAI Classification in Catastrophically Traumatized Holocaust Child Survivors'. *Attachment and Human Development*, 5, 4, pp. 381–397.

Lacter, E.P. (2011). 'Torture-Based Mind Control: Psychological Mechanisms and Psychotherapeutic Approached to Overcoming Mind Control', in Badouk Epstein, O., Schwartz, J., and Wingfield Schwartz, R. (eds), *Ritual Abuse and Mind Control: The Manipulation of Attachment Needs.* London: Karnac, pp. 57–141.

LeDoux, J.E. (2015). *Anxious: Using the Brain to Understand and Treat Fear and Anxiety.* New York: Viking.

Liotti, G. (1999). 'Disorganization of Attachment as Model for Understanding Dissociative Psychopathology', in Solomon, J., and George, C. (eds), *Attachment Disorganization.* London: Guilford, pp. 291–317.

Liotti, G. (2004). 'Trauma, Dissociation, and Disorganized Attachment: Three Strands of a Single Braid'. *Psychotherapy: Theory, Research, Practice, Training*, 41, 4, pp. 472–486. https://doi.org/10.1037/0033-3204.41.4.472.

Liotti, G. (2006). 'A Model of Dissociation Based on Attachment Theory and Research'. *Journal of Trauma and Dissociation*, 7, 4, pp. 55–73.

Lyons-Ruth, K., Yellin, C., Melnick, S., and Atwood, G. (2005). 'Expanding the Concept of Unresolved Mental States: Hostile/Helpless States of Mind on the Adult Attachment Interview Are Associated with Disrupted Mother-Infant Communication and Infant Disorganization'. *Development and Psychopathology*, 17, 1, pp. 1–23. doi:10.1017/s0954579405050017.

Main, M., and Hesse, E. (1990). 'Parents' Unresolved Traumatic Experiences Are Related to Infant Disorganised Attachment Status: Is Frightened or/or Frightening

Behaviour the Linking Mechanism?', in Greenberg, M.T., Cicchetti, D., and Cummings, E.M. (eds), *Attachment in the Preschool Years*. Chicago, IL: University of Chicago Press, pp. 161–182.

Mesman, J.M.H., van IJzendoorn, M.H., and Sagi-Schwartz, A. (2008). 'Cross-Cultural Patterns of Attachment: Universal and Contextual Dimension', in Cassidy, J., & Shaver, P.R. (eds), *Handbook of Attachment: Theory Research, and Clinical Application*. New York: Guilford Press, pp. 790–815.

Middleton, W. (2013). 'Ongoing Incestuous Abuse During Adulthood'. *Journal of Trauma and Dissociation*, 14, 3, pp. 251–272.

Middleton, W., Sachs, A., and Dorahy, M. (2017). 'The Abused and the Abuser: Victim–Perpetrator Dynamics'. *Journal of Trauma and Dissociation*, 18, 3, pp. 249–258.

Mikulincer, M., and Shaver, P.R. (eds) (2007). *Attachment in Adulthood: Structure, Dynamics, and Change*. New York: Guilford.

Miller, A. (2012). *Healing the Unimaginable: Treating Ritual Abuse and Mind Control*. London: Karnac.

Moss, E., St-Laurent, D., and Parent, S. (1999). 'Disorganised Attachment and Developmental Risk at School Age', in Solomon, J., and George, C. (eds), *Attachment Disorganization*. London: Guilford, p. 160.

Motley Crew (2011). 'What's It Like? Alters/Parts'. *Multiple Parts*, 1, 1, p. 12.

Reinders, A.A., and Veltman, D.J. (2021). 'Dissociative Identity Disorder: Out of the Shadows At Last?'. *The British Journal of Psychiatry*, 219(2), pp. 413–414. https://doi.org/10.1192/bjp. 2020.168.

Richardson, S. (2010). 'Reaching for Relationship: Exploring the Use of an Attachment Paradigm in the Assessment and Repair of the Dissociative Internal World'. *Attachment: New Directions in Psychotherapy and Relational Psychoanalysis*, 4, 1, pp. 7–25.

Sachs, A. (2007). 'Infanticidal Attachment: Symbolic and Concrete'. *Attachment: New Directions in Psychotherapy and Psychanalysis*, 1, 3, pp. 297–304.

Sachs, A. (2013). 'Still Being Hurt: The Vicious Cycle of Dissociative Disorders, Attachment & Ongoing Abuse'. *Attachment: New Directions in Psychotherapy and Psychanalysis*, 7, 1, pp. 90–100.

Salter, M. (2017). 'Organized Abuse in Adulthood: Survivor and Professional Perspectives'. *Journal of Trauma & Dissociation*, 18, 3, pp. 441–453. https://doi.org/10.1080/15299732.2017.1295426.

Salter, M. (2023). 'Presidential Editorial: The Facts and Fantasies of Dissociation'. *Journal of Trauma & Dissociation*, 24,: 1, pp. 1–7. doi:10.1080/15299732.2022.2157620.

Schimmenti, A. (2017). 'Traumatic Identification'. *Attachment: New Directions in Psychotherapy and Psychanalysis*, 11, 2, pp. 154–171.

Schore, A. (2003). *Affect Regulation and Disorders of the Self*. London: Norton.

Schore, A. (2012). *The Science of the Art of Psychotherapy*. London: Norton.

Schwartz, H.L. (2013). *The Alchemy of Wolves and Sheep: A Relational Approach to Internalized Perpetration in Complex Trauma Survivors*. London: Routledge.

Sinason, V. (2017). 'Dying for Love: An Attachment Problem with Some Perpetrator Introjects'. *Journal of Trauma and Dissociation*, 18, 3, pp. 340–355.

Sinason, V. (2020). *The Truth About Trauma and Dissociation: Everything You Didn't Want to Know and Were Afraid to Ask*. London: Confer Books.

Steele, H. (2002). 'Multiple Dissociation in the Context of the Adult Attachment Interview: Observations from Interviewing Individuals with Dissociative Identity

Disorder', in Sinason, V. (ed.), *Attachment, Trauma and Multiplicity*. London: Brunner-Routledge, pp. 107–121.

Steinberg, M., and Schnall, M. (2001). *The Stranger in the Mirror, Dissociation – The Hidden Epidemic*. New York: HarperCollins.

van der Hart, O., Nijenhuis, E., and Steele, K. (2006). *The Haunted Self: Structural Dissociation and Chronic Traumatization*. London: Norton.

van der Hart, O., and Dorahy, M.J. (2009). 'History of the Concept of Dissociation', in Dell, P., and O'Neil, J.A. (eds), *Dissociation and the Dissociative Disorders*. London: Routledge, pp. 3–26.

Chapter 1

Using an Attachment-Based Model to Understand and Work with People with Dissociative Identities

Mark Linington

Introduction

I have trained with Una McCluskey, a psychoanalytic psychotherapist, researcher and author, for more than ten years in an attachment theory model that has developed from the work of Ainsworth (1979; Ainsworth et al., 1978), Bowlby (1969, 1974, 1980, 1988) and Heard and Lake (1997). The training uses one's own relational experience and attachment and object relations theory to understand and work with the operation of attachment-based systems in relationships. A key element of the training is the use of one's own supported explorations and those of others, in understanding and supporting a person to develop the operation of their attachment-based systems across the life cycle and to understand the diverse ways in which these systems can function in relationships. A fundamental consideration within these explorations is the ways in which these systems do or do not function to support one's sense of security and well-being in the external world and in relationships with others.

Through these explorations the understanding and theory which underpins this attachment model continues to develop. As further experiences and thinking are explored, more can be understood about the diverse ways in which these attachment-based systems can function in oneself and in relationships is achieved. I have been particularly interested throughout this training to explore how this model might be used therapeutically with people who are living with dissociative identities. It has been recognised that this remains an area that needs to be further understood. In Heard, Lake and McCluskey (2009), after some research, the authors decided that "dissociation is too big a topic to discuss in this book" (p. 73).

A Manipulation of and Attack on the Human Need for Attachment

We all have a need to attach to another person. Many people's dissociative identities have arisen from chronic and severe traumatic, abusive interpersonal

DOI: 10.4324/9781032696720-2

experiences, often involving other people or someone with whom the person has a significant, often primary, attachment relationship. These dissociative identities rarely originate in a single abusive experience but are a consequence of repeated abusive experiences taking place in early life and continuing over a prolonged period, often into adulthood. Some people with dissociative identities still have contact with others in which they are severely abused. This may not solely be because we might all have a tendency to seek out familiar patterns of relationships, especially if we have not been helped to find alternative patterns of relationships. We also know that perpetrators often intentionally manipulate the people they abuse in a way which maintains these abusive relationships. Such perpetrators can sometimes utilise, or even deliberately develop, the fragmented aspects of a person's dissociative identities to ensure the continuation of this abuse-based attachment.

We know that people with dissociative identities have many aspects of their selves severely damaged and fragmented by terrible abusive experiences with others. We also know that the dissociative aspects, whereby one identity does not know consciously about the abuse that has occurred, but rather this knowledge is held by another identity (or identities), have often helped to ensure the person's physical and psychological survival in extreme circumstances. "Survival" here means both the best attempt at preserving one's own mental health and well-being and the preservation of the best possible attachment relationships, even where these are with someone who is abusive.

Attachment-Based Systems and Dissociative Identities

The work of Dorothy Heard and Brian Lake (1997), and then later including and further developed by Una McCluskey (2005; McCluskey and O'Toole, 2020; Heard et al., 2009), originated in the work of John Bowlby (1969, 1974, 1980), who explored the nature and functioning of human relationships from an attachment perspective. Bowlby's focus was specifically on the interactions between the careseeking system, most often that of an infant or a child, and the caregiving system of someone who is their primary attachment figure (most often a parent). In addition, he explored the operation of the fear (self-defence) system.

Heard, Lake and McCluskey (2009) developed this thinking to include further considerations of adult relationships, with an inclusion of further attachment-based systems. These included the interest sharing and sexuality systems which shape interactions in peer relationships, in which neither partner, in Bowlby's terms, is "older and wiser".

The seven attachment-based systems are: careseeking, caregiving, self-defence, interest-sharing, sexuality, the internal environment and the external environment. I have described them as attachment-based systems, because each of these systems, whilst being biologically hard wired through evolutionary processes, are also significantly shaped by our experiences in our early attachment relationships, that is, the relationships in which we receive care as careseekers, as well as other later experiences in relationships. In this context, system means an internal organised pattern of feelings, thinking, behaviours and relational expectations. Although the organisation of the different systems may well appear disorganised in the way it manifests in relationships, even this disorganisation can be understood as meaningfully patterned, in the context of earlier abusive relational life experiences.

Caregiving

Caregiving is the provision of help in response to another, who is either careseeking or looking to explore. There are two broad types of caregiving:

- Type 1: The provision of help to another who is in a state of emotional dysregulation and who needs some soothing or comforting of those emotional experiences. This type of caregiving is sometimes expressed as providing a "safe haven" (Powell et al., 2014).
- Type 2: The provision of a secure base that supports the person in the exploration of their internal or external worlds. This form of caregiving can be present as interest, delight, attention, guidance and encouragement to the person, in their autonomous but relationally connected explorations in the world.

One can see how these two forms of caregiving might be especially important with regard to providing psychotherapy and how giving the wrong type of care is often at the foundation of interpersonal experiences of misattunement for a person. Another aspect of caregiving that I have found to be important in work with people, especially with those who have had the sort of abusive trauma experiences seen in people with dissociative identities, is to consider how the caregiving system provides care to other identities internally.

Careseeking

This system is apparent in the way that a person seeks help when they are in a state of need. Many people with dissociative identities have experienced relationships with frightening attachment figures (Slade, 2013). The careseeking patterns of avoidant, anxious and disorganised attachment (Main et al., 1985, 2005; Main and Solomon, 1986) are relevant here, emerging as a result of the caregiver's responses to them repeatedly, over time.

The goal of this attachment system is to have one's needs responded to and met as this system, like the caregiving system, is goal corrected (Bowlby, 1969). When the goal of careseeking is met, the system stops being active and the person in a secure relationship experiences relief and becomes exploratory. Where people have had a fear-filled experience of caregiving, this system may fail to reach its goal and a person may continue to seek care in a distressed way. For some people with abusive experiences, their careseeking system can be entangled with their self-defence system, as caregiving which appears to be satisfying may well have been a prelude to sadistic abuse.

Self Defence

The fear system is part of the self defence system, the defensive or protective self. The instinctive responses of fight, flight, freeze, fawn (pleasing others) and collapse, are biologically based strategies that are used by human beings. These strategies are used for survival in frightening situations when no supportive caregiver is available for help. As with all of the systems, but perhaps most noticeable with the self defence system, is the tendency we might all have, particularly if we have experienced repeated abusive relational trauma from a young age, to utilise the same ways of protecting ourselves that we employed when we were younger. Sometimes these strategies are used in situations which are not necessarily as threatening as the past, but which might feel, sometimes unconsciously, to be so. Awareness of this possibility can be an important part of providing psychotherapy to a person with childhood abusive experiences.

Over time and with the right support we might begin to be able to utilise different ways of protecting ourselves that are more effective. Most importantly, the development of a more effective and supportive careseeking system is key to managing frightening situations in a different way.

Interest Sharing

This system can be considered both regarding interests engaged with alone, and interests shared in peer relationships. The goal of the system is to experience a satisfying closeness in peer relationships based upon a common interest, or the engagement with interest alone. An important feature of this system is that it is to some extent distinct from the attachment dynamic, although it is also influenced by earlier relational experiences of careseeking to caregiving. For people who have had traumatising experiences of attachment it is sometimes emotionally and relationally easier to engage in this system, as it can provide a way of avoiding the distressing dynamics that are associated with the operation of the caregiving and careseeking systems.

In work with people with dissociative identities, the development of the interest sharing system can provide a path to a relationship in which there is some respite from the painful experiences of the earlier abusive caregiving–careseeking relationship. This has often been the case in which the person has experienced being trapped in an abusive relationship as a child, where being able to find some interest has been a welcome refuge from the terrifying and painful abuse.

Sexuality

This system is concerned with sexual identity, sexual feelings and sexual behaviour. The goal of this system is to have a close and satisfying sexual relationship. Often, given the experience of many people with dissociative identities of sexually abusive relationships, this area can feel a very frightening self-system. Where a system is experienced as frightening because of its connections to severe abusive trauma, there can be a confused entanglement between systems, or where one system functions as a screen system for another system. For example, where the sexual system is entangled with careseeking where the person is trying to have their needs for help met through the use of sexual behaviour. Another possible way of managing difficulties with this system, where the experience of sexuality, due to sexual abuse, has become overwhelmingly frightening, is to segregate the system from consciousness or to deactivate it completely (Bowlby, 1962). Although both of these segregation and deactivation strategies might be utilised within any system that is felt to be frightening, it seems most common in work with people with dissociative identities for these strategies to be used in relation to both the careseeking and the sexual systems.

Internal Environment

The internal environment develops from a person's relational and lived experiences. A key shaper of the person's internal environment is the early attachment experiences with their attachment figure. People who have had abusive experiences of attachment, and have developed structural dissociation as a result, have a segregated, internal environment, where there can be a lack of connection between different aspects of themselves and their mental representations of relationships. A frequent feature of the internal environment for people with dissociative identities is that there can be harsh, critical, sometimes persecutory, internal relationships and messages. Such internal relationships and messages can have a protective relational function. The person may blame themselves and become the object of their own anger, to safeguard the good representation of their attachment relationships (cf. Fairbairn's "moral defence", 1952). Helping the person recognise and understand this harshness in their internal environment, with its self-protective function, can be an important area within therapy.

The internal environment can reflect the operation of the different attachment-based systems and messages about the person based on real, relational experiences. For example, there can be an internal, harshly critical caregiver who is punishing towards different aspects of the person; and/or an internal distressed careseeking part that is frightened that close relationships cause harm; and/or an internal message that the person does not deserve to share their interests with another, as well as other internal messages, or working models of relationships that negatively influence the operation of their different attachment-based systems.

External Environment

The function of this system is to create a safe, external environment that supports the well-being of the self or selves. This system is concerned with how our home, or the external environment we have created for ourselves, supports our well-being. Often the external environment can become a location into which we project our internal environment and attachment experiences. For example, we might neglect our external environment as a representation or parallel of the neglect we have experienced in our attachment relationships.

Keystone Systems

> A further development in the understanding of the internal and external dynamics of the seven attachment-based systems, has been that of the *keystone system*.
>
> (McCluskey and O'Toole, 2020)

> The idea of a keystone system allows us to think that a person may function primarily from the basis of using one of the biologically based aspects of the relational self to sustain well- being. The person will prioritise that aspect of their life at the expense of all others. For example, someone with an unresolved caregiving self might prioritise caregiving to others. In this case the caregiving self becomes their keystone system.
>
> (McCluskey and O'Toole, 2020, p. 8)

For a person with dissociative identities, it often seems that the different attachment-based symptoms have become located singly in different identities as that particular identity's keystone system. For example, often a protective role will be adopted by one or more identities and a distressed careseeking role by another. Sometimes the predominance of one system has been manipulatively induced in a particular identity as a sort of "job" for them to do.

The work with different identities' keystone systems involves the recognition of the ways in which specific identities may be making use of a particular system to try, as best they can, to ensure the safety and well-being of either themselves as an individual identity, or some or all of the other internal identities. Having recognised how each identity makes use of their keystone system, it can then become possible to reflect on whether this is truly effective in ensuring the well-being of themselves and other identities, and whether there is a post-traumatic constriction in place, whereby other systems, for example supportive careseeking, might also be developed to ensure a higher degree of safety and well-being.

The Restorative Process: The Aim of Psychotherapy

The restorative process (Heard, Lake and McCluskey, 2009) is the way (in which) the seven systems outlined above work to attempt to restore a person's security and well-being in whatever threatening environment they find themselves. If the environment is interpersonally threatening, that is, the person is not in a secure environment (cf. Bowlby's "environment of evolutionary adaptedness" Bowlby, 1969), the systems can find a way in response to the caregiving available to ensure the best possible well-being and continued survival in that environment. The operation of the systems in this original childhood environment often do not work well to ensure their well-being in a new adult environment. In therapy we try to help the person find "a new developmental trajectory" (McCluskey and O'Toole, 2020) for the operation of their seven attachment-based systems whereby the systems function in the current environment to support the person's well-being.

People with dissociative identities have usually developed them as a way of protecting themselves from often terrifying situations and the way they negatively impact on their well-being. As with the operation of their attachment-based systems, their dissociation, with its different features, whilst it may have helped in the original abusive traumatic situations, is often not helpful to them in their present-day, adult life. Given these attempted restorative adaptations, the therapeutic relationship aims to find and create a more adaptive model in their experience of their present day emotional and relational life. This may include some of the following psychotherapeutic tasks.

- To recognise the different keystone systems of the different identities. The keystone system is often the way of relating for a person or identity which provided the greatest security in the relational environment in which it developed. Empathically recognising with each of the person's different identities, the significance to them of this system, its purpose in their early life, and the way in which it functions in their life now, can become *a locus of connection* between the therapist and the identity.
- From this initial establishment of security with the person, it can become possible to begin to explore with the person's identities other attachment-based systems. An understanding can be built together about how they operate in their current life and relationships, how these systems operated, and the function they served, in their earlier relationships, including in interpersonal abusive situations.
- Understanding with the different identities, and between identities as carefully shared knowledge, how the self defence system becomes active and operates, and particularly its relationship to the careseeking system. Of particular importance is the relationship between the way the self-defence system operates for survival when no safe caregiver is available to

provide help leading to the use of fight, flight, freeze, fawn and collapse, and the person's ability, often truncated, to seek care.

- Alongside this therapeutic process, supporting the development of more connected and supportive relationships between the different identities and empathically recognising with them the attachment-based systems that each of the identities use, and how they use them with each other and others in the external world, is vital to developing more effective, present day ways in which well-being can be restored. This part of the therapeutic process needs to take careful account of any dissociative barriers that exist between identities. Overall, a guide to this development of internal connection, communication and collaboration can be that the different identities indicate they are feeling secure enough to explore this area.

In exploring with each identity and across their self-system (Sullivan, 1954) the ways in which the attachment-based systems can develop to promote increased well-being, two aspects of this new developmental trajectory seem to be important. Firstly, the development of the *range* of systems which operate within each identity. For example, where an identity is very focused on self-defence by making use of angry fighting, or a frightened running away, the development of an increased operation of the other systems in a healthier way can be supported.

Secondly, enabling the development of the *supportive* rather than traumatised or unsupportive characteristics of the attachment-based systems to operate in relationships can also make an increased contribution to a more secure sense of well-being. This can be developed for example by reflecting with the identity on the impact on their well-being, and that of other identities, of using a system in a particular way and by exploring the historical relational origin of this system's way of operating.

Assessment of the Attachment-Based Systems

As part of any assessment of a person with dissociative identities, or indeed anyone who is considering psychotherapy as a form of help, it can be very helpful, in my experience, to consider what is known about the operation of the different systems for their different identities as far as they are known at any point. As part of this assessment, together with a more general psychotherapy assessment that considers family history, history of any known trauma, risk areas and so on, and an assessment of their dissociative symptoms using the Structured Clinical Interview of Dissociative Disorders (SCID-D), each identity that is known is assessed regarding how the seven attachment-based systems function for them. The keystone system for each identity is recognised where possible. Each system is considered concerning whether it functions effectively to support the self as a whole and their well-being, whether it is unsupportive to their well-being and whether it operates in a way that is indicative of past relational trauma.

Clinical Example: Bridget

In the following clinical example, I describe my work with Bridget and her different identities through the lens of the attachment-based systems outlined above. I have divided the work into three periods, as a way of trying to show the developments that took place over time. I have represented the relationship between Bridget's different identities and the different attachment-based systems diagrammatically.

Referral and Assessment

Bridget was a 35-year-old white woman, with a mild to borderline intellectual disability whom I saw for five and half years, twice a week, as part of my private work as an attachment-based psychoanalytic psychotherapist. She has given me permission to talk about her and our work together in a non-identifying way.

Bridget was referred by her psychiatrist who was concerned about the increasing amount of time Bridget reported not knowing what had happened in her day-to-day life. The psychiatrist wondered if there might be a dissociative aspect to these experiences. He was also concerned about Bridget's ongoing contacts with an ex-partner who had been violent towards her and her neglect of herself concerning aspects of life such as eating enough and bathing. Bridget had reportedly made suicide attempts earlier in her life by taking overdoses and threatening to throw herself under a train. She had had periods where she had cut herself severely enough to require medical attention. It was unclear as to how current these risks might be. Bridget was described as a very secretive person, who could not always be trusted to tell the truth about things that were happening in her life. She had a part time job as a cleaner in a health centre and one day a week she attended a local farm as a volunteer where she looked after animals with other people.

The psychiatrist thought I might be able to help Bridget, as I had some experience in providing psychotherapy to people with intellectual disabilities who also struggled with complex mental health issues and abusive trauma. At this time there were no known abusive traumas in Bridget's very early life. It was known that she had had some very difficult loss experiences and that she had experienced sexual abuse by a neighbour in her young teenage years. Both of her parents had died: her mother from pancreatic cancer when she was a young girl aged nine, and her father when she was in her twenties and still living with him. In addition, Bridget was also able to describe difficulties with a past abusive relationship with a partner, to whom she was believed periodically to return. She knew she tended to contact others who might cause her harm and had got into difficulties several times with men that she had met on the street. In the assessment she described how she would often lose track of exactly how she ended up having contact with such men, saying that she had experience of a sort of "dark fog" coming down and then later found herself in dangerous sexual situations with these men.

Although Bridget's dissociation and her identities were not clearly apparent at the point of referral, one potential indicator, along with the descriptions of losing time and the "dark fog", were how her first attempts at coming to see me for an assessment were thwarted by her going into an apparently dissociated state. She described having known that she had an appointment with me, falling asleep, then waking in a panic, and when she set off on the bus to see me there was a moment as she came near to the clinic when she said the fog came down, and she found herself sometime later looking at dolls and prams in a shop.

We were able to speak together on the phone about this experience and make a new appointment. She later told me that she was able to come to the new appointment with me, because I had not angrily punished her for not coming, had understood that she was probably frightened about coming to see me, and had reached out to her to make contact. These three features: a strong expectation of punishment, the significance of empathy, particularly for fearful feelings, and the responsiveness of me as an attachment figure, continued to be significant throughout my work with Bridget and with her other identities as they eventually came forward.

In the assessment, we considered her potential dissociative experiences, including the five symptom areas of amnesia, depersonalisation, derealisation, identity confusion and alteration. When asked about the experience of whether there were others, or a sense of struggle inside, she was able to describe how she was aware that sometimes she could hear an internal conversation going on, often with a huge amount of angry feelings. She was able to describe some of her different identities, or "the other ones inside". She was able to tell me that the identity whom she thought communicated these angry feelings was someone she called "She-Wolf", and that there was also another who wanted to go out to contact men. She had experienced hearing something from these others since her early life.

She said she had not talked about this before in her contacts with mental health and social services, because she was concerned that people would think that she was "mad" and that she would be "locked up again". She also said no one had ever asked her these sorts of questions before. Bridget said that she had previously been admitted to a mental hospital when she had had a "breakdown" after her father died from a heart attack when he was at the supermarket. She described how she lost a lot of time after this shock and ended up living on the streets. Somehow, she became involved with a drug gang and was picked up by the police. Following this, she had a vague memory of going to a mental health hospital, but she was not able to describe many details about how she came to be admitted.

As part of this assessment, I noted that it was possible to see the operation of the different attachment-based systems including across her different identities. These are summarised in Table 1.1.

It is apparent from this initial assessment that:

a there seem to be different keystone systems held by different identities.

b that despite the abusive trauma and difficult experiences of loss, some of Bridget's and her other identities' attachment-based systems functioned in a way that supported their well-being.

c there seemed to be some ways in which these systems operated insecurely and did not support Bridget and the others' well-being. In addition, there were more severe examples of the systems operating in a way that seemed a repetitive consequence of the trauma they had experienced.

Table 1.1 An initial assessment of Bridget's attachment-based systems

System	Supportive	Unsupportive	Traumatised
Careseeking	Some ability to ask for help	Some identities unable to seek help from others	Highly distressed careseeking is active in an infiltrating way in other systems, e.g., sexuality
Caregiving	Cares for animals and expresses care for other people in a general sense	No internal caregiving process seems apparent	Very angry verbal attacks on caregivers for their failures
Self Defence	Has a desire to protect themselves from further harm	Anger in relational interactions disproportionate to the real situation	Unable to protect themselves in dangerous situations; aims "fight" at body/other identity as self-harm and suicide attempts
Interest-Sharing	Shares interest in animals with others	Anxious that others are not as interested as them	Sometimes withdraws from interests
Sexuality	Has the desire for a warm and affectionate sexual contact	Cannot read relationships regarding others' sexual interest in them well	Replaying of abusive sexual situations
Internal Environment	Has some awareness of some features of their internal environment	Disconnected in their internal environment with low levels of compassion and high levels of criticism	Punishing internal environment with messages about blame and feelings of shame
External Environment	Is concerned to make their external environment more supportive and has made some attempts to achieve this	Has periods where they are unable to attend to their external environment	Sometimes other identities do destructive things to their external environment

First Period of Work

Following the assessment, we agreed that we would start working together. From the beginning of the work, Bridget began to describe a number of different identities with whom she was familiar. Her known identities at this time were herself as Bridget, an identity called She-Wolf, and Bride. She described She-Wolf as "very angry" and "scary". She said She-Wolf would often shout at people, especially men she had had romantic relationships with, and sometimes inside She-Wolf would shout at her and blame her for getting into relationships with these men. She thought it could be She-Wolf who harmed her/the body. She also described the identity she called Bride, whom she said she knew less, but whom she thought was very lonely and always looking to try and find a man to marry her. She thought it was this identity who made different contacts with men and got them into difficult situations in which Bridget thought, based on injuries she noticed, that they were sometimes, perhaps frequently, sexually assaulted. Bridget described often feeling angry with Bride for getting them into these situations, although she thought that she would also like to have a close relationship with a man at times.

Figure 1.1 is a visual representation showing what I knew of the different identities during this first period of the psychotherapy. It shows the attachment-based systems which seemed to be operating as keystone systems for each of these identities, and the apparent dissociative barrier that seemed to have some permeability at times, and which appeared to be in place regarding the relationship between Bridget and Bride. She-Wolf also seemed to have no connection with Bride at this time.

Work with She-Wolf

During this time, I worked with She-Wolf to reflect on and understand more about her fear and hatred of others, both external and internal, and her

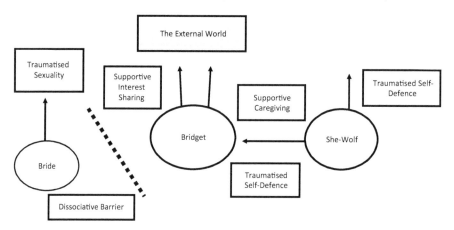

Figure 1.1 Period 1: Bridget's identities and attachment-based systems

behaving in a verbally aggressive, and at times physically violent, way towards others that she thought might represent a threat to her. This expression of defensive anger included me as her psychotherapist; indeed she initially strongly expressed it towards the idea of having psychotherapy at all, at external others, most strongly men, and at Bridget.

She-Wolf saw Bridget as responsible for having put them into all harmful abusive situations in the past because she was not able to see the dangers in situations or understand that other people can be dangerous. Understanding the function of this feeling, thinking and behaviour with She-Wolf as a way of protecting herself/themselves from harm and thinking with her about possible other ways in which she might protect herself, and others inside, from such danger and injury gradually began to reduce the aggressive way in which She-Wolf related, and raised the question of seeking help from others. In attachment-based systems terms this was about the development of the careseeking system.

Establishing a relationship with her in which she felt empathically better understood, and her value recognised, took about a year and a half. Having established this more secure relationship with me and being able to think about the way she interacted with me in detail over many sessions, including thinking about the connections to her relational history, gradually began to broaden out to the way she related to others externally. At the same time, it was noticeable that she might still return to an aggressive way of relating in situations in which she was particularly fearful of violence.

Work with Bridget

I looked first to find the locus of connection with Bridget to begin to develop a secure enough relationship with her. This involved first making a link with the two relatively supportive keystone systems of *interest sharing*, apparent in her relationships with others at the local farm where they would share knowledge and experience about the animals, and *caregiving* towards the animals. It was noticeable that she could recognise and respond to animals when they were in need; although she sometimes saw others as being neglectful of them and their needs, which would elicit a deep fury in her. Interestingly, in this volunteer work, she seemed able to see and understand some aspects of the seven attachment-based systems in relation to the farm animals for whom she cared. She would notice their need for comfort (careseeking), their response to appropriate caregiving, their play (interest sharing) and their responses to having a good place to live (external environment), and the effect on them of historical mistreatment and current misattunement (self-defence). Making this connection allowed us to explore the different attachment-based systems at a safe distance from herself, and then, as relational security was further developed, to begin to think about how these things might also operate in human beings generally, and then to think of how they might be operating for her.

Work with Bride

When Bride became present in the psychotherapy sessions, she initially approached me in what seemed to be a flirtatious way. She was interested in whether I was available for a romantic relationship. I noticed that I would often feel significantly afraid when Bride became present in the sessions and sometimes would also feel an uncomfortable feeling of dread before a session, thinking about the possibility of her becoming present. To at least some extent this seemed to be connected to my being put into a sort of perpetrator-like position and was perhaps an indication of how the sexuality, careseeking and self-defence systems were all operating simultaneously.

When Bride began to understand that I was not available for some sort of sexual or romantic relationship, it seemed as though she experienced a sense of relief. Although for a long time she would keep returning to this as a possibility for our relationship, often it seemed at times of anxiety or fear. The role of fawning as part of the self defence system seemed to be operating at these times.

One development in the work in this period was that Bride and Bridget started to communicate together, initially in writing through a communication book which they set up, and then beginning to be able to have a conversation inside. They began to share something of their interests together: Bride in having some form of close relationships and Bridget in her enjoyment with animals and some of the people with whom she shared an interest in animal behaviour and their well-being.

Second Period of Work

Work with She-Wolf

In this middle period of our work together (shown in Figure 1.2), She-Wolf began to tell me more about the knowledge she held of abusive experiences she/they had in their past. This included rape by the father throughout her childhood and into her twenties, when living together with her father. She told me that her father used to regularly rape her and treat them like they were a "sort of wife" and used to sell her to his friends, who would violently sexually assault her. They still experienced significant distress about this abuse and had frequent flashbacks of some of these violent, sexual assaults. We worked together on gradually developing ways to be comforted in these experiences using type 1 caregiving and then began to work on a process of introducing them into their internal environment. During this period, She-Wolf began to seek care from me more effectively, rather than just being angry, frightened and self-defensive in their sessions. This development of the careseeking system, which was eventually developed with all identities in the psychotherapeutic relationship, provided a more secure relationship in which the processing of trauma could continue.

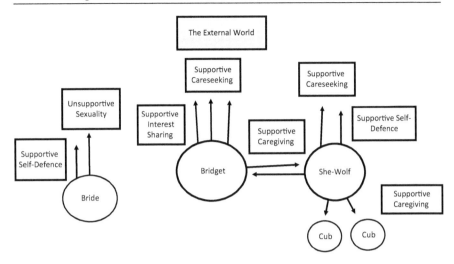

Figure 1.2 Period 2: Bridget's identities and the development of their attachment-based systems

Work About the Cubs

Over time, She-Wolf began to talk to me about her caring for her "cubs"; these seemed to represent child-like traumatised parts. She talked to me about their histories and the traumas they had experienced and how at times they struggled with flashbacks on the inside, which could in turn have an impact on She-Wolf's well-being and levels of distress. At this time, I did not meet these child-like identities, because She-Wolf was not sure if it was safe for them to come out into the external world. She said the only time they came out for short periods of time was when there was no one else around. We began by exploring what these identities needed and recognising how the caregiving provided by She-Wolf could meet their needs. She was most focused on type 1 caregiving, with an emphasis on providing comfort at times of distress. We gradually began to explore the possibility of a different sort of caregiving (type 2) that could perhaps support them in their ability to play and explore.

Work with Bridget

During this period Bridget noticed that the relationship with She-Wolf was beginning to change. Harm to the body reduced significantly and She-Wolf began to communicate with Bridget in a calmer way. They both seemed to recognise that if they could be connected in a different way and collaborate about keeping themselves safe through joint supportive self-defence and mutually supportive careseeking and caregiving, they could begin to feel better internally and their external life could also improve. Bridget began to reciprocate She-Wolf's caregiving towards her by also wondering what her needs might be. She became more able to understand She-Wolf's angry communications with her as an indication of fear about something and would either take action to make something safer, explain that the threat was perhaps not as significant as it might seem without being dismissive, and begin to explore with She-Wolf whether she might need something. She also began to draw She-Wolf's attention to the pleasure there was in the connection with the animals and the other people, and invite her to share in these good feelings.

Work with Bride

During this part of the work Bride continued to come to the psychotherapy sessions. She began to enjoy the communication with Bridget, feeling that she had someone who understood her and was concerned about her safety. She began to develop some insights into how her relational pattern of making connections to men through the sexual system was tangled up with her also wishing to find someone who might care for her. As we reflected about how the operations of these systems had been shaped by past experiences in relationships, she began to make connections to her relationship with her mother and the loss of her in childhood. She described times when her mother had cared for her in ways that fostered a strong connection, but at the same time described her mother's complicity in the abuse by her father and her profound anger that her mother had failed to protect her from her father's sexual assaults.

Third Period of the Work

Work with She-Wolf and the Cubs

During this third and final period of the psychotherapy (shown in Figure 1.3), She-Wolf began to feel safer to seek care, and a consistency began to develop in her ability to do this. As the goals of the careseeking system are met in interactions with an attuning and empathic caregiver, the feelings of relief and satisfaction that come with this feed back into the system to develop its operation in a more consistently supportive way.

In addition to this development in careseeking, she became more able to bear experiences of misattunements, or challenges in life and relationships, without going into the self-defence/ fight system. Her capacity for reflection on interactions and the supportive responses of her own attachment-based systems increased. For example, in the earlier periods of our work if I did not respond to a written communication from them quickly enough, she would take this lack of responsiveness as an indication of my not being available and not caring for her, which would elicit feelings of very angry distress.

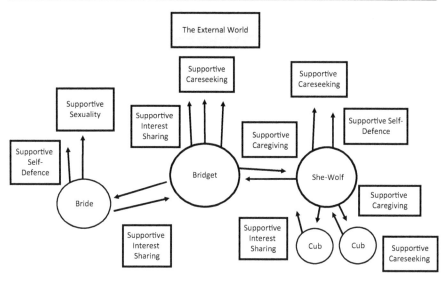

Figure 1.3 Period 3: Bridget's identities and the further development of their attachment-based systems

This distress was frequently based on the working model expectation that my caregiving was a manipulation of their attachment needs, and that my delay in responding was an indication of my sadistic pleasure in hurting her. As we were able to reflect more on such interactions, including thinking about the relationship between her careseeking system, self-defence and the messages in her internal environment, so the need to fight as a way of trying to both protect herself and get her needs met diminished.

In parallel to these developments in the way She-Wolf interacted and her ability to reflectively explore, her cubs began to emerge in the psychotherapy sessions and we were all able to consider the quality of their relationships, their historical experiences of abuse and what might develop to support their sense of well-being. The cubs were significant in further developing and understanding the role that interest sharing, often in the form of play, had for the well-being of all identities. She-Wolf was able to develop her ability to provide supportive care for her cubs, in parallel with her development of a more supportive relationship with both Bridget and Bride.

Work with Bridget

Working with Bridget to help her feel safer about having increased connection, communication and collaboration with different identities across the range of attachment-based systems was a very significant development. This process of establishing a form of internal intersubjectivity, where internal identities are related to not just as internal representations of dissociated traumatic experience, but as subjects with their own current and historical lived experience, all sharing the same physical body, was an important development step in being able to change the quality of the relationships internally.

Most notably, the relationship with She-Wolf began to change significantly. Moving from a relationship where the self-defence system, in a form of aggressive fighting, was their only form of connection and communication, an inclusion of the interest sharing systems developed between the two of them. She-Wolf was able to begin recognising Bridget's interests, her feelings of joy that could emerge when she was relating to animals and the growing development of positive friendships with other people who shared the same interests.

Work with Bride

Bride began to be able to differentiate in herself between her careseeking needs, her wish for an affectionate relationship and to understand how the representation of these needs in a sexual form were connected to some extent to her experiences of sexual abuse when she was younger. With Bridget's support, she was able to begin to develop friendships with the people at the animal farm that Bridget attended, so that this experience of interest sharing became a joint, safer and satisfying experience for them as connected identities. With this combination of developments of her attachment-based systems Bride began to have an increased sense of well-being.

Conclusion

Of course, there are many more aspects of this attachment-based work with Bridget and others that could be explored further. These could include the significance of the counter-transferential communications and relational enactments, and the use of these as part of the development of the psychotherapy, how hearing about the terrible abusive experiences worked to allow for an increased sense of recognition and empathic understanding that allowed for further development of the attachment-based systems.

The understanding of attachment-based approaches in psychotherapeutic work with people with dissociative identities is continuing to develop. For the most part, understanding of how to work with the different attachment-based systems as described in the work of Heard and Lake (1997), Heard, Lake and McCluskey (2009), McCluskey (2005) and McCluskey and O'Toole (2020) has not yet been much utilised in the work with people with dissociative identities. Hopefully this chapter offers some further understanding of how this application of attachment theory as attachment-based systems can be helpfully used in the work with those experiencing dissociative identities with a history of severe interpersonal trauma.

References

Ainsworth, M.D.S. (1979). "Attachment as Related to Mother-Infant Interaction", *Advances in the Study of Behavior*, 9, pp. 1–51.

Bowlby, J. (1962). "Defences That Follow Loss", in Duschinsky, R. and White, K. (eds), *Trauma and Loss: Key Texts from the John Bowlby Archive*. London: Routledge, pp. 17–63.

Bowlby, J. (1969). *Attachment and Loss*, Vol. 1. *Attachment*. London: Hogarth Press and the Institute of Psycho-Analysis.

Bowlby, J. (1974). *Attachment and Loss*, Vol. 2. *Separation: Anxiety and Anger*. London: Hogarth Press and the Institute of Psycho-Analysis.

Bowlby, J. (1980). *Attachment and Loss*, Vol. 3. *Loss: Sadness and Depression*. London: Hogarth Press and the Institute of Psycho-Analysis.

Bowlby, J. (1988). *A Secure Base: Clinical Applications of Attachment Theory*. London: Routledge.

Fairbairn, W.R. (1952). *Psychoanalytic Studies of the Personality*. London: Routledge.

Heard, D., and Lake, B. (1997). *The Challenge of Attachment for Caregiving*. London: Karnac.

Heard, D., Lake, B., and McCluskey, U. (2009). *Attachment Therapy with Adolescents and Adults: Theory and Practice Post Bowlby*. London: Karnac.

Main, M., Kaplan, N., and Cassidy, J. (1985). "Security in Infancy, Childhood, and Adulthood: A Move to the Level of Representation", *Monographs of the Society for Research in Child Development*, 50, pp. 66–106.

Main, M., and Solomon, J. (1986). "Discovery of a New, Insecure-Disorganized/Disoriented Attachment Pattern", in Yogman, M. and Brazelton, T.B. (eds), *Affective Development in Infancy*. Norwood, NJ: Ablex, pp. 95–124.

Main, M., Hesse, E., and Kaplan, N. (2005). "Predictability of Attachment Behavior and Representational Processes at 1, 6, and 19 Years of Age: The Berkeley Longitudinal Study", in Grossmann, K.E., Grossmann, K., and Waters, E. (eds), *Attachment from Infancy to Adulthood: The Major Longitudinal Studies*. New York: Guilford Press, pp. 245–304.

McCluskey, U. (2005). *To Be Met as a Person: The Dynamics of Attachment in Professional Encounters*. London: Karnac.

McCluskey, U., and O'Toole, M. (2020). *Transference and Countertransference from an Attachment Perspective: A Guide for Professional Caregivers*. London: Routledge.

Powell, B., Cooper, G., Hoffman, K., and Marvin, B. (2014). *The Circle of Security Intervention: Enhancing Attachment in Early Parent-Child Relationships*. New York: The Guilford Press.

Slade, A. (2013). "The Place of Fear in Attachment Theory and Psychoanalysis", in Yellin, J., and Badouk Epstein, O. (eds), *Terror Within and Without: Attachment and Disintegration: Clinical Work on the Edge*. London: Karnac, pp. 39–57.

Steinberg, M. (1994, 2023). *The SCID-D Interview: Dissociation Assessment in Therapy, Forensics and Research*. Washington, DC: APA Publishing.

Sullivan, H.S. (1954). *The Interpersonal Theory of Psychiatry*. New York: W.W. Norton.

Chapter 2

An Exploration of the Relational Dialogue Between Client and Therapist

Catherine Holland

Introduction

I want to express my deep appreciation for the hard work and dedication that has gone into organising this important Bowlby Centre conference. Bringing together professionals, experts and individuals with lived experience to discuss dissociative identity is very welcomed and I do recognise, validate and honour the huge reservoirs of courage and expertise that those living with dissociative identities have.

It was a natural progression in my career to work therapeutically with those living with dissociative identities and their families. My ongoing interests in neuroscience, and the link between early disrupted attunement and primary defences against anxiety, as well as discovering the impact of implicit memories on altered states through trauma-informed practice, has led to me embracing this area of work.

However, it took me quite some time to feel confident and capable enough to give myself permission to consider working with this client group. The idea of being able to create a safe enough clinical space to contain and work with the complexity of multiple identities/parts in one body was more frightening than the reality. Many of us are afraid of the unknown and carry our own bias. It is important to slow down and take time to notice and explore our responses to things we have yet to understand.

Working with those living with dissociative identities is an exploration into the void. Like all relationships, we seek to understand. As clinicians, we undertake a therapeutic dance moving between the exploration of an issue, noticing the activation/affect and then consolidating new perspectives that our clients have discovered as they make mindfully informed choices.

I am often asked: what is it that you actually do in a session? Well, like most therapists, I am in the moment with whatever is happening, without 'memory or desire' (Bion, 1967). I may or may not know the history, but for me, the story is less important. I aim to work with gentle curiosity, clarifying what is being said or not said. I look for patterns that are emerging and take time to slow down any activated energy or what some people call triggers,

DOI: 10.4324/9781032696720-3

both in myself and in the client in the transference/countertransference. I unpick past from present and use my relational self to understand dynamics.

> Attachment based therapists or those working with a trauma informed practice will be well versed in this methodology when working therapeutically. So, what is different about dissociative identity? We all dissociate. It is a normal everyday experience that ranges from mild forms of daydreaming and spacing out. The more severe forms that we find in complex PTSD and complex dissociation are different in nature and entail a different approach so that clients can learn to engage their prefrontal cortex as they discover themselves through parts work.
>
> (Fisher, 2017, p. 157)

Dissociative identity is yet again different because the presence of two or more separate individual self-states or identities within an individual. These identities are distinct, have their own unique experiences, memories, thoughts, emotions and behaviours. These self-states may have different names, accents, ages, genders, interests and physical health conditions.

My First Encounter with Dissociative Identity: Jan

To put some context around my own journey leading to working with this client group, my first encounter with dissociative identity happened when I met Jan. I recognised how accomplished she seemed to be at everything. She studied medicine, was gifted musically, excelled at sports, enjoyed the arts, was socially adept, politically astute and knew how to party. Jan came from a prominent family and had quite a comfortable lifestyle.

I had got to know Jan when we worked together one summer. Jan discovered that I was going to university in the same city where she was training and convinced me that we should share a flat instead of following my intention to go into halls of residence. I bought into the idea, and everything was easy and wonderful for a while. Jan was my flatmate, and I was 19.

Slowly I began to feel bewildered by her rapidly changing plans. I felt blindsided by the incongruence between the person I thought I knew and the one that I was now sharing a flat with. I did not think much of it until Jan's level of unpredictability and anxious behaviour became rather extreme and her distress began to disrupt my own studies and social arrangements.

Despite all of Jan's achievements and advantages, I noticed how she struggled with feelings of inadequacy and dissatisfaction which belied how she presented to the outside world. She would often speak about how she felt she was not living up to her full potential and that she was never truly happy. I began to wonder what was going on as one moment there was unbearable distress and the next, Jan was living the dream, energised and competent with whatever she was turning her mind to, indicating no connection to the previously felt state. To say I was discombobulated would be an understatement. Jan certainly assaulted my reality of who I thought she was, but I considered her a friend and continued to try and understand what was unfolding.

Everything felt rather confusing to me but one day I got frightened when she showed me her hidden scars and told me about her suicide attempts. The unthought known became known as I listened to the unspoken (Bollas, 2017). Jan had islands of conversations that were disconnected and often not remembered. I felt suffocated by Jan's contradictory perspectives, as I struggled with frustration and anger in trying to figure out what was going on. I began to walk on 'eggshells' to prevent reactive outbursts. I withdrew and began to make plans to take flight to halls of residence. I wanted out of this situation and did not want the responsibility of Jan's mental health issues.

It was at this point a part of Jan made themselves known to me and tried to explain what I now have language for: parts with different identities. This was at a time where there was no internet and no access to the understanding we have nowadays. There was very little information available then for what at that time was known as multiple personalities. It was a time when those living with dissociative identity were called 'liars' or misunderstood and mis-diagnosed as psychotic or personality disordered. It was not a safe time for women, who are thought to be nine times more likely than men to have this condition, to seek supportive help, as historical stigmatisation, misdiagnosis and mistreatment of traditional gender roles as well as social stigma conspired to oppress perspectives and challenges of women's mental health awareness.

I stayed.

Throughout the next year, I learnt from experience how to engage and communicate with whichever identity was making themselves available. I made mistakes. I discovered that you do not share with one part what you have learnt from another as this causes severe distress. Jan had no idea that she had multiple identities. All she knew is that she often could not remember things. I began to realise the enormity of amnesic states and how their presence can make it difficult for those living with dissociative identities to maintain consistent relationships, employment and other aspects of daily life. These amnesic states may be a protective mechanism helping to manage traumatic experiences or may act out something that is unresolved and not in conscious awareness.

I also discovered that it was an extreme adverse childhood experience that activated the first split off part and subsequently learnt how other parts were 'born' to provide what I now understand to be a protector function against stress and overwhelm. I developed a compassion for the distress and whilst I did not have words for the part who got on with normal life, I did have a very lived experience of being relationally alongside dissociative identities.

Being friends with Jan was challenging. It was difficult at times to navigate the various parts and find ways of maintaining consistent communication and continuity in the friendship.

This had the following impact:

- I became rather hypervigilant.
- I was tentative about self-expression as I did not want to activate a trigger and cause dysregulation.
- Boundaries and expectations of being a supportive friend were confusing.
- I felt isolated and totally out of my depth and wondered about my own sense of the world.
- For those of you in friendships/relationships or living with dissociative identities do consider seeking additional support from a skilled counsellor or therapist to help build effective communication and coping skills.

At the same time, friendship with Jan was also remarkable and interesting. When she was not distressed, she was capable of incredible achievements, and I gained much from those 18 months of discovery that has informed my therapeutic work with those living with dissociative identities.

The Function of Parts with Different Identities

The function of parts can vary depending on the specific needs of the person with dissociative identity. Some parts may be created to cope with specific traumatic events or emotions, while others may evolve to perform specific functions in the person's life, such as managing day-to-day activities or interpersonal relationships.

In many cases, parts can also serve as protectors, helping the person to manage their emotions and experiences in a way that feels safe and manageable. For example, a child part may be created to help manage feelings of fear and vulnerability, while an angry part may be created to help manage feelings of rage or helplessness.

Fronting and Masking

While parts can be helpful in managing overwhelming emotions and experiences, they can also cause difficulties in a person's life, particularly if they are not aware of their parts or are unable to control when certain parts come to the forefront, termed 'fronting'.

Fronting refers to the experience of a particular identity taking control of the body and behaving as if they are the primary personality. This can be triggered by a variety of internal or external stimuli, such as stress, memories or social situations.

Masking is a related concept in which a part attempts to conceal their identity, or true feelings and behaviour, to avoid drawing attention to themselves or to maintain an appearance of conformity. This can include suppressing emotions, changing speech patterns or behaviour, adopting a persona that is consistent with the expectations of the situation, or pretending to be another part. The process of masking and fronting refers to the switch of control between different identities.

Both fronting and masking can be adaptive coping strategies that allow individuals with dissociative identities to navigate their daily lives, but they can also be a source of distress and confusion. This is not a choice or planned but a reaction to the situation. Each part will develop organically in their perceived way of managing their own individual role. In therapy, the intention is to help the parts within the system communicate and work collaboratively, which will then help reduce the need for masking or fronting.

Working with dissociative identities typically involves the agility and flexibility of being always in the moment as the therapist must be able to recognise and understand when these shifts are happening, and sense (or by sensing) the impact on the therapeutic process. It is important that all parts understand that they are welcomed.

This can present ethical dilemmas for the therapist, as they may have to work with parts who have conflicting goals or conflicting perceptions of experiences and/or events; for example, the dilemma of whether and when to share information between parts to support understanding within the system.

The process of working with dissociative identities often involves building a therapeutic relationship with each part, including those who may be hidden or covert, to create a safe and supportive space for each part to express their experiences and emotions. At times this involves addressing underlying trauma which helps develop greater awareness and control. This process takes time but gradually builds a sense of working together and wholeness. The therapist must also take care to help the individual understand and make informed choices on whether they choose to integrate the different parts of their identity or opt for collaboration as a realistic goal when the individual is ready. Timing is important!

Through increased internal communication, the parts can learn to accept and trust one another, express their feelings and experiences more openly, and work together to achieve shared goals. As a clinician my intention is to help the parts develop new, healthier coping strategies and find ways to integrate their experiences and identities in a way that feels safe and authentic for them.

An Example: Sky's System

I want to honour Sky's system and Star for letting me share our work.

Sky is the 'apparently normal part of the personality' (van der Hart, Nijenhuis and Steele, 2006) for the system, and I shall use this name when I speak about the part that is getting on with everyday life. Sky self-referred having been assessed as having dissociative identities at one of the two specialist centres in the UK for people with dissociative conditions.

Sky was aware of having some parts and came to therapy as they expressed a desire to be able to hold down a relationship and have a significant other in their life. It is Sky who predominantly shows up in the therapeutic space.

As a clinician, I try and create an understanding of the mind–body connection by speaking about the autonomic nervous system, using psychoeducation to provide a platform from which we can work. So many systems have been rendered powerless at some point so it is important that they feel they have agency in the therapeutic space. There will be parts who will think we, as clinicians, are coercing, tricksters or manipulators but that gives opportunities for further work.

Whilst I try and initially use the language that the client uses, I slowly introduced Janina Fisher's (2017) language of parts, Dan Siegel's (Siegel and Schore, 2021) 'Window of Tolerance', Stephen Porges' (2011) polyvagal theory, as well as Schwartz's (2021) internal family systems framework. Peter Levine's (2010) focus on sensation, imagery, behaviour, affect and meaning (SIBAM) to process trauma enabled self-regulation. Further techniques I used with Sky included classical psychoanalytic interpretation, sensorimotor techniques (Ogden and Fisher, 2015) and Eye Movement Desensitisation Reprocessing (EMDR) (Shapiro, 2001). As Sky's system began to trust and collaborate more, sessions of Deep Brain Reorienting (DBR) (Corrigan and Christie-Sands, 2020) were introduced and shifted symptoms that evolved from unresolved attachment shock from early adversity and trauma. In addition, developmental resourcing for attunement wounds further progressed developmental healing Parnell (2013). Sky's system uses art and poetry to express different parts.

Introducing Sky's System

- Sky: Gets on with everyday life but can easily withdraw when there is too much stress.
- Star: Passionate. Sex 'n' Drugs and Rock 'n' Roll. She is awesome and wanted you all to know that.
- Sunni: Academic. Double 1st from a top tier university.
- Forest: Sensible, practical, stoic, concrete.
- Rock: Rules orientated. Very traditional 'old school' where gender specific roles suggest obedience and deference to need to autocratic authority.
- River: Quietly brave, endures.
- The Pebbles: The children.

Sky is extremely bright so takes flight into intellectual defence easily. They have a strong sense of responsibility for their extended family who have become a priority, often at the expense of Sky's own life opportunities. Sky's relatives live in Sky's country of birth, a homeland where there is masculine bias and women suffer from a lower status compared to men who are expected to provide.

Sky's History and Aims in Therapy

Sky witnessed and experienced intergenerational psychological and physical violence. Sky's father was ambitious and moved from country to country to make money. He would terrorise the family into submission, asserting dominance and control with threats of abandoning them all. He often acted out his own adverse childhood experiences, blaming Sky and their mother for his frustrations. Beatings were everyday experiences. Father had an idea that Sky's life was his, that they reflected him and needed to both comply and obey to his will. It was planned that Sky would succeed at a top tier university so that they could financially provide for him when they became an adult. Father died before Sky went to university, but money earned now provides for their relatives' lifestyle.

Sky presented as wanting to work on securing an adult relationship so that they did not go through life on their own but stated that they didn't know how to negotiate the different needs within their system and all their relationships kept being problematic.

Different parts wanted different things. The Pebbles just wanted someone to play with and care for them and would fall in love with the first person that was kind to them. The Rock wanted a 'proper' heterosexual whom they could cook and care for. Star did not want to be tied down to anyone as they were having too much fun flirting and loved the art of seduction and conquest. Sky identified as pan-sexual and occasionally began relationships with both genders which put Star and Rock into active masking mode so that difficulties would arise from sabotage and the relationship would end.

The Process of Therapy with Sky's System

A year ago, Sky was feeling desperate and forlorn. I had been working with Sky and their system for about 18 months and a level of safety had evolved. Open communication had been encouraged and accountability around who was fronting and listening had been established. Sky was having what Knipe (2014) describes as 'board level' conversations and/or negotiations to invite the system to enter a healthy adult monogamous relationship, but Star was determined to live a non-committal sexually active life and would not comply to the pleas of the others.

One of the Pebbles came out and told me that Star would not let anyone eat. Star felt that Sky was going to the gym too much and was feeling good about their body that was developing muscles. This was interfering with Star's need to be small, petite and feminine. There was no way Star was going let Sky become masculine! During the session, when Sky fronted again, I asked Sky if they were having increased periods of amnesia. Sky nodded and shared they had been in a committed monogamous relationship but said that their body had had so many unexplained bruises from sexual play with others, they were constantly finding excuses not to meet up with their significant other as it would be obvious that their body was being harmed in sexual encounters with other people.

I asked Sky if Star would be prepared to come to therapy for a few sessions, perhaps fronting with Sky and allowing the others to listen in. I commented that I hoped that Star was listening now, and I was concerned that there was some tension in the system: competing needs were disturbing the getting on with normal life. I also wondered if something else was going on for Star. I expressed that I was aware that various parts were getting angry and blaming Star and how difficult that would be and wondered out loud if Star might be feeling quite lonely. Apparently, Star did not like my saying that and told Sky that I did not understand, and the system was ruining everything for them. I was holding in mind that Star was re-enacting early adverse experiences, trying to overcome something that they were not processing. I had previously thought that one of the Pebbles was carrying the memory of early abuse but could see that perhaps Star held that function.

Star arrived at the next session, with a glass of red wine and cigarette in hand. They were glamorous and bold, very Mae West in their style radiating sublime control. I said I was curious about a couple of things and appreciated their coming to session. Firstly, I wanted to understand what was distressing them to the point that they were not eating, and secondly, they really seemed not to want to be in any relationship.

In this moment, there was just Star and me. I held the belief that Star was carrying something for the system that they were tired of doing. Despite the bravado, I saw quite a vulnerable person. Star believed that they were bringing everybody down but felt unsafe about being in a relationship. They explained that they felt trapped and terrified of being exploited. I asked if this was why they liked to endure pain, exerting control, and bearing the unbearable as a form of conquering others. Yes, they replied. Star got very emotional at being blamed by the system, dropping into quiet tears. I slowed everything down so that they could notice their feelings. I noticed and reflected out loud how brave and stoic they were and how much they had endured alone. I asked if this was always the case?

Star was trying to make sense of something and was acting out the pain of not being in control. Star explained that they were protecting everyone in the system and the system just saw them as being difficult. I validated their feeling of being misunderstood and asked where they felt that in their body. We then began to work through somatic symptoms of unusual pain tolerance, self-sabotage and betrayal of loved ones using EMDR, DBR and various sensorimotor psychotherapy techniques. These approaches aided a process of transformative stabilisation and symptom reduction, working with traumatic implicit memory, and then re-integrating discovery into the system. Star had compartmentalised and adapted to abusive adults as a child and these patterns of self-destructive and addictive behaviour in the present were their attempt to get some relief from internal conflicts. Janina Fisher (2017) beautifully describes the legacy of traumatic experience and autonomic symptoms of post-traumatic conditions which aligns to Star's re-enactment behaviour of unresolved traumas. She highlights the importance of stabilisation within the clinical space so that the standard of 'No Part Left Behind' can be embodied (Fisher, 2017, p. 142) to support the understanding and healing of the intrapersonal conflicts and struggles experienced within the system.

Star had been hijacking the process of getting on with normal life as they were terrified of loving and getting close to anyone. They were finding it difficult to regulate impulsivity and their level of suspicion and mistrust escalated. Equally Star desired closeness and longed to be appreciated, liked and validated. Star could not live in the past, present or future. Instead, they were living with a memory of one perfect day that they felt good when they were 22 years of age. Star wanted to return to that one day when they felt alive. They shared that they could not tolerate any real feeling other than pain as they were unable to bear the overwhelming emotions of pleasure and enjoyment. Star felt that they needed to be in control so that they would not be humiliated or rejected. Star was driven by fight/flight responses that gave them a sense of control. Their adaptive behaviour provided relief from trauma-related feelings and sensations, but their sense of their self in relationship was malnourished and impoverished.

Returning to the tasks of the therapist, I provided some psychoeducation around what Star was carrying for the system, inviting them to explore how to differentiate between past and present, and identify triggers that protected them from the traumatic overwhelm they experienced as a child. Star created appropriate strategies for them all to be able to get support from one another. Further EMDR on specific memories was required as well as some homework to help facilitate internal conversations so that Sky and the others could appreciate what Star had endured for so long. Connection with the other parts began to feel safe for Star once they realised that they could process their unresolved feelings and allow all their selves to mourn their lost childhood.

Sky had been living with the chronic conflict between approach and avoidance that they had been unable to resolve and synthesise as a child; their care givers had let them down. Star was born out of structural dissociation of their defensive system. She was phobic of relational attachment, pseudo-independent and disconnected from self-needs. Whilst other parts yearned for connection, striving to fulfil a sense of loss, struggling with bullying, being made the unacceptable 'other' and inability to be alone, Star existed to contain and take flight into pain.

Star is now present full time alongside Forest and Sky and 'getting on with normal life', keeping the system safe and functional. Rock is going through quite a bit of distress but is being met with compassion and empathy. Rock is supported by Star as Rock grieves and finds a new way to live as they adjust to the lifestyle that the system is designing for itself. Sky, overall, is stable in the here and now, differentiating from the past and interfacing with the external world in a more sustainable and satisfactory way, leaning into the strength of the parts without giving up fronting the system.

Sky has now secured a committed and supportive relationship in which both they and their partner are committed to creating a safe and stable environment where understanding of dissociative identities and their impact regularly gets explored.

What the Therapist Needs to Do in Work with Dissociative Identity

- Help clients develop a language to explore their conflicts, behaviour, implicit and explicit memories, intrusive emotions, or reactions that are out of proportion to current day experiences.
- Explore the concept of blending and un-blending between parts (Schwartz and Sweezy, 2020; Fisher, 2017).
- Be aware of differentiating past and present, parts and whole to promote developmental growth.
- Be committed to understanding and respecting boundaries.
- Develop empathy not only for your client but also for the different parts within yourself which may get activated.
- Develop willingness to learn and grow together. No two systems are alike.

It is my experience that working with a person with dissociative identities is like embarking into the unknown, heading to a new frontier where beauty and pitfalls unfold as the journey is navigated.

When the Client Is Unaware of Different Identities

It is important for the therapist to be sensitive and empathetic when working with clients who may not be aware of their other identities. It is important to prioritise the client's safety and well-being in all interactions. What you can do:

1 Assess the client's readiness. Before addressing the presence of parts, the therapist should assess the client's readiness to explore this topic. It is important to be mindful of the potential impact that this information could have on the client's mental and emotional well-being.
2 Normalise the experience. The therapist can help the client to understand that having parts is a normal part of dissociative identity and that many people with dissociative identities are not initially aware of them.
3 Educate the client. The therapist can provide education and resources to the client about dissociation and the role of different parts of the personality in the system.

4   Explore the presence of different identities. The therapist can gently explore the presence of parts with the client, without overwhelming them with too much information too quickly. This may involve asking the client questions about their experiences and encouraging them to pay attention to any feelings or sensations that arise.

5   Develop a collaborative approach. The therapist should work collaboratively with the client to develop a plan for exploring the presence of other identities and should be respectful of the client's pace and preferences.

Conclusion

Working with individuals with dissociative identities requires a high level of skill, sensitivity and creativity from therapists. The process can be challenging, but with the right approach, it can lead to significant improvements in the individual's mental health and well-being.

It is an area of work that I have found challenging and rewarding. It is heartening that there is so much interest at The Bowlby Centre conference. I welcome ongoing collaboration with experts who live with dissociative identity, grateful for the Centre for Dissociative Studies and of course appreciative of one of my training homes, The Bowlby Centre, who are not afraid to explore new frontiers.

Recently a client, called Odette, was yearning for relief, just to be 'normal'. She asked if I had ever worked with a system who managed to have all their parts integrated. This was a painful moment as the grief of her experiences of confusion, lost time amnesia, and sense of alienation was taking its toll on Odette's system. Whilst I could not give Odette's system the answer they were looking for, I was able to share that I have worked with systems whose parts, as they began to process both individual and collective understanding of the various functioning self-states, had become a collaborative high-functioning team. I said it was all about communication and trust, where competing and conflicting needs could be shared, perspectives articulated, and a way forward negotiated and agreed upon without one part dominating the journey. Odette relaxed into her chair and said 'I'd really like that... that means there is hope for us'.

References

Bion, W.R. (1967). 'Notes on Memory and Desire'. *The Psychoanalytic Forum*, 2, pp. 272–280.

Bollas, C. (2017). *The Shadow of the Object*. London: Routledge.

Corrigan, F.M., and Christie-Sands, J. (2020). 'An Innate Brainstem Self-Other System Involving Orienting, Affective Responding, and Polyvalent Relational Seeking: Some Clinical Implications for a "Deep Brain Reorienting, Trauma Psychotherapy Approach"'. *Medical Hypotheses*, 136, pp. 1–10.

Fisher, J. (2017). *Healing the Fragmented Selves of Trauma Survivors*. London: Routledge.

Knipe, J. (2014). *EMDR Toolbox*. New York: Springer.

Levine, P. (2010). *In an Unspoken Voice: How the Body Releases Trauma and Restores Goodness*. Berkeley, CA: North Atlantic Books.

Ogden, P., and Fisher, J. (2015). *Sensorimotor Psychotherapy: Interventions for Trauma and Attachment*. London: Norton.

Parnell, L. (2013). *Attachment Focused EMDR: Healing Relational Trauma*. London: Norton.

Porges, S.W. (2011). *The Polyvagal Theory: Neurophysiological Foundations of Emotions, Attachment, Communication, and Self-Regulation*. London: Norton.

Schwartz, R.C. (2021). *No Bad Parts: Healing Trauma and Restoring Wholeness with the Internal Family Systems Model*. Boulder, CO: Sounds True.

Schwartz, R.C., and Sweezy, M. (2020). *Internal Family Systems Therapy* (2nd edn). New York: Guilford Press.

Shapiro, F. (2001). *Eye Movement Desensitization and Reprocessing (EMDR)* (2nd edn). London: Guilford Press.

Siegel, D.J., and Schore, A.N. (eds.) (2021). *Interpersonal Neurobiology and Clinical Practice*. New York: Norton.

van der Hart, O., Nijenhuis, E.R.S., and Steele, K. (2006). *The Haunted Self: Structural Dissociation and the Treatment of Chronic Traumatization*. London: Norton.

Chapter 3

What Are We Doing?

Stabilisation Work with a Mind Control[1] System of Altered Identities

Emma Jack

Introduction

The International Society for the Study of Trauma and Dissociation (ISSTD) recommend a three-phase approach to treatment following a formal diagnosis of dissociative identity disorder. The phases work to establish safety, stabilisation and symptom reduction; working through and integrating, processing and integration of traumatic memories; identity integration and rehabilitation (Chu et al., 2011).

My proposition is that the Phase 1 stabilisation work is not merely something to be worked through to get to Phase 2 trauma processing but is a crucial part of the therapy to be returned to throughout the work. I intend to elaborate the idea that stabilisation is not something that the client alone needs to achieve but could also be thought of as the stabilisation of the therapist and the relationship between the therapist and the client.

The chapter presents some of the work I have done with a client who has been in intensive twice-a-week therapy with me for around eight years. The client has a large system of altered identities and fits the profile of a mind control style of dissociative identity (Lacter, 2008).

The work with this client to date has involved all three phases of the treatment model. The interventions I describe are all from about seven years into the work and so, although the set of altered identities I talk about here were new to me, the system was not. To begin with I will share some of the clinically important presenting details to bear in mind when treating any client with dissociative identities.

Assessment

At assessment and in the early months of treatment it is helpful, if possible, to begin to form a view on the following:

- What was the type of childhood abuse situation: familial/external, individuals/groups, ritualised/opportunistic?

DOI: 10.4324/9781032696720-4

- Are there installed altered identities who have been subjected to mind control techniques such as torture?
- Are there comorbid factors such as addiction, chronic suicidality and/or self-harm, depression, anxiety?
- Do they have support in the real world that is genuinely helpful?
- Is the abuse historic or ongoing?

Knowledge of any of the above can be useful in informing the therapeutic approach you might adopt. In particular where the work would be best pitched from a more supportive stance to a more in-depth or analytic therapeutic engagement. To be clear about this, forming a clinical view on any of these queries could give an indication of the client's ability to tolerate dysregulation and their current ability to re-regulate. Dysregulation is inevitable. This needs to be accepted at the outset.

It is also important to evaluate the dissociation-specific considerations:

- What is the general level of amnesia? How much co-consciousness is there? Are there amnesiac barriers and, if so, what does the therapist know about how they operate or why they are there?
- What is the style of switching (the change from one identity to another)? Is it spontaneous or co-operative? Is switching within someone's control internally or externally, or is it situation dependent, for example, the altered identity who goes to work. Is it known why this is?
- Who has brought the system to therapy and why? Is that person here for another reason or do they have full knowledge of their dissociative condition?
- What does the person arriving in therapy know about structural dissociation? How comfortable or not are they with the idea of their dissociative symptoms?
- What is their predominant attachment pattern (Bowlby 1997)? Are they able to make relationships and use them to regulate themselves? This could be different from one altered identity to another.

At the outset of treatment, attention needs to be paid regarding any knowledge of the above in order to calibrate interventions to best accommodate what is known but also to allow for what is not known. Careful and accurate assessment of one's countertransference is key (Davies and Frawley, 1994, pp. 149–166), with the aim of providing a secure base (Bowlby 1988) to enable the work of therapy to commence.

The ISSTD state that:

In the initial phase of treatment, emphasis should be placed on establishing a therapeutic alliance, educating clients about diagnosis and symptoms and explaining the process of treatment. The goals of Phase 1 treatment include: maintaining personal safety, controlling symptoms, modulating affect, building stress tolerance, enhancing basic life functioning and building or improving relational capacities.

(Chu et al., 2011, p. 136)

Although this is a reasonable description of the aims of Phase 1 of the treatment model, it does not describe the way in which this is not just a phase to be passed through to get to Phase 2 trauma processing. Phase 1 work is needed throughout the treatment of clients with dissociative identities. The undervaluing of this stabilisation work or premature movement into Phase 2 trauma processing can undermine the entire therapeutic endeavour.

In addition, the therapist working with a client with dissociative identities needs to be prepared to modify their use of the core conditions of empathy, congruence and unconditional positive regard considerably to meet a client with multiple altered identities. I say this because frequently primary trainings lead us to believe that simply providing these three things will automatically create a therapeutic alliance. It is important to accept that stabilisation is not straightforwardly the creation of a therapeutic alliance.

In the work with clients with dissociative identities it is key for the therapist to keep in mind at all times that they may be in the presence of a number of individual altered identities who all think, believe and know different things. Our interventions need to leave space for other points of view. This can be very difficult, to seek to come alongside both the deeply hurt and traumatised, the internal persecutors, the deniers and the outraged.

In Ocean Vuong's novel *On Earth We Are Briefly Gorgeous*, he writes:

Sometimes being offered tenderness feels like the very proof that you've been ruined.

(Vuong, 2019, p. 113)

This describes beautifully the way in which the empathy of another can be very hard (if not initially impossible) for the severely traumatised person to receive. Dissociative clients are frequently mired in a painfully shamed state. Not least because often, an exchange has had to be made.

Briefly, Fairbairn's (1943) moral defence describes the unconscious exchange of *badness*; the child believes they must be bad in order for the caregivers to remain good. This makes it possible for the child to attach to abusive caregivers. It is a persistent and maladaptive strategy, but it also works to ensure the survival of the child. Beneath the moral defence lies terrible grief and shame (Grotstein, 1994, pp. 116–118).

The therapeutic task could be seen as work that returns the *badness* to the caregivers and for the client to mourn all that this means. This is an understandably slow and painful process that is likely to be enacted in the therapeutic relationship. It is obviously more complex where abuse is ongoing.

Working with clients with dissociative identities requires the therapist to be prepared to inhabit being a bad object (Greenberg and Mitchell, 1983). They need to be able to openly explore this without collapsing or retaliating and to demonstrate in some way who they really are. An opaque, blank or bland therapeutic stance is not suitable for the dissociative client.

A Clinical Example

I am going to describe some of the work I have done with a dissociative system of altered identities that I have been working with for the last eight years. To give you a very brief sketch of this client: The client's body is female aged 42. The presenting client is married and works full time in a dynamic and responsible job. The client's husband does not know any of the altered identities, nor does he seek to know them. The client is not open about her dissociative condition. The client is still apparently being abused by numerous external abusers. The presenting client is not allowed to know about the above abuse. In the first year of therapy, it became apparent that the client met the DSM-V criteria for a formal diagnosis of dissociative identity disorder (diagnostic code 300.14). Furthermore, it transpired that there is a large system of altered identities that could be described as a ritual abuse / mind control style of system (Miller, 2018).

The presenting client is divided from the rest of the system by an entirely amnesiac barrier. Although she is aware of some narrative details concerning familial abuse, she is not aware that the abuse is ongoing and facilitated and participated in by her mother (her father died some years ago). The system of altered identities is made up of babies, toddlers, older children, teens and adults both male and female. They tend to form small groups and very few of them are able to move around freely. There are two sides to the system of altered identities, and they do not interact. The left side do not appear to know the father, only the mother, and they have been abused within the family and in a group religious setting. The right side appear to know both the mother and the father and some of them have been abused within the family and by an organised abuse group. The work described belongs to a group of altered identities on the right side of this system. The group are: Nevar aged 13, Baby Boy 6 months, Charlie aged 7, Jamie aged 5 and Jamie Boy aged 2.

The first therapeutic goal is to get the client into therapy. This is the same with any client, but it can be more pronounced in the dissociative client. Although there is a client in the consulting room, they may not be ready or able to do anything that looks or feels like conventional therapy. In a client with dissociative identities, it is very likely that a number of their altered identities will not want to be in therapy or may even think they are not allowed to be. This a common 'rule' in a mind control system of altered identities. Seven years into the work with this dissociative client, following my usual summer break, I got the following text message:

> Hello I'm fine. I might not need therapy anymore. I'm feeling better in myself. Thanks.

This was not the first time an attempt to end the therapy had been made. From previous experience I suspected that a shift in the system had occurred, and a return to more stabilisation style interventions would be needed, despite having been working for some time in Phase 2. While this sounds like a huge backward step, my working hypothesis in this kind of situation is always that all the work that we have done in therapy will have trickled through the system, if not narratively then in a felt way. Meaning that I am generally hopeful that it will be possible to work with them to get the therapy back on track.

My reply to this text sought to speak to both the altered identity that sent it and the system behind. My suspicion was that this message was an attempt to impersonate the presenting client and I reminded the messenger that our agreement was that the presenting client would need to see me in person to end the therapy. There followed a bit of a text tussle between us in which I made it clear I would not accept an ending by text or Zoom and that attendance in my consulting room was necessary. They continued to express a desire for the therapy to end, but they also began complaining that they were alone with a number of child altered identities who were upset. I saw an opportunity to be quite straightforwardly helpful and said:

> If the little kids and babies are hurt and crying, they need talking to softly and comfortingly and they need to be cuddled or rocked.

To which they replied:

> I'm not the loving type. Tough love they are used to it... They don't cry they fucking scream, I can't stand it. I do hit, it works with the small baby and the blind fucker. The other three are caged awaiting lessons.

This exchange alerted me to a number of possibilities. This altered identity was probably the victim of torture and was doing the only thing they knew to stop others crying; the use of violence. The last line indicated to me that this situation had probably been caused by an external perpetrator group. However, I also noticed they were daring to tell me small details that were probably confidential. This encouraged me to feel a bit hopeful so I moved towards the desperation in what I hoped would be perceived as a pragmatic way, that is, not too emotional:

> OK. Well if you come tomorrow, I can try to stop the screaming and crying. Even if you only come for an hour, I can help with this, and I'd like to tell you a bit of what I know. The lessons are where the pain is.

Although I couldn't really guarantee the settling of the little kids, I had been able to do this before, so it seemed like a fair offer. I included the last line to let them know I was at least aware of bad things in the real world and prepared in an uncomplicated way to mention it. To which they replied:

Won't I be collaborating with the enemy. Anyway, I need to end therapy.

My thought here was that they are uncertain who I am since perpetrator groups are known to have people pose as therapists, but the expression *won't I* leaves a little space that appears to be seeking my engagement. I decided to keep to the pragmatic tone and short messages:

I'm not the enemy and we won't be doing therapy. It's called Littles Management.

Perpetrator groups frequently tell the systems of altered identities under their control that therapy is a negative or dangerous thing. In my clinical experience many of the new altered identities I have met during the course of therapy have initially been frightened of me and believed I was going to harm them in some way. I thought it would be better for now to move right away from any idea of therapy. I thought this altered identity might understand *Littles Management*.
    They replied:

What are you going to use hypnotherapy?

to which I replied straightforwardly:

No, I don't know hypnotherapy. Just simple things that quieten a baby.

Keeping the message simple and factual but leaving some space for their curiosity. I deliberately used the word *quieten* rather than *comfort* to try and remain more alongside them. They replied:

OK I'll come if it'll shut the fuckers up… can you send your address, how long does it take to drive to you.

I replied:

It's about 30 mins from your house. This is me holding a baby.

The inclusion of a photo of me with a baby is an unusual intervention and I would be unlikely to use something like this with a system I did not know well. I used the photo as a message to other identities in this system that know me well, to remind them of who I am. However, this image could definitely be frightening to some altered identities. Rupture is never far away in this work. In this instance the gamble paid off and Nevar arrived in my consulting room, and I was able to quieten the little ones.

This began what has been 18 months of work with him and a series of young male altered identities connected to him. Initially the work was all about just getting Nevar to come to the sessions and helping him to move away from hurting others inside to nurturing them. We moved from Littles Management to therapy slowly but steadily.

Having met Nevar I suspected he was an altered identity who had been subjected to mind control techniques. There were some red flags:

- The name Nevar is Raven backwards. Backwards names are common in mind control systems of a ritualised type.
- He arrived wearing religious jewellery he called identification.
- In the room he performed various repetitive hand movements.

In terms of the stance needed to work with him in therapy, I kept in mind information I know about others in the system as this is likely to apply to him. This altered identity will:

- have been tortured
- have had near-death experiences in which an attachment figure has both inflicted the near-death event and saved them from it possibly causing infanticidal attachment (Sachs, 2002)
- have been made to harm others
- be following instructions to the letter believing that to do otherwise could cause something very bad to happen to himself or others
- have a very polarised view of the world where people are either victims or perpetrators
- be full of supressed rage and shame
- have survived the unimaginable.

I am stating these things as facts even though I do not know them to be facts, not to pre-emptively know something (not knowing is a big part of this work) but more to inform my therapeutic stance around him. In other words, to remind myself that his opinions and behaviours will have emerged as a result of these kinds of experiences and it could feel terrifying for him if I were to rush into challenging them. The work commenced with all this held lightly in mind. However, these are not light things and the desire to dissociate oneself, to push these unimaginable facts away, is an ongoing battle. The 'unimaginable' needs pulling to the front of one's mind frequently in order to attune more accurately.

This leads to a second therapeutic goal that I call *tipping point*. Every intervention made in the therapy has to work to gently move the altered identity, in this case, Nevar, from the place I suspect he is in: highly controlled and quietly terrified, to just *off the track* enough to look back and see things in a different light. In other words, to allow him to become aware of the mind control programming. To do this, I need to attune to where he is now, including the things to be kept in mind above. I also need to make sure to leave space for other altered identities that I can't see and not forget that I don't know who Nevar is or what his role is within the system. If I can make space for all of this, in my experience, there is the potential for something to *loosen* and some of the conditioning or pro-gramming to begin to fall away and the reactivation of attachment needs to become possible (Richardson, 2002).

It may also be necessary to create a tipping point in the system as a whole, in other words working to move to a place where more of the altered iden-tities are interested in being in therapy than not. Until this tipping point is created very little can happen. This is one of the key goals of stabilisation. At the point I met Nevar, I had achieved this on the other side of the system so I was fairly confident I would be able to reach him.

To reach him or altered identities like him, it is necessary to create a therapeutic space that feels qualitatively different to other spaces they may have been in. At the outset, the work is concerned with demonstrating the reliable container of both the room and me. This involves the creation of materials, games, symbols, activities and shared experiences, with a focus on the reactivation of attachment behaviour. None of this is learned technique. It is individual, bespoke, real, spontaneous and deeply meaningful to both them and me.

Daniel Stern poses the question 'How can you get inside of other people's subjective experience and let them know you have arrived there without using words?' (Stern, 2003, p. 138). This is a question that bears regular reflection regarding any client, but none more so than the client with dissociative iden-tities. It is important to seek to occupy this challenging non-verbal space. Stern also says, 'The sharing of affective states is the most pervasive and clinically germane feature of intersubjective relatedness' (Stern, 2003, p. 138). This is enormously important in the work with dissociative clients and brings us to a key part of building a therapeutic alliance with them.

'Companionable relating' (Heard and Lake, 1997) describes a dynamic between caregiver and careseeker that promotes exploration. When compa-nionable relating is employed clinically in such a way that an alongside relationship can flourish, there becomes the possibility that the client can begin to move away from the defensive prohibition of attachment needs.

Holmes and Slade (2018, p. 47) quoting Winnicott argue that playing offers a means to 'relaxed self-realisation' discovering and elaborating what is in one's mind. Winnicott was of course largely talking about the lives of real children. However, play can become a key tool in the work with dissociative clients.

The toy gun battle as a way to get into therapy was something Nevar and I developed about six weeks after the text conversation above. Nevar found ordinary empathic enquiry repellent. He would squirm and become angry at the beginning of therapy sessions. Equally, silence enraged him. I knew I had to find some kind of alongside activity that we could get into to help him relax relationally and get used to being with me.

Guns, the air force and superheroes were all interests he had shared with me, so it wasn't a big leap to think about getting a toy gun. Once I mentioned the possibility, he was ecstatic, did lots of research and soon we had a little toy gun that fired foam rods at high velocity.

Nevar came up with the cans as targets and he chose the places all around my consulting room to balance them. Some were easy and some were hard. The game was simple: whoever uses the least number of bullets to shoot the targets down wins. He was usually great at it, and he got a lot out of this feeling of skill. I was not very good at it and allowed him to see my real disappointment when I missed the target. In this small way he began to know who I really am. He loved that he was better than me at it, but he also celebrated my good days. We were in it together.

Clinically important in this experience is the feeling of power and agency, the feeling of competence, self-belief, the genuine experience of me, the discharge of anxiety about being in therapy and possibly the safe expression of hatred and anger. None of this needed putting into words or interpreting, it was just how we started every session and it worked because following this he would settle and allow other things to happen.

The other young male altered identities, Charlie, Jamie, Jamie Boy and Baby boy arrived in the therapy later, through a series of flashbacks that Nevar struggled to understand. I am not going to talk about the flashbacks here, except to say they were incredibly gruelling for all these boys and involved near-death experiences. Once each of the boys made themselves known through the flashbacks, they became like younger brothers to Nevar. Initially he hated them. He was angry with them for, as he saw it, forcing these images into his head. They didn't belong to him they didn't have anything to do with him. A new therapeutic imperative emerged: to help these boys get along together and be able to support and take care of one another.

I returned to the work I had done with Nevar when he arrived, showing him with soft toys the sorts of things that might soothe a child who was upset and crying. He had a go and it worked. A new feeling began to grow in Nevar: being a big brother, looking out for them and beginning to show an interest in their interests. He bought things in line with their interests. Jamie Boy loves birds and so Nevar bought him books with birds in the story and a set of books with buttons that activated bird songs.

Jamie loves stories, in particular ones that he could elaborate. Nevar and I spent time collaborating around what they might like but also at times about what they might need. Nevar had noticed problems in the internal world around specific beliefs that had been engendered by the perpetrator group. For example, all of these boys were terrified to express any preference or desire. They had no agency whatsoever.

The book *You Choose* (Sharrat and Goodhart, 2018) became a great resource on a number of levels. It is a regular book not intended for working with a mind control child altered identity but this is how it worked for all of these boys. The book is a series of highly coloured illustrations of lots of different things like modes of travel, clothes, houses and so on. On each page, it asks you to choose a thing.

This book worked clinically on a number of levels. Firstly, it offers a very simple experience of choice. In most dissociative presentations, and certainly in a mind control system, the ability to choose has been denied, twisted and, where it has been allowed, has often led to deadly consequences. This little book began to give a small 'as if' experience of choice in a relational context. To begin with, all of the boys were too terrified to choose anything, so I began choosing, pointing at things and elaborating what the choice might mean. They became engaged in this and excited by the possibilities, so they began by very sweetly commandeering my finger to choose things, holding my hand and pointing *my* finger at the things they wanted. Jamie Boy still does this, but Jamie has now graduated to choosing for himself. Important in this experience is that there are no adverse consequences as a result of choosing. This activity has allowed them to experience something going on in the mind of another and they continue to like to hear my choices and why. They can also make a different choice every time we look at it. This entirely contradicts the programming they have been subjected to in a very gentle way.

Obviously as an activity it is in line with Winnicott's 'relaxed self-realisation' (Holmes and Slade, 2018) and is naturally aiding the development of a new attachment relationship with me. It is also, crucially, an experience for them of being in the body, with an adult who is not harming them.

Internal collaboration is very much part of Phase 1 work and for this group of boys this has been a big piece of work that in the present has created a useful template for them to negotiate the collaboration needed in the more difficult Phase 2 memory and trauma processing work. The collaboration has been both between me and each of the boys individually but also between all of them inside. *Penelope's Feathers* is an original story by me, Jamie, Jamie Boy and Nevar. It came about because Jamie loves me to tell him an original story. If the story captures his imagination, he will seize upon it, elaborate it a bit internally with the other boys and bring it back to me. Jamie Boy loves birds so this story was especially exciting. With the best ones we have written them down and Nevar is illustrating them. They have become a properly co-created thing that we are all very proud of. *Penelope's Feathers* also provided an opportunity through its narrative content to help the boys think about envy, working together and learning not to be judgemental.

Over the years I have been working with this client we have employed, enjoyed and co-created many resources. Nearly all of them are working therapeutically at a number of levels; in the service of reactivation of attachment behaviours, being in the body in a new and positive way, relaxed self-realisation, collaboration and sharing, and to soothe and distract when traumatised.

Lacan (1997) states that: 'the therapist is not 'the one who knows' but has an open mind, is deeply curious working on the assumption that there is meaning to be made and found however provisional and subject to revision' (cited in Holmes and Slade, 2018, p. 50). This is the stance I am always striving for.

The Final Intervention

The final intervention I would like to describe is right in the centre of this open-minded 'deeply curious' place that Holmes and Slade (2018, p. 47) are describing.

Les Misérables (Hugo, 2003) has become a very important and pivotal motif in our work together. I do not believe we have entirely understood its meaning yet; it continues to deepen and evolve. The music of *Les Misérables* became very important to everyone on the other side of the system, in particular the song 'Can You Hear the People Sing' (Schönberg, 1998) which tells of a group of people full of anger who refuse to be enslaved any longer. This song became part of therapy, a tool to help ground various altered identities in the therapy room and to lessen dissociative symptoms in times of acute dysregulation following flashbacks. We listened to it and sang it together. It became synonymous with the idea *you're in the therapy room, you're safe, you're with Emma*. It's been a long time since I have worked with that side of the system, so it was quite a surprise when, out of the blue, Nevar watched the musical film and told me how much he loved it and wanted us to watch it together, which we did. We also watched a television adaptation (Davies, 2018) and saw the stage show.

Les Misérables has prompted lots of questions in Nevar, which have been fruitful in terms of providing safe material to explore issues that feel very pertinent to Nevar's emerging sense of what has happened to him and others in the system and to dare to think differently about why that might be. His questions have been around the motives of some of the characters, the nature of good and bad, why some of the characters are cruel to others and what makes some of the characters vulnerable to exploitation.

I suspect the answers to these questions mean a lot to many altered identities in the system and that this material may represent the first thread of connection between one side of the system and the other. It may also form part of the way we might link the whole system and break down some of the fundamental controls that have been imposed on them all.

Three months after first meeting Nevar I received a text from him:

I was just about to die and I realised there were others whose lives matter. I was just about to die and then I heard the baby crying and it made me pause. I was just about to die and then I remembered Emma.

This was a very moving text to receive. I think this conveys well something of where Nevar has reached in terms of the goals of Phase 1 treatment. Alongside the obvious suicidal ideation, he is also expressing his understanding and acceptance of his multiplicity, a new, more collaborative, way of being with those inside and the reactivation of attachment behaviours through his relationship with me.

We have continued to use the resources we co-created, we have elaborated them and frequently return to them alongside the Phase 2 trauma work that we are now engaged in. They help to re-regulate when distressed but they are also crucially giving this system the beginning of a new life outside of an abuse group.

Note

1 Mind control has existed in different forms for centuries. Its varieties do not always involve the presence of altered identities. Harvey Schwartz (2000, p. 315) describes it thus: 'The essential goal of mind-control programming is the creation of a population of sub-consciously programmed individuals, motivated without their knowledge and against their wills to perform in ways in which they would not otherwise perform'.

References

Bowlby, J. (1988). *A Secure Base: Clinical Applications of Attachment Theory*. London: Brunner-Routledge.

Bowlby, J. (1997). *Attachment and Loss*, Vol. 1: *Attachment*. London: Pimlico.

Chu, J.A., Dell, P.F., Van der Hart, O., Cardeña, E., Barach, P.M., *et al.* (2011). 'International Society for the Study of Trauma and Dissociation Guidelines for Treating Dissociative Identity Disorder in Adults, Third Revision'. *Journal of Trauma & Dissociation*, 12, 2, pp. 115–187.

Davies, A. (2018). *Les Miserables* (six-part television adaptation of V. Hugo, 1862). London: BBC.

Davies, J.M., and Frawley, M.G. (1994). *Treating the Adult Survivor of Childhood Sexual Abuse: A Psychoanalytic Perspective*. New York: Basic Books.

Fairbairn, R. (1943). 'The Repression and the Return of Bad Objects'. *British Journal of Medical Psychology*, 19, pp. 327–341.

Greenberg, J.R., and Mitchell, S.A. (1983). *Object Relations in Psychoanalytic Theory*. London: Harvard.

Grotstein, J.S. (ed.) (1994). *Fairbairn and the Origins of Object Relations*. London: The Guilford Press.

Heard, D., and Lake, H. (1997). *The Challenge of Attachment for Caregiving*. London: Routledge.

Holmes, J., and Slade, A. (2018). *Attachment in Therapeutic Practice*. London: Sage.

Hugo, V., and Wilbour C.E. (Translator), (2003). *Les Miserables.* Sterling Publishing, New York.

Lacter, E. (2008). 'Mind Control: Simple to Complex', in Sachs, A., and Galton, G. (eds), *Forensic Aspects of Dissociative Identity Disorder.* London: Karnac, pp. 185–195.

Miller, A. (2018). *Healing the Unimaginable Treating Ritual Abuse and Mind Control* (2nd edn). London: Routledge.

Richardson, S. (2002). 'Will You Sit by Her Side', in Sinason, V. (ed.), *Attachment Trauma and Multiplicity: Working with Dissociative Identity Disorder* (2nd edn). London: Routledge, pp. 150–165.

Sachs, A. (2002). 'As Thick as Thieves or the Ritual Abuse Family', in Sinason, V. (ed.), *Attachment Trauma and Multiplicity: Working with Dissociative Identity Disorder* (2nd edn). London: Routledge, pp. 75–82.

Schönberg, C. (1998). *Les Misérables: A Musical.* London and Milwaukee, WI: Alain Boublil Music. Exclusively distributed by H. Leonard.

Schwartz, H.L. (2000). *Dialogues with Forgotten Voices: Relational Perspectives on Child Abuse Trauma and Treatment of Dissociative Disorders.* New York: Basic Books.

Sharrat, N., and Goodhart, P. (2018). *You Choose.* London: Puffin.

Stern, D. (2003). *The Interpersonal World of the Infant.* London: Karnac.

Vuong, O. (2019). *On Earth We Are Briefly Gorgeous.* London: Penguin Press.

Chapter 4

On Being With

Working Creatively with Clients with Dissociative Identity

Orit Badouk Epstein

Introduction

Theories are wonderfully enriching and helpful, as each generation puts forward a noble idea, working it to its core until the next generation comes along, elevating the idea with the next layer of scaffolding. In moving from the residues of previous centuries to the emergence of this century we need to remind ourselves that it is the pain of the past that motivates us to harm less in the present. Thus, in shepherding all that I have learnt, in this chapter I would like to focus my attention to give the therapeutic relationship a chance and multiply it with the perspective of intersubjectivity and creativity that helps the self combat fear, and maintains coherence and continuity.

Advances in Attachment Theory

Throughout the 20th century, attachment theory and research have helped us recognise evolving changes in emphasis on caregiving:

1   Survival: Until the discovery of Penicillin in 1928 (which was the first mass produced drug that could clear bacterial infections) parental concerns were about keeping their offspring alive.
2   Material care giving: With the growth of the industrial revolution and improved longevity, the emphasis was for parents to provide better external living conditions.
3   Secure relationships: In the field of attachment theory, infant research and neuroscience that has flourished since the mid-20th century, the arrival of the digital revolution has helped increase awareness about the quality of intersubjective relatedness and the necessity for caregivers to be aware of the need for empathy, sensitivity and attunement to facilitate healthy autonomy and exploration.

The neuroscientist Antonio Damasio (1999) informs us about the philosophers Descartes' and Boyle's error in thinking that human cognition is separate from

DOI: 10.4324/9781032696720-5

our bodies and that just sitting and thinking would provide us with all the answers. The Cartesian view of duality is no longer viable today. Both mind and body influence consciousness and are critical to human homeostasis. The abundance of research in the field of neuroscience has taught us that infant brain development is asymmetrical. We can see that the right hemisphere is functioning from birth, involving facial recognition and the expression of emotions, whereas the left hemisphere develops over the first few years of life. This is the work of Allan Schore (1994) who emphasised the regulatory system of right brain to right brain communication. The research also shows how implicit/procedural memory is closely linked to attachment processes and relationship behaviour is held in neural networks created through lived experiences that are largely anchored in the right hemisphere. This type of memory function is what Bowlby (1969) called the Internal Working Model of attachment relationships.

In the *Master and His Emissary*, the psychiatrist and philosopher Ian MacGilchrist (2009) wrote at great length about the importance of right brain communication to our intuition and survival. The right hemisphere helps us understand the world with emotions; the left hemisphere gets hold of the world and conveys certain pictures with certain representations. It helps us manipulate the world; it is not wrong, however science without intuition and imagination is limited. Therefore, in the words of the poet Layli Long Soldier: "It is our responsibility to develop our intuition because it makes you a good relative" (Naimon, 2018).

Modes of Care: The Secure Base Offered in Therapy

As an attachment-based psychoanalytic psychotherapist, I have come to understand secure relationship as consisting of modes of care that I try regularly to practice within the world surrounding me. These modes are not devoid of interpretation rather their emphasis is on the aetiology surrounding the quality of care the client once received as a child. The modes of care are as follows:

1   Confidence: meaning the caregiving relationship can provide safety, reliability, and availability. It is within the context of secure attachment that the caregiver's unavailability can be tolerated.
2   Connection: meaning the caregiving relationship can offer empathy, affect validation, sensitivity, attunement, nurturing language and safe touch.
3   Collaboration: meaning the intersubjective space between caregiver and careseeker can offer intersubjective negotiation, co-operation and exploration. It is within this context that misattunement, rupture and repair will take place and can be tolerated.

For the purposes of this chapter, I focus on collaboration as a mode of care that will demonstrate how being with has helped open vistas of creativity previously unknown to the very traumatised client. Collaboration, in Daniel Stern's way of thinking, is a synchronised dance:

> The infant is a virtuoso performer in his attempts to regulate both the level of stimulation from the caregiver and the internal level of stimulation in himself. The mother is also a virtuoso in her moment-by-moment regulation of the interaction. Together they evolve some exquisitely intricate dyadic patterns.
>
> (Stern, 2002, p. 133)

In less optimal conditions, collaboration always includes the diversity of our inner and outer realities. Just as in music, collaboration means that we have a kind of score to begin with, but we are open to changes that can happen from moment to moment and what happens within those moments. This is what the Boston Group (Stern et al., 1995, 1998a, 1998b)[1] called "moving along". This process is filled with back-and-forth negotiation, attunement and misattunement. The secure relationship is not an ideal, rather it is like an improvised jazz band, being open with a degree of vulnerability to inputs that are outside our control and help expand our imagination without fear in non-rigid and creative ways. These improvisatory moments of interaction, according to Daniel Stern, are not prescriptive and happen on unfamiliar ground and cannot be guided under the guise of any established doctrine or technique. This is what the Boston Group also termed procedural memory and is in the realm of the sub-symbolic where infants in the pre-verbal phase interact with caregivers on the basis of a large amount of implicit relational knowledge.

> This implicit knowing is registered in representations of interpersonal events in a non-symbolic form, beginning in the first year of life.
>
> (Stern et al., 1998a)

When a caregiver can adequately provide this, the pathways towards autonomy and exploration are then flexibly paved.

The Impact of Fear on the Attachment System

Traumatic events we know will activate the fear system in disproportionate measures and can change the perception of time, space, language, and desire long after the traumatic event. A lot has been said about the impact of fear on the attachment system. Bowlby (1969), Mary Main and Judith Solomon (1990), Giovanni Liotti (2004), and other pioneering researchers have shown us the paradoxical part that attachment and fear play as motivational systems in the mind and body of a child. We usually see it clearly when working with the more insecure and traumatised clients. These clients have sadly missed critical developmental opportunities which disable their sense of safety, connectivity and exploration in the world surrounding them.

When a child grows up in a family where a culture of control and violence is the governing force, while having no other choice but to depend on them, such dyads can be the most rigidly hypervigilant and reactive to the tiniest expression of relationship affects. Fear rigidifies the self, increases control and hinders exploration. Bowlby (1980) used the word "deactivation" to describe one of the psychological defences against disorganisation in the face of attachment loss. This deactivation involves the exclusion of all affects and thoughts that might activate attachment behaviour and feelings.

> The magnitude of effect on personality functioning of a behavioral system being deactivated will clearly depend on the status of the system within the personality.
>
> (Bowlby, 1980, p. 66)

We often encounter this defensive exclusion with clients who come from the most traumatic and insecure backgrounds.

> Attachment theory privileges fear as a major elemental drive that activates our attachment system, regulates physical and psychological proximity seeking and contact maintenance and shapes the organisation of mental life.
>
> (Slade, 2013, p. 39)

The impact of fear in the context of attachment relationships can be summarised as follows:

- There is the fear of an infant who doesn't know the world around them, but they know the arms that safely hold them – secure attachment.
- There is the fear of the infant who doesn't know the world around them and whose ground is easily shaken from underneath them – insecure attachment (still organised) as seen in avoidant and ambivalent attachment patterns.
- And then there is the fear of the infant who knows the world mostly through fear where there is nowhere to hide except within themselves, as seen in cases of child abuse with disorganised and cannot classify status.

A secure relationship is the antidote to fear and control. However, for reasons of survival, whether a caregiver is good or abusive, a child will seek proximity and be dependent on their caregiver. Furthermore, when childhood experiences are drenched with fear and accumulative frights and not a single solution is provided, in its paradoxical way, the conjunction of fear and proximity will provoke dissociation to be the best protective mechanism to survive such betrayals.

But at what cost?

In healthy development a child who is frightened or upset seeks a safe haven with their caregiver for comfort and protection. On gaining proximity, fear will subside if the caregiver's response is soothing. Yet, when the response is rejecting, relentlessly abusive, shaming and sinister, the child's fear will not subside. More so, since unpredictability is the bedrock of the frightening dynamics, the child's fear will not subside even when the parent is not actively abusing. The interpersonal trauma that is located within this dyad gives rise to what is termed by Main and Solomon (1990) as disoriented/disorganised attachment status.

I have coined the term "scaregiver" to describe the way a frightening, alarming and unpredictable caregiver behaves in their relationship with their child, leading to the child suffering pernicious emotional, physical and sexual abuse (Badouk Epstein, 2015, 2017, 2019, 2021). We know that this invariably leads to a process of dissociation in the child as a means of survival. In this relational landscape of fright without solution (Main and Hesse, 1998, 2005), the child's fear system will simultaneously engage in three core dissociative processes:

1   Heightened vigilance
2   Heightened communication
3   Heightened alienation.

Heightened Vigilance

This is where the child is still dependent and focused on following the scaregiver's unpredictable behaviour.

> Disorganized infants may represent a special category; hypervigilant of the caregiver's behavior they use all cues available for prediction and may be acutely sensitized to intentional states and thus may be more ready to construct a mentalized account of the caregiver's behaviour. We would argue that in such children mentalization may be evident, but it does not have the central and effective role in self-organisation which characterizes securely attached children… they may have the skill but fail to integrate this with their self organization.
>
> (Fonagy and Target, 1997, p. 691)

Heightened Communication

Devoid of secure emotional bonds, even when the "scaregiver's" response is not actively abusing, the dissociated child engages incessantly with the parent in a placating, false self-manner, which does not match their true feelings. Smiling can be co-opted by the fear system as a form of placation (Crittenden and DiLalla, 1988).

An example of what I have called these heightened-communication strategies might be the child saying: "Daddy, shall we play your favourite game? Daddy, shall I take your shoes off for you? Daddy look it's your favourite car!" Such hypercommunication will mitigate the fear system while trying to protect the child from the unpredictability of the scaregiver. During therapy such representation can be seen when the traumatised client incessantly talks at us rather with us, hardly noticing us yet fearing our judgment.

Heightened Alienation

Through the many frightening interactions with the scaregiver, the child has learnt to read the scaregiver's mind but not know their own minds and feelings, since according to Fonagy and Target (1997) "The child may know what the other feels but care little or not at all about this; alternatively, this information, for some youngsters, may be an issue of survival" (p. 681). This is happening while a dissociated part of the child is feeling emptied of emotional connection and experiencing a profound sense of detachment.

For example: A client who used dissociation extensively in her survival had been in three years of three times a week therapy when she described the following. On arriving at her parent's/scaregiver's home she noticed two things – she was frightened, her heart was racing while having a nice cup of tea with them. She also noticed how one of her "Not Me parts" took over to help her to be with them. She said: "she took over, I felt nothing but knew I had to act nice and finish drinking my tea".

Figure 4.1 explains the paradox of proximity and fear.

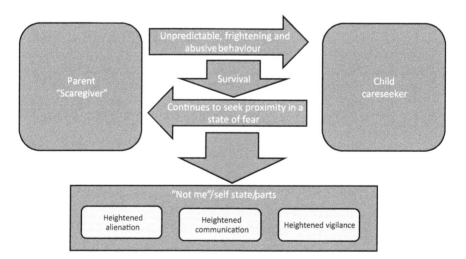

Figure 4.1 The paradox of proximity and fear in disorganised attachment

The Importance of Language

Growing up in a family that corrodes freedom by using subordination and possession as a means of communication will usually leave a child with imaginary abilities that are mostly geared towards survival, but which confine their space to trust their imagination to have meaning, texture, pleasure and to play without fear.

For example, a client with a dissociative identity used to write the most beautiful love poems only around Valentine's Day. During therapy we learnt that the part who could write had to prove her love to her abuser around this time of year.

Metaphor, according to Jeremy Holmes:

> … is inherently mentalising in that an image, while containing an important psychological truth, is by definition in the mind rather than out of reality… metaphor-making enhances playfulness and the use of transitional space as the participants add to and creatively modify each other's imagery. But for someone in equivalence mode, metaphor can also be confusing, merely adding to the breakdown of reality testing rather than strengthening it.
>
> (Holmes, 2010, p. 23)

It took a few years for the client to be less afraid and recognise her poet self as the one who saved her but one that was geared towards survival. The freedom to express her creativity in the presence of empathic witnessing and creative appreciation has helped her move on to exploring different styles of poetry written at different times that are more associative than dissociative.

Humans are a language-using species. We are born into language that precedes us and shapes our values as social beings. But language is also a function of the body. Before language is formed, the first sound the infant hears and feels is their mother's heartbeat. This is not just a plain sound, but rather an embodied sensation. In health the mother's heartbeat is syncopated with structure and flow, its rhythm is anticipated. Secure attachment means that from its inception the relationship the child has with their caregivers will afford many syncopated moments of rhythm and flow, as well as fewer unsyncopated moments and moments of misattunement. As the child grows and learns to respond to the caregiver's words it is with nurturing language that we come closer. The values and narratives we develop throughout childhood are always constructed within the context of the social system, namely the family in which we cohabit; thus, language is a form of relationship making. We tend to use words that are borrowed from our external landscape and that are reflected in what Bowlby termed as our Internal Working Models; an imprint of the relationship we carry with our caregivers and with ourselves. Yet as we hear from our clients, when they don't always have a language to describe how they are feeling, when the space they occupy is filled with psychic pain and no words to tell another, but worse when they are not allowed to participate in language as a form of self-expression, then the internal turbulence of confusion, shame and dissociation begins to dominate.

More so, "It has been argued that adversity becomes traumatic when it is compounded by a sense that one's mind is alone" (Fonagy and Allison, 2014, p. 379). For the mind-controlled child the language of love is deeply enmeshed with the language of terror, coercion, guilt and shame. This is a deliberate manipulation of the child's attachment needs, and the abuser's attempts to divide and control them, since according to Fonagy and Target (1997), "In abusive families the meaning of intentional states may be denied or distorted. Abusive parents may claim beliefs and feelings at odds with their behaviour" (p. 693).

We often meet the brutality of the abuser reflected in the narrative of the parts the client, in order to survive, has had to mimic and internalise. For example, one of the parts of my client acts in a racist, supremacist and xenophobic manner. During childhood this part was not allowed to mention the existence of difference within the world surrounding her. She was told about the cruel erasures which were needed for people who embody those differences. The words recognising their diversity and humanity had to stop existing in her mind. Everything connected to being inclusive had to be obliterated. For example, just mentioning to her family that there were Black children in her school and any mention of social discrimination was met with utter condemnation and corporal punishment. In therapy, the mind control that she had endured regularly and the family values of white supremacy were assuaged by my reading her a chapter from the book *The Memory Police* by Yoko Ogawa (1994): "And what will happen if words disappear? I whispered to myself, afraid that if I said it too loudly it might come true" (p. 26). This made a difference to the client's own experience.

What Happens to Creativity When Words Disappear and When Language Creates a Distorted Version of Reality?

In her Nobel Prize speech (1993), the writer and poet laureate Toni Morrison wrote about how the different iterations of European values impact on language. She gives voice to an imagined figure of a blind, wise, elderly woman descended from slaves to say:

> She is worried about how the language she dreams in, given to her at birth, is handled, put into service, even withheld from her for certain nefarious purposes. For her a dead language is not only one no longer spoken or written, it is unyielding language content to admire its own paralysis.
>
> … She is convinced that when language dies out of carelessness, disuse, indifference, and absence of esteem (or killed by fiat), not only she herself, but all users and makers are accountable for its demise. In her country

children have bitten their tongues off and use bullets instead to iterate the voice of speechlessness, of disabled and disabling language, of language adults have abandoned altogether as a device for grappling with meaning, providing guidance, or expressing love. But she knows tongue-suicide is not the only choice of children, it is common among the infantile heads of state and poor merchants whose evacuated language leaves them with no access to what is left of the human instincts for they speak only to those who obey... oppressive language does more than represent violence: it is violence... Sexist language, racist language, theistic language – all are typical of the policing language of mastery and cannot, do not permit new knowledge or encourage the mutual exchange of ideas.

(Morrison, 1993)

What Morrison is palpably conveying is that language is a vessel for communication of love as well as failed communication of power.

The American linguists Lakoff and Johnson (1999) perceived language partly as the language of the "Strict Father Metaphors". We have become so used to the construct of patriarchy that we are blind to the prejudice at its core. Following on from the philosopher Kant, Lakoff and Johnston state:

In fleshing out the Family of Man metaphor, by imposing upon it a Strict Father interpretation in which the family moral authority is the father, the father's commands are the family moral laws, and nurturance is the nurturance needed to become morally strong.

(1999, p. 420)

What patriarchy has taught us is that when our perspective is largely shaped by the gaze of the strict father, our mode of care for ourselves, for our children and for others is continuously compromised in linguistic binaries of good and evil, sin and punishment and perpetual violence. This is partly how we have become accustomed to ignoring our attachment needs and vulnerabilities.

Furthermore, the medical jargon developed in the West during the nineteenth and twentieth centuries that was often used against traumatised individuals has its own exclusivity and dominance and can be pathologising and objectifying. When we pathologise the other we automatically distance ourselves. Calling traumatised people: psychotic, schizophrenic, narcissistic, hysterics, paranoid, crazy and so on, is all part of a non-mentalised language that serves the need for binary power of patriarchal values and profit-based puritanism of the observing strict father. Through this way of seeing the client we name, shame and blame as a way of maintaining a degree of social and moral control that allows distance othering and the continuation of being trapped and stuck in a negative loop of affect and language.

As a man of his time, Bowlby's sensitivity to language nonetheless was always in line with his child-centric approach to life. In some correspondence between Bowlby and Mary Main, Bowlby suggested Mary Main use the word "inexplicable" rather than "irrational" in relation to the behaviour she was observing in the Strange Situation (Main, 1987).

"How well will I write if I were not here", said Calvino (1981, p. 34). True empathy is the ability to inhabit another person's perspective, yet as empathic therapists, by fully identifying with the client, we also hold the risk of abolishing the experience of the observer since sometimes the observer's subjectivity can be overtaken by the observed experience. This is what Freud referred to as countertransference entanglements. Moreover, the tension created between the observer and the observed usually happens when we feel threatened and fail to mentalise while rushing to perceive any othering as bad or abnormal. A mentalised life according to Fonagy and Target (1997) would mean to notice oneself in the context of the other, the world, and the environment surrounding us.

> They emphasised especially disorganized attachment relationships may anticipate to hinder the integration of imagination and understanding.
>
> (Duschinsky, 2021, p. 115)

For that we need a degree of feeling safe.

But we also have cultural expectations that can stand in contrast to emotional expectations. How do we evaluate the different dimensions we are operating from?

> Winnicott (1960) distinguished the notion of the subjectively conceived and objectively perceived self and other as interacting components within human perception and urged that only when these are brought together mental life is experienced as "alive and creatively usable".
>
> (Duschinsky, 2021, p. 127)

Most of our clients arrive in therapy after they have lost the capacity to imagine what it is to be in the proximity of a comforting and safe other. For example, a very traumatised client was invited by a kind friend for a Christmas lunch which she felt would be triggering. The client got herself into an internal turmoil, almost harming herself, since she could not negotiate a place within herself where she could deal with the triggering Christmas lunch without disappointing the friend. During therapy, anchoring the key scenes of her traumatic experiences in the past while reiterating the safety of the present while addressing her failed grief gradually helped her distinguish past from present. Yet she later reported that what really helped the client was carrying in her pocket the Christmas card I gave her, a reminder of our safe connectivity and that "'Was' is not 'is'" (Shakespeare, 1603).

Attunement

I am often asked how to attune to the suffering of a person whose multiple presentations arrive in polyrhythmic imprecision and unease. I use this metaphor to describe switching. Can the talking cure and its language sufficiently express what it's supposed to do? How do we position new words to reveal something that is felt but cannot be expressed? How can we listen to the music of a mind that was deliberately shattered to the point of total annihilation? And when is a good time to say something or say nothing. In truth, there is never a right moment to express the unsaid, particularly when the unsaid is being carried in segregated pockets of not knowing. With the help of the Boston Group (Stern et al., 1998a, 1998b), we have learnt about the domain of "implicit relational knowing" where changes necessarily occur in the non-verbal realm. As infants we begin recognising pitch changes based on the way caregivers use their voices to soothe and engage with us. It is the recognition of the vocal rhythm and tender tonality of caregiving (perceived as warmth) that carry emotional qualities of interaction relevant to developing attachment (Beebe and Lachmann, 2014, p. 33).

When our first conversation is soothing and calming, we develop an ear for implicit melody and a sense of belonging.

> These are present moments that make up their flow... The vast majority of therapeutic change is found to occur in this domain.
>
> Of particular importance is "the moment of meeting" in which participants interact in a way that creates a new, implicit intersubjective understanding of their relationship and permits a new "way-of-being-with-the-other". We view "moments of meeting" as the key element in bringing about change in implicit knowledge, just as interpretations are thought to be the key element in bringing about change in explicit knowledge.
>
> (Stern et al., 1988a, p. 300)

It is the many micro-moments of positive interaction between the therapist and the client that enable the client to move to other spheres of interiority. This is the most important part of the therapeutic dyad, when we are not only accessing the neglected dissociated child parts, but we also enable new developmental opportunities.

"Polyphonic dialogism" (Badouk Epstein, 2021) is a metaphor I use whenever listening to the chorus of the dissociated client's different voices where each part conveys something important to the process of communication and collaboration. Polyphonic dialogism can help put words and meaning to everything that the body knows but cannot express. And when words are not enough, it is silence, music, a favourite smell, or safe touch that has the power to envelop our space. For example, one client commented with a grudging tone that feels intrusive: "I see you are wearing a new jumper"; I listen to the threat in her voice and with that, her need to intrude and control me. As Liotti (2004) has taught us, by the time the disorganised child has reached the age of six they will have developed "punitive controlling strategies" towards self and other.

I take a deep breath and say:

> I guess you are the one who used to be left in the car waiting for what felt like an eternity while mother went for her daily shopping trips. To you, I am just like her possessing a new jumper and you also feel like her possession.

Another voice then enters the conversation, she feels the shame of her intrusion and she apologises. And so, with increased co-consciousness and empathic understanding we continue to bridge key scenes from past to present.

The modes of creativity vary in therapy; in essence they are modes of care that help the client construct their moral imagination to work in opposition to dominant forces that continue to define them even after the parent has died. In seeing creativity as an antidote to control, we try to attune to our very traumatised clients on levels they have never encountered – away from the power dynamic, and the self-reliant and self-imposed rules of ruthless patriarchy.

Since we are all subjectively motivated, each client and each therapist are unique. None of us is identical and will require different modes of nearness and different modes of distance. The therapist's own attachment history also arrives with an emotional constellation of the different shades of attachment patterns and relationship interactions. So how as therapists can we practice these modes of care with our clients without it being self-serving, infantilising or rescuing? I will illustrate this by sharing aspects of my relationship with the client who I have named Lilly.

Lilly: A Survivor of Mind Control

Lilly is a skilled professional in her late forties who arrived to therapy with a formal diagnosis of dissociative identity disorder and was not using any medication.

Growing up in a family submerged in sexual abuse and mind control experiments, where deliberate amnesia was planted, things were made to seem as if nothing had happened, so no one could recall what had taken place. In one early session Lilly was sobbing: "I can't remember me". In the words of Harvey Schwartz: "When mind control is successful there is no memory left and no story to tell" (Schwartz, 2013, p. 80).

Yet Lilly was left living with hundreds of parts, which her front or apparently normal personality (ANP) (Nijenhuis and Van der Hart, 2011) was too amnesiac to recognise. Living against the backdrop of terror and in close proximity to her parent's denial about the abuse, Lilly's fear system never

ceased being activated and she would spend days in a fog, her dissociation a veil of secrecy over both past and present. In this unmoored state, a part reported finding herself wandering the streets barefoot in the middle of the night, mumbling: "I only know what nobody knows". Lilly's regular night terrors caused her nights to become filled with morbid preoccupation and she found it increasingly difficult to function at work. "What is life to me without me?" a part regularly pondered during the first year in therapy. The feeling her dissociation produced was not one of general melancholia but one that was stored in different pockets of her being, each with a separate and distinct existence.

Unable to vocalise her feelings, it was her depersonalised body that would do it on her behalf. I then witnessed her body's sensation of feeling broken, followed immediately by a sensation of shivering, sweating, jolting or going into a hypnotic trance state. Her diminished self was mostly preoccupied with her mother's stream of messages and any vitality petered out; all I could see was a shadow of a shadow, desperately trying to gather some coherence. Lilly was lost in time, and could not consider its passing to be real, for her body was mostly in the "then and there" in some forest or church, a farm, or a stately home when she was tortured in the name of her badness. Worse still, they told her she loved it. Their words penetrated deep and played like a requiem on her broken mind. Awash with shame she whispered: "I am evil, I like it". Schwartz writes (2013): "When a child's sense of self has been undermined to this extent, all forms of mind control are possible" (Schwartz, 2013, p. 82).

During childhood Lilly's stolen subjectivity meant that many parts were trained to follow the family rituals unthinkingly and so by becoming a "psychic slave" (Schwartz, 2013, p. 81) she remained both highly loyal and highly dissociated. Her fear of her parents nonetheless was constant and alloyed with her admiration for their social piousness and false integrity. The rapid switching that took place during many sessions left us both in a dizzying haze. Unable to probe the gap between perception and reality, Lilly's traumatic life didn't allow her to have a two-person perspective, since a child who is compelled to only read their parents' mind will know little or nothing at all about their own mind. Lilly was always left feeling trapped in some crisis, leaving her in her need for survival to cling to the methods of the past. Lilly could not survive and be curious at the same time. Moreover, it was survival which made her store her love for others in separate parts within herself. I heard the poet and activist Dionne Brand (2022) say: "you can't live and love at the same time". My small addition to that would be that we can't survive and love at the same time. What we want is to be able to live and love at the same time. It was never safe for Lilly to open her heart to others and so I saw it as my role to enable these parts to come out of their hiding places and slowly participate in living and loving.

Lilly and Me

For the child survivor, the tension between being needed and not being wanted is what makes relational therapy suffer moments of breathless subjectivity, these are moments of failed mentalisation and enactment for therapist and client alike and in these moments, we feel overwhelmed to the point that we can hardly breathe. For example, for the client it might be experiencing gestures of nurturing kindness which can be so unfamiliar to their dysregulated system. For the therapist, on the other hand, to comprehend the extent of the atrocities perpetrated upon an innocent child can evoke fear, helplessness and panic, discouraging the therapist from wanting to work with such intensity, leaving the therapist feeling they can't do this job.

Cultural rituals essentially are a symbolic expression of social relations that help create a sense of togetherness. In families like Lilly's though, rituals are a concrete reminder of the requirement to put duty above care that is geared to activate fear and guilt to no purpose. Lilly's loyal parts would appear around certain anniversaries and significant dates, even after she minimised contact with her family.

Through Lilly's hypervigilance she had learned to register the speed of her parents' changing moods. It was clear that they too had dissociative identities themselves but chose perpetration over healing. Living in the thrall of extreme surveillance all her life, Lilly developed an intense external locus of control, which inevitably I too was subjected to through her controlling punitive behaviour. With the failure of separating time and space and when the past is in every corner of the present, Lilly's loyal parts would sometimes see me as her mother because her imagination did not have the space to see me as another subject.

A "Now moment", according to Daniel Stern (2004), is a "present moment" that suddenly arises in a session, it is a charged moment that can put the therapeutic relationship into question. A "now moment", nonetheless, is an emergent property of the "moving along process". It was during those multiple "now moments" that I would be taken off guard, as Lilly asked me questions about my private life, since her hypervigilance had taught her not to trust anyone not to abandon her. She also threatened to quit therapy, particularly before I went on holiday or when I was sick. These were the voices of the different parts, some of which were helpless children's parts, and some were the imitating family parts who incessantly tried to control us both.

Jean is one of the loyal daughter parts of Lilly who denies any abuse and who has a sharp eye for the negatives. But Jean was also protecting Lilly from possible disappointments, that to her felt intolerable. Then there were the parts who are pretty much clones of her mother and father and would shred the therapy to pieces to empty their feeling of instability as their only way of regulating.

The internalised father part would appear with his Nazi values spewing hatred towards people of colour and different gender identities. As a member of a minority myself, I would find these sessions the hardest to attune to and with my failed mentalisation I would roll my eyes in sheer despair, which only inflamed these parts, encouraging them to quit therapy. I sometimes would use a mirror while asking Lilly to reflect on what she was seeing, and she would report back the name of the part she saw in the mirror. Another time when words failed us, I would offer her a straw and would ask her to breathe out slowly through it – what we called "kind air". These ways of communicating were helpful but not enough to stop the ferocious attacks of the internalised parent parts.

What brought a lasting change was helping the parts better negotiate between themselves and others. During one session I was conversing with the parent parts who insisted that Lilly should go back home. Listening and dialoguing with each part, I then asked the mother part what she missed about her daughter the most. The mother part replied: "I don't know why you are asking this; a child belongs with their parents". The father part then added: "A daughter belongs with her mother!" I then asserted that Lilly is no longer a child and is working hard on becoming more autonomous. The mother part replied angrily: "But without me she doesn't exist!"

Whenever talking to one part the therapist needs to remember that there are always other parts who are lurking behind. Looking at her directly, I then called for other parts to pluck up the courage and tell us how they felt. "Afraid", a young voice whispered. I reassured her that I was there with her and that the internal parents are what Sullivan (1954) termed as "Not-Me" parts who were created to maintain control and loyalty in the subjugated child. I went on to reading to her a short article from a newspaper weekend supplement:

> When asked what you owe your parents the children's author and illustrator Cressida Cowell replied: "A lot – but not as much as they think I do. One of the differences between my parenting and my parents' is that I think my children owe me less".
>
> (Cowell, 2020)

I recall the dismay shown on Lilly's face. She lifted her head, to meet mine and the freedom of that present moment.

When working with survivors of extreme abuse, it is not only the memory recovery that is helpful to our work with them, rather it is a new way of being with other intersubjective exchanges when a growing sense of "I know you and you know me" slowly helps shape relational form and texture.

Being a survivor of mind control and seeing the world only through the eyes of her parents, Lilly found it almost impossible to get out of her mental maze and her gaze was often glazed over and lost in depths beyond reach.

While some parts yearned for closeness, others were terrified of being controlled. After all, seeing the light through a kind person's eyes can feel equally threatening to seeing darkness through her family's eyes. Lilly's fear of attachment meant that she risked herself becoming someone else's marionette and I became aware of the risk of being perceived as her new puppeteer. Time and again I reiterated to the parts who were anti-therapy that they have the freedom to end therapy or choose other forms of therapy. And so, while listening and having a back-and-forth negotiation with each part, my relationship with Lilly's divided system had a Russian doll quality of polyvocal perspectives where different modes of care are expressed through this kind of polyphonic dialogism.

It was during the Christmas period when the internal mother and father parts turned up lashing out abuse at their daughter and me. Their attacks went on for a while, until the internalised mother part asked me to intervene: "Are you not going to do something about that useless slob, what are we paying you for?" I decided to take her up on her offer and with soft tonality I talked to the emotionally battered child part telling her that no child should be treated like this, not even her parents who once were also abused children themselves. The mother's looming angry stare then shifted/switched and became tearful. Speaking as the ANP, Lilly then reported: "It's gone quiet inside; I think everyone liked what you just said". This is what Stern named as "a moment of meeting", when Lilly's interior clashing came to a halt to find a safe shelter away from the terrorising relentlessness of her "now moments" (Stern et al., 1998a, p. 304).

As time progressed, Lilly's dreams grew to be a more symbolic and contained conversation with the family that showed less fear and more self-empowerment. The increased consciousness between parts also made her realise that the power her parent held over her was not as imprisoning as they made her believe. In one collaborative session, I read to her two lines by the poet Solmaz Sharif:

Thank you fear. That's enough now.

(Sharif, 2022, p. 112)

She asked to keep these lines in her jacket pocket.

Conclusion

We never know which part of the personality will turn up on our doorstep. It is through multiple moment-to-moment interpersonal interactions between the therapist and the client that we gradually notice the formation of anticipated patterns of unpredictability. For example, the client's birthday is usually an anticipated trigger that will invite fear and rage to interrupt the flow of the safety of the therapeutic relationship. It is important not to react to the intensity of their rage but to see it as a form of self-protection against the terrorising relationship they had endured, and furthermore to anticipate that some of it will be repeated the following year. However, with growing security and decreased intensity we continue to move along.

Abuse is the cipher of fear, and control is the cipher of the imagination. Thus, albeit a creative mechanism for survival, dissociation nonetheless presents the survivor with a great deal of lack of safety and compromised living. It is through dissociation that the past rules the present. It is through dissociation where the client maintains unhelpful proximity to the abusers. It is through dissociation that self-harm and suicidal ideation continue to be around. It is through dissociation that clients struggle with everyday relationship(s), and it is through dissociation that their exploration and creativity are restricted.

Sometimes we make a new world with a single sentence, in moving away from the strict father metaphor, perceiving language as a mode of care, we can take control of the narratives handed over to us by patriarchy. The more we insist on a nurturing and textured language the less we experience binary outcomes, and the more there is the growth of connectivity with each other.

In a world of inequality, wars, natural disasters and disembodied digital disappearances, it is the security of our embodied relationship that binds us all. Having the creative freedom to love and think outside the constraints of the client's straitjacketed life, I believe, is what helps them and us to be creative collaborators.

Attachment-based therapy is a "we space" formation, where collaboration means including the diversity of our emotions. Intersubjective relatedness involves many present moments, a great deal of embodied creativity and mutual interactions that no mind control programming or interactive machine can fully track.

My work with Lilly continues to be intense yet displays gestures of a growing trust, such as meeting my eyes with a soft gaze and warm smile at the end of a session feels more decisive than the terrorised stare I first encountered.

> Epilogue
> In the beginning there was no me
> just we
> now that my imprinted fear
> is soaked in reformed love
> I can
> see you
> and a world without you
>   By Sia[2]

Notes

1 The Boston Group, founded in 1995, is a small group of psychoanalysts, developmental theorists and researchers including Daniel Stern, Louis Sandler, Edward Tronick and Karlen Lyons-Ruth (Stern et al., 1998a).
2 Reproduced with permission from Sia, a part of the personality of a client with dissociative identity seen for therapy by the author.

References

Badouk Epstein, O. (2015). "Cross the Bridge to Redefine the Pain". *Attachment: New Directions in Relational Psychoanalysis and Psychotherapy*, 9, pp. 290–294.
Badouk Epstein, O. (2017). "The Occupied Body". *Attachment: New Directions in Relational Psychoanalysis and Psychotherapy*, 11, pp. 257–272.
Badouk Epstein, O. (2019). "The Most Tender Place in My Heart Is for Strangers: Sexual Addiction, the Fear System and Dissociation through an Attachment Lens". *Attachment: New Directions in Relational Psychoanalysis and Psychotherapy*, 13, pp. 43–60.
Badouk Epstein, O. (2021). *Shame Matters*. London: Routledge.
Beebe, B., and Lachmann, F.L. (2014). *The Origins of Attachment*. London: Routledge.
Bowlby, J. (1969). *Attachment and Loss*. Vol. 1. *Attachment*. New York: Basic Books.
Bowlby, J. (1973). *Attachment and Loss*. Vol. 2. *Separation: Anxiety and Anger*. New York: Basic Books.
Bowlby, J. (1980). *Attachment and Loss*. Vol. 3. *Loss, Sadness and Depression*. London: Hogarth.
Brand, D. (2022). *Between The Covers: Conversations with Writers in Fiction, Nonfiction & Poetry* [Podcast], 1 October.
Calvino, I. (1981). *If on a Winter's Night a Traveller*. New York: Harcourt Brace.
Cowell, C. (2020). "Cressida Cowell: 'My Favourite Smell? Babies, Roses, and the Wind by the Sea'". *The Guardian*, 19 September. www.theguardian.com/lifeandstyle/2020/sep/19/cressida-cowell-my-favourite-smell-babies-roses-and-the-wind-by-the-sea
Crittenden, P.M., and DiLalla, D. (1988). "Compulsive Compliance: The Development of Inhibitory Coping Strategy in Infancy". *Journal of Abnormal Child Psychology*, 16, pp. 585–599.
Damasio, A. (1999). *The Feeling of What Happens*. London: Vintage.
Duschinsky, R. (2021). *Mentalizing and Epistemic Trust*. Oxford: Oxford University Press.
Fonagy, P., and Allison, E. (2014). "The Role of Mentalisation and Epistemic Trust in the Therapeutic Relationship", *Psychotherapy*, 51, pp. 372–380.
Fonagy, P., and Target, M. (1997). "Attachment and Reflective Function: Their Role in Self-Organization". *Journal of Development and Psychopathology*, 9, pp. 679–700.
Holmes, J. (2010). *Exploring in Security*. London: Routledge.
Lakoff, G., and Johnson, M. (1999). *Philosophy in the Flesh: The Embodied Mind and Its Challenges to Western Thought*. New York: Basic Books.
Liotti, G. (2004). "Trauma, Dissociation and Disorganized Attachment: Three Strands of a Single Braid". *Psychotherapy: Theory, Research, Practice, Training*, 41, pp. 472–486.
MacGilchrist, I. (2009). *The Master and His Emissary*. Boston, MA: Yale University Press.
Main, M. (1987). "Letter to John Bowlby, 15 March 1987". Wellcome Trust Library Archive, PP/BOW/B.3/35/1 MM1983–87.

Main, M., and Hesse, E. (1998, 2005). *Frightened, Threatening, Dissociative, Timid-Deferential, Sexualised, and Disorganized Parental Behaviour: A Coding System for Parent-Infant Interactions.* Unpublished Manuscript, University of California, Berkeley.

Main, M., and Solomon, J. (1990). "Procedures for Identifying Infants as Disorganized/Disoriented During the Ainsworth Strange Situation". In Greenberg, M.T., Cicchetti, D., and Cummings, E.M. (eds), *Attachment Beyond the Preschool Years: Theory, Research and Intervention.* Chicago, IL: University of Chicago Press, pp. 121–169.

Morrison, T. (1993). "Nobel Lecture". Nobel Prize Outreach AB 2024. www.nobelprize. org/prizes/literature/1993/morrison/lecture/.

Naimon, D. (Host). (2018). *Layli Long Soldier: Whereas. Between The Covers: Conversations with Writers in Fiction, Nonfiction & Poetry* [Podcast], 2 December. https:// tinhouse.com/podcast/layli-long-soldier-whereas/.

Nijenhuis, E., and Van der Hart, O. (2011). "Dissociation in Trauma: A New Definition and Comparison with Previous Formulations". *Journal of Trauma & Dissociation*, 12, pp. 416–445.

Ogawa, Y. (1994). *The Memory Police.* London: Harvill Secker.

Schore, A.N. (1994). *Affect Regulation and the Origin of the Self: The Neurobiology of Emotional Development.* Mahwah, NJ: Erlbaum.

Schwartz, H.L. (2013). *The Alchemy of Wolves and Sheep.* London: Routledge.

Shakespeare, W. (1603). *As You Like It*, Act 3 Scene 4.

Sharif, S. (2022). *Customs.* London: Bloomsbury.

Slade, A. (2013). "The Place of Fear in Attachment Theory and Psychoanalysis", in Yellin, J., and Badouk Epstein, O. (eds), *Terror Within and Without.* London: Karnac, pp. 39–57.

Stern, D.N. (1995). *The Motherhood Constellation: A Unified View of Parent-Infant Psychotherapy.* New York: Classic Books.

Stern, D.N. (2002). *The First Relationship.* Boston, MA: Harvard University Press.

Stern, D.N. (2004). *The Present Moment.* New York: Norton.

Stern, D.N., Sander, L.W., Nahum, J., Harrison, A.M., Lyons-Ruth, K., Morgan, A.C., Bruschweiler-Stern, N., and Tronick, A.Z. (1998a). "The Process of Therapeutic Change Involving Implicit Knowledge. Some Implications of Developmental Observation for Adult Psychotherapy". *Infant Mental Health Journal*, 19, pp. 300–308.

Stern, D.N., Sander, L.W., Nahum, J., Harrison, A.M., Lyons-Ruth, L., Morgan, A. C., Bruschweiler-Stern, N., and Tronick, A.Z. (1998b). "Non-Interpretive Mechanisms in Psychoanalytic Therapy". *International Journal of Psychoanalysis*, 79, pp. 903–921.

Sullivan, H.S. (1954). *The Psychiatric Interview.* New York: Norton.

Winnicott, D. (1960). "The Theory of the Parent-Infant Relationship". *The International Journal of Psychoanalysis*, 41, pp. 585–595.

Chapter 5

When the Alleged Abuser Is Famous

Some of the Problems in Dealing with Alleged VIP Abuse

Valerie Sinason

Introduction

Adult mental health professionals hearing a disclosure of past rape or assault in childhood from an adult can feel frightened as well as empathic. If they have not experienced it themselves, they can feel in their minds and bodies the impact of the cruelty they are hearing about; the invasion of space, of security, of ordinary living. If they can lend themselves out to bearing it, they can imagine what the impact would be on themselves and those they love. They can feel frightened that any living perpetrators who harmed the person they are listening to might come to attack them. A sense of safety and a just world can be broken. If they have experienced it before themselves, it can reawaken past trauma that needs further processing. This is before we even consider the fact of VIP allegations.

Working with a small person, a child, disclosing contemporary rape or assault can be even more difficult. We see the size of the small being who should have been protected, the size of the child against the size and power of the adult. Sometimes it makes us remember our own painful childhood experiences and even become too overwhelmed with them to continue. We do not grow painlessly from childhood to adulthood. We contain imprints from each age inside us. Among other opinions, it was the view of the late John Southgate (2002) that we are all multiple, containing aspects of every age we have passed through. The only difference is whether we are associating or dissociating multiples.

In my primary school in 1956 there was a popular joke making its whispered rounds in the playground. It was because of the changed behaviour of the headteacher and some of the form teachers in the face of a forthcoming school inspection. Enormous attention was suddenly being paid to the state of the desks, the tidiness of the piles of books, our socks, our hair, our spelling. Punishments increased as did the raised level of voices. Here is the joke.

SON CRYING: "Mum. Mum. I feel too scared to go to school. The teachers don't respect me and the children hate me".

MOTHER: "Now son, you are the headmaster. You have to go to school".

DOI: 10.4324/9781032696720-6

At ten years of age, we were able to understand something of the unresolved inner child experiences that could be triggered in adults in difficult situations and the fact that adults could be frightened as well as frightening. Even though children in the UK could be subject to legal physical assault by teachers in the classroom up to 1986 in state schools, 1998 in private schools and (unlike in the rest of Europe) can still be subject to "justifiable chastisement" in the home, children slowly become consciously aware of the fears of their parents as opposed to somatically only. Somewhere, societally, that was forbidden knowledge. It meant knowing what you are not supposed to know (Bowlby, 1988). Fear enters centre stage at the thought of losing body autonomy accompanied by its partner shame. A most powerful combination.

Historical Context

In 1962 a leading American paediatrician, Henry Kempe, pointed out that there was no "clumsy child" syndrome. Instead, there was a "battered child" syndrome. Injured children whose parents or guardians ascribed their bruises and broken bones to clumsiness were in fact children who had been physically abused (Kempe, 1962). It was not therapists who uncovered this. There is fear in considering what has happened to a child we are working with as well as shame we could not stop it. As Lloyd de Mause (1976, p. 1), the late psycho-historian, sharply reflected:

> The history of childhood is a nightmare from which we have only recently begun to awaken. The further back in history one goes, the lower the level of child care, and the more likely children are to be killed, abandoned, beaten, terrorized, and sexually abused.

Most mental health conditions in adulthood come from what the brave child had to bear. Indeed, dissociative identity is, par-excellence, a brave response from a creative child to a mad world. Success in our relatively new international field of trauma-informed therapy and understanding of dissociative identities hides the huge societal gaps in training and understanding of emotional, sexual and physical trauma that weaves its way through childhood and adult psyches, wreaking destruction in its wake. However, even with training, the professional can and will be knocked off course.

One brave social worker in the 1980s was able to realise:

> the terror the child I was working with experienced waiting for something bad to happen to her at night got right inside me. I realised I was feeling like a frightened child waiting for my line management to sack me for doing too much or not doing enough or that the child's alleged abuser would come to my house and kill me.

(Permission to give quote anonymously)

When dissociated inner-child fear enters multiprofessional systems of trained adults it increases the lack of security in multiprofessional trauma work.

The early few who tried to grasp this nettle, initially Freud (1897), and then Ferenczi (1988), were shocked at the level of vitriol they received. Ferenczi continued although scapegoated, but Freud could not bear the implications of all the influential middle class neighbours he knew being guilty of abuse, including possibly his own father. He never gave up on the toxic damage of early abuse but it was not his focus. Professionals over 100 years later find it just as hard despite the greater awareness, especially when the abusers are respectable and even more so when they are upper class or aristocratic. And, thinking of Freud's predicament, even harder when they are close neighbours or colleagues. Having to deal with suspected abuse within a hospital or unit setting by a professional colleague or colleagues is devastating as Jennifer Freyd has shown with institutional betrayal trauma (Freyd, 2023).

Noting abuse within the most deprived social classes has always been more acceptable to consider than abuse within the middle, upper and aristocratic classes. Even though the British public have slowly become aware of "boarding school syndrome", the impact on intimacy, attachment and sexuality as a result of separation from parents at the tender age of eight, and vulnerability to abuse by older boys and teachers in such schools, the impact on MPs who rule the country is hard to digest. It is hard to accept the pain, however unintentionally caused, that is felt in circles of that level of power and privilege.

Consider the impact on the future King Charles III when we see the small boy, formally shaking his mother's hand when she returned from an overseas trip, knowing already he was not allowed to run and hug her. Loving aristocratic and upper-class mothers have wept as they sent their eight-year-olds off to boarding school, hoping they would come through alright. That was the culture. How much did such experiences lead to parliamentary inability to put children first? Each culture has its equivalent of footbinding, scarification, cliterectomy, circumcision, beating... the rituals carried out to make someone a proper disciplined part of the group. Not all trauma is intentional. However, we do not want to see reflected in our society the pain we all loyally bear or dish out through attachment and compliance because the fear of being excluded and abandoned is too big.

Has the Climate Changed?

I consider that the tensions Freud faced are fundamentally no different today over 100 years later, except that he was more isolated than any of us have been. Possible abuse by attachment figures is hard to bear in itself and intentional abuse by well-known "good" citizens is equally difficult and frightening as it threatens our concept of our society. We are also aware of the threat to livelihood, or even life. As many have said at whistleblowing meetings all over the country: "I have a mortgage to pay. I need my work. I do not feel free to say anything about my supervisor / Head of Department even though I have doubts about his behaviour and ethics". If we add to this the way many abused children and adults can only speak to the extent they feel they will be heard, we can see the vicious circle of being silenced.

Despite the greater social recognition of the existence of abuse, therapists, like other professionals, can internalise the fear of speaking out. Will a supervisor support the work or be frightened, especially if the disclosure is of organised ritual crime or the disclosure comes from someone with dissociative identities? If the disclosure involves a famous and powerful person how much harder will it be? The negative treatment of professionals working with marginalised groups adds to the concerns. Beatrix Campbell (2023) has unpacked the levels of lies, secrecy and disinformation behind the attacks on the professionals following the medical diagnosis of child sexual abuse in Cleveland in 1987.

In the climate created by #MeToo there are hints of improvement. In the UK the Government accepts that 1 in 4 adults will experience abuse within their lifetime. 11 million adults. But how much do we all dissociate from the social implications of that? 11 million people. If being a victim of abuse meant joining a political party it would be the largest political party in existence and could transform the world. However, shame and silencing limit humans and that is why the increased visibility of survivor professionals and experts by lived experience is so important.

In addition, we have safeguarding procedures, guidelines, police training. Yet those who dare to make allegations, who break through the silence, are still all too often left unsafe and unheard.

Victim withdrawals from prosecution due to failings in the legal system, backlog of cases and lack of support add to the problem. I consider the issue of VIP abuse is strongly a cause of this. We have not yet even returned to the 2016 levels of charging and convictions for rape, the government's own low target. The majority of survivors do not report to the police because of lack of trust and therapists are facing a range of tick-box approaches to disclosures which can also cause breaches in trust.

From 2015 to 2020, 599,747 adults disclosed rape but only 2,012 got to court compared with 3,043 the year earlier. At each stage in the criminal justice system the numbers have dropped so far that Dame Vera Baird, the former Victims' Commissioner for England and Wales 2019–2022, said "we are witnessing the decriminalising of rape". Only 4% of all rape cases reported to the police were even referred to the crown prosecution and only 3% of rape claims in London result in a conviction. Only 1 in 65 survivors gains justice. Dame Vera Baird ended her term of office on 30 September 2022 and remains active on this subject. On 9 November 2023 she wrote on her website (https://verabaird.com), "criminal justice is so bad that over a third (34%) of victims who had been through the process said they would not report a crime to the police again". Although the government accept the true level of abuse this shocking figure of minimal prosecutions is rarely explored. This gap is caused by shame, fear, being silenced, disbelieved and discredited.

If several million adults in the UK, a fortunate Western country not at war, have a history of child abuse, how does the impact of untreated perpetration and long-lasting abuse show itself? How much are depression, suicide, breakdown of immune systems, crime, war, violence, mental illness, somatic breakdown and unhappiness a symptom of past untreated and unaddressed abuse? How does it affect the generation of babies born into betrayal and toxic environments? How would it affect our sense of ourselves as a country if we really faced it? A nation of collusion and delusion.

There is the fear, based on pragmatic experience, that if the victim is vulnerable due to disability or dissociation they will not be adequately listened to. There is the fear of the therapist, used to listening attentively and intuitively, suddenly feeling frightened that they are in a legal situation and do not know what to do. There is fear surrounding the unbearable understanding that abuse is not restricted to one class or one religion. It is ubiquitous. It breaks down the defensive "them and us" barriers.

Additionally, and the focus of this chapter, there is the fear of someone powerful and famous being named and especially if they are named *before* they die. The therapist and patient can then unconsciously and/or consciously face the fear of their child self and adult self being damaged now in real time as punishment for hearing and providing an emotional home. This fear extends into the general population.

It is a measure of our fear that Savile, Epstein and Cyril Smith could only be truly seen nationally for the extent of their corrupt and abusive acts after their deaths. All these issues need to be unpacked and faced to consider the safety of the therapy dyad and the wider team when abuse by someone famous is disclosed. And fear of what might happen, which has already happened in the past, is linked closely to the painful experience of shame, the feeling of having done something wrong in the face of authority, for which there will be public humiliation.

"Do You Know Who I Am?"

By using these words, a famous perpetrator, as a way of getting rid of his own terrors, can frighten the victims by warning them of the public attacks they will receive if they ever dare speak of him. DARVO is Jennifer Freyd's seminal term for the usual response of an offender when confronted: Deny, Attack, Reverse Victim and Offender (Freyd, 2023). DARVO is the usual response of an offender when confronted: "You pathetic bad damaging liar – you want attention by using my status to try and hound me and pull me down. I will pull you down instead".

In the face of such issues, living in a small village, sheltered housing, hospital ward or island such as Jersey poses extra confidentiality fears to patient and therapist alike when abuse is disclosed. However, living in a larger area, when you disclose abuse to a therapist or counsellor as an adult you can feel anonymous. Even though your therapist has a supervisor or a supervision group you can feel that no-one knows your abuser. Their name is usually unknown. If you live in an urban area not only are the names you mention usually unknown, but also the addresses. Public places mentioned are often so large it does not feel personal. Everything feels private in the consulting room.

The task for the therapist is made easier by the anonymity of the perpetrators even though it can be hard to speak of and listen to the details of a crime. However, if someone is named that you know and have feelings and assumptions about, how does that affect your clinical judgement? If you like that person and personally do not believe they could ever be guilty of such a crime how does this affect you in the therapy room? Or if you dislike them? Some of us carry around a litany of names, not knowing who was guilty, where there was disinformation and what was true. This is where a police investigation is essential.

If someone discloses bedwetting or nightmares there is no demand to forensically check if it is true, but when a rape is disclosed, a crime, we enter a legal area. This is an area of complexity for everyone even before fame enters the picture or ritual abuse or dissociative identity, and then it becomes even harder.

The clinician is not a police officer or judge and jury but empathically and actively listens and responds. When the clinician hears disclosures of a crime and is asked desperately, "Do you believe me?" there is a danger of the scared clinician abusing the concept of neutrality by trying to take up a rigid position.

As experienced colleagues helpfully say:

> clinicians should not reflexively accept or reject as fact a client's initial report of uncorroborated abuse. However, by maintaining neutral stance clinicians may fall short of therapeutic honesty and transparency, may fail to promote reality testing and may not perform the necessary step of bearing witness.
>
> (van der Hart and Nijenhuis, 1999, p. 37)

When a patient asks, "Do you believe me?" I can honestly reply "I believe horrid things have happened to you and you are the evidence of that, but we may never find all the details". With some patients with dissociative identities there is the added problem that part of the personality A does not believe any abuse ever happened and disputes everything part of the personality B says. This is before we even consider whether the perpetrator is known to us or not.

When Mr and Mrs Smith of Smith Street, whose names and addresses are not familiar to us, are alleged to have abused a patient of ours, we can feel safe in our therapeutic relationship, neutral. Even then, some therapists will find it hard that these alleged perpetrators are alive and dissociate from those external details in order to emotionally focus on the relationship in the room. Survivors making allegations about publicly unknown relatives face the internal and external judge and jury of their family and themselves. However, survivors alleging abuse by famous individuals face the jury of public opinion, social media, articles from the famous supporting their besmirched friend, rallying of false memory groups and others, let alone their own self-criticisms, and feel concerned at the public attacks on their therapist.

In other words, where the name is known the therapist cannot so easily focus clearly and intently in the room. We are, after all, listening to a possible major crime that has been ignored. The whole issue of police involvement for a past or current crime is an ethical mess where the therapist risks an unconscious bias to aiding the client to seek police help or to avoid it. With children there is a clear rule that social services have to be informed but the safeguarding issues for vulnerable adults are fraught with difficulties, even if the perpetrators are unknown to us.

The UK, just a decade ago, was energised by a sudden mushrooming of disclosures and major police investigations. It was split into different camps, victims and survivors and their friends and supporters had hope that we were entering a new stage of enlightenment. Friends of alleged perpetrators felt fear we were entering a McCarthyite era where allegations became public without any trial. Other citizens felt either pride we were getting to grips with such massive wrongdoing or felt shame that our country was perpetuating trauma. And perpetrators?

A focal point was 2012 when Tom Watson MP, Deputy Leader of the Labour Party, used parliamentary privilege to point to a powerful paedophilic network linked to parliament and No 10. This was linked to the paedophile Peter Righton. This was also the period when hidden bombshells from the 1980s were unpacked: Jimmy Savile and Cyril Smith were being revealed as serial abusers. Home Secretary Theresa May began an independent inquiry, and more disclosures came, including from people with dissociative identities. There were missing government files and an enormous amount of knowledge about Cyril Smith but even when police felt they had succeeded in catching him, he would be released. Indeed, Lord Tebbit, former Conservative cabinet minister, said with shocking honesty that the instincts at the time were to protect "the system" and not delve too deeply into allegations. "At that time, I think most people would have thought that the establishment, the system, was to be protected and if a few things had gone wrong here and there that it was more important to protect the system". The few "things" that had gone wrong were the dispensable children, destroyed by abuse (Tebbit, 2014).

I heard from many survivors at that time who were really grateful for MP Tom Watson's intervention. The media provided a very different response and a huge attack on Tom Watson began. The attack then moved into an attack on police investigations into allegations against the powerful and a plethora of different police investigations.

Police Investigations

The police investigations fragmented into multiple small groups. As well as Operation Hydrant and Operation Conifer there were Operation Midland, Fairbank, Fernbridge, Athabasca, Yew Tree, Jersey and several more.

Operation Yewtree was a Metropolitan Police investigation launched in October 2012 into sexual abuse allegations, predominantly the abuse of children, against television presenter Jimmy Savile and others. A report into Savile's alleged abuse was released by the Metropolitan Police in January 2013.

Operation Jaguar was an investigation conducted by Greater Manchester Police into allegations made over decades against the late Sir Cyril Smith, who died in 2010. He was a prominent local councillor in Rochdale and then Liberal MP. He was never prosecuted.

Operation Fairbank started in 2012 as a scoping umbrella exercise into child sex abuse claims involving high-profile figures including politicians. It led into other inquiries, including Operations Fernbridge and Midland. Operation Midland was set up by the Metropolitan police to examine claims that boys were systematically abused by a VIP paedophile ring at locations across southern England, including Dolphin Square estate in Pimlico, southwest London, an area popular with politicians.

Operation Fernbridge was launched by the Metropolitan Police in February 2013 to examine allegations of abuse in the early 1980s at Grafton Close children's home in West London and at Elm Guest House in Barnes, south-west London. Two men were charged in connection with Grafton Close, including a guilty Catholic priest after which Fernbridge was closed and investigations into Elm Guest House were taken over by Operation Athabasca. The late Cyril Smith, former MP for Rochdale, was said to have visited the Elm Guest House in Barnes, south-west London.

What I want to give extra attention to in this chapter is that in 2015, in the wake of the Savile scandal, an investigation was set up to specifically look into allegations against the former conservative Prime Minister Sir Edward Heath, who led a Conservative government from 1970–1974 and died in 2005. The investigation's objectives were:

> to identify and safeguard children and vulnerable adults who may be at risk of abuse today; to seek the truth about the allegations of child abuse made against Sir Edward Heath through an objective and proportionate investigation; through the course of the investigation, identify, and where possible bring to justice, any surviving offender.

As Sir Edward Heath lived in Wiltshire, it was agreed Wiltshire police should lead for Operation Hydrant.

Operation Hydrant was not a specific investigation into child abuse but the name given to a co-ordination hub for allegations of child sexual abuse within institutions or by people of public prominence. The Hydrant team revealed police across the country were investigating more than 1,400 men, including 261 high-profile individuals over allegations of historical child abuse.

Through the need for a co-ordinated response based in Wiltshire under the leadership of the Chief Constable Mike Veale it became Operation Conifer. Mike Veale was quite clear that were the former Sir Edward Heath still alive there would have been enough grounds to question him. Apparently, he would have been questioned over seven of the total of 42 claims if he had been alive when they came to light, but that no inference of guilt should be drawn from this. Of the seven allegations deemed most credible the victims were five boys and two men (college.police.uk).

As there was no prospect of a prosecution involving Sir Edward Heath, lines of enquiry did not have to be completed to the evidential standard required by a court of law. However, there is an ethical issue as to whether that is adequate. When an allegation is made against such a major figure there is a danger of either their reputation remaining unfairly besmirched or unfairly intact.

However, I have a different purpose here in naming some of the major investigations that began at that time. Savile, Smith and others were found guilty. Some victims were identified who were validated even though their abusers were dead and could not be brought to trial. Then, something even more salutary and worrying happened here, concerning the treatment of a false witness.

Anger at police investigations naming Sir Edward Heath and other well-known public figures led to a new Metropolitan Police investigation into Operation Midland. This was largely due to an accuser, Carl Beech, being imprisoned for falsely accusing public figures of murder and child sexual abuse following a 2016 report by retired High Court judge Sir Richard Henriques, who found more than 40 failings in Operation Midland. Two other accusers were seen to be liars but were not prosecuted (Sir Richard Henriques, Report. www.net.met.police.uk).

Beech, referred to as "Nick" during Operation Midland, was a former NHS paediatric nurse, who was working as a hospital inspector with the Care Quality Commission. He was also the governor of two schools in Gloucestershire where he lived. Originally seen as a credible witness (unlike many vulnerable individuals) he was subsequently convicted of making false claims of sexual abuse and child murder about a VIP group.

As a result of his evidence, the homes of Harvey Proctor, Lord Bramall, former chief of the defence staff, and Lord Brittan's widow, Lady Diana Brittan, were searched. He also named Sir Edward Heath, Lord Janner and Leo Brittan MP (both of whom died in 2015). The narrative he expressed was one provided by other survivors who have not been discredited in this and other inquiries, like the Independent Inquiry into Child Sexual Abuse (IICSA), but these allegations purporting to come from his owned lived experience were held to be lies. Carl Beech also said his stepfather Major Beech abused him and pimped him at VIP parties. A final concern was that he was also found to be downloading child abuse imagery and filming a teenage boy. There was no adequate evidence provided by him, and there were contradictions and inconsistencies. Public support for all survivors naming VIP abusers dwindled and a stronger attack on such survivors began.

Carl Beech received a prison sentence of 18 years, longer than for murder. A mad logic entered the public narrative that if Carl Beech had lied, then all victims talking of VIP abuse were liars. If Carl Beech had lied about murderous acts against boys by VIPs, then none of it existed. All the people he named must be innocent of anything and everything. If he told these lies in therapy, then all therapists were colluding in lies. This is quite separate from the arguments of those who felt he was being scapegoated.

Trauma therapists witnessed a damaged response in survivors. We can also see this in the dramatic decrease in numbers coming forward. Almost every trauma professional I have known in this period has reported survivors saying: "I will be accused of being a fantasist, a liar and then my abusers will have won in the court of the land".

Where is the forensic interest in why such lies would be given, if they were all lies? Where is the public curiosity at seeking to understand how telling a lie is committing a crime that is worse than murder? To be wrongly accused is to be abused and has a terrible impact. But whose reputation is so important that an attack on them deserves such disproportionate penalties?

Every time a survivor truthfully discloses abuse and police, the Crown Prosecution Service or court responses are profoundly unhelpful, there is huge reputational damage to that survivor. Millions of them. There is also the media reputational hurt to all those who work with survivors alleging VIP abuse. Yet in this instance the reputational hurt caused to the tiny number of people he named was considered worth a prison sentence longer than for murder. What message does that give? A police investigation is crucial and reputational damage is appalling damage but there is a disproportion in whose reputation really matters.

A group of us were so concerned that a letter from 32 professionals was published in *The Guardian* which expressed concern about the anger directed at Tom Watson MP, the police and Carl Beech after his trial. The letter argues that there are lessons to be learned from Beech's case and that trauma and abuse evoke powerful feelings that need to be understood. We said the kind of scenarios Carl Beech described were familiar to us, that "fantasists" need to be understood, that to be wrongly accused is to be abused but the number misnaming abusers is very small compared to the huge numbers abused and the tiny number who gain justice. We quoted a survivor who said: "When Tom Watson spoke I felt I could vote and visit parliament. But if he is attacked for doing the right thing – and 'Nick' is imprisoned for so long, what would happen to me?" (Sinason et al., 2019).

Milgram and Obedience

The issue of VIP abuse involves attachment, class, gender, hierarchy and obedience.

Stanley Milgram, while at Yale and still in his twenties, conducted some truly frightening experiments showing the speed with which people obey someone who appears authoritative (Milgram, 1974). With actors playing the victims and an authoritative experimenter, students were asked to give what they thought was a powerful electric shock (although it was all acting); 65% gave these shocks even though they were uncomfortable. It does not take a long journey from obeying authoritative figures to committing violent acts. If police and MPs are publicly vilified for supporting a survivor's narrative and considering that there is sufficient evidence to investigate, what happens to the genuine survivors who lived through it or the professionals who heard such disclosures?

When a name is known to us and is in the media too and we experience the feelings of shock and terror in a client a boundary is crossed in us. The consulting room cannot be a place impervious to all that is going on in the outside world. We need our nest, our calm space in which to think and relax. However, when the name stays with us wherever we go we get a sense of the helpless anger of many survivors who cannot alter the stories unravelling on TV, radio and social media. Many colleagues, like me, will be hearing from survivors who disclosed abuse by Savile but did not feel safe to give later evidence after the prison sentence handed to Carl Beech.

A Real Life Example

I have experienced hearing many disclosures about people I have heard of. Here is a composite situation for us to consider.

The man in question was a key figure in the mental health field and I had been so proud when friends told me he had recommended a book of mine at a large conference. I will call him Dr Liar. However, we had not actually ever met face-to-face at the point where I heard more about him.

Lara, a young woman in her twenties who had dissociative identities, lived with her loving mother. Her father had died. She had a history of abuse from infant school which led to stays in hospital and self-harm in her teens. No perpetrator had ever been arrested. Her mother was devastated by her fluctuating states as much as by the trauma she continued to suffer and had wanted a further assessment. It was not long-term therapy that was wanted, just this one meeting.

The mother rang early in the morning of the assessment worrying Lara might not turn up as she had quietly left the house after her mother had fallen asleep and had not come back. "I can't keep her locked up", she said.

At the meeting Lara presented as a pale blonde waif with startling blue eyes and a look of complete exhaustion. T is Therapist; P1 is Lara; P2 is Lana.

T: You look tired.
P1:   Yes

A stronger voice then took over.

P2:   So would you if you'd had the night I did. Dr Liar is a randy old sod.

She laughed.

T: Dr Liar?
P2:   Yes. You probably know him. Thinks he is a big cheese at all these conferences.

I felt a chill run through me. This sounded like the Dr Liar I knew of.

T: Doesn't sound like you think he is a big cheese.
P2:   Well he smells like one (laughing) under all that fancy cologne he just stinks.
T: Doesn't sound like a very nice night then.
P2:   Course it wasn't. But I can cope.

There was a pause.
Quiet Lara reappeared.

P1:   I don't want to talk too much because Lana will hear and she will hurt me.
T: Lana?
P1:   You were just talking to her. She can hear what I am saying.

There was a pause.

T: Lana, it would be very helpful if you could let Lara speak.
P2:   Oh she is a fucking cry baby. No wonder Dr Liar only wants me.
T: Sounds difficult. You have sex with him but you think he is a bit smelly and you don't want Lara to speak.
P2:   OK. I will let her. She will soon come snivelling back. Nothing changes with these stupid meetings anyway. I have had more assessments than you have had hot dinners.
T: Thank you Lana. Lara, Lana gives you permission to speak.
P1:   Dr Liar is one of the men who hurt me ever since I can remember. I get school and hospital all mixed up. I said his name to the police when I was little and no-one listened. They said he was a nice man trying to help me. And they put me in a hospital where he carried on hurting me. And so now I am telling you because I want something done. Before I die. They got Smith and Savile even if they didn't get Heath and they can get Liar.

P2:   Ooh – who is trying to sound all strong and brave. It doesn't work. You won't get anywhere with the police. Nor did my Mum. It will all just carry on.

I got permission from both of them and a child personality to speak to safeguarding and a vulnerable victim co-ordinator. I also got their permission to speak to their mother.

T: They said Dr Liar was the name of the main man who abused them.
MOTHER: Yes. I didn't want to name him until you heard her name him herself because I was pretty sure you would have heard of him and I didn't want to be accused of putting ideas in your head. As you might guess, wherever I go they are ready to say everything is a false memory.

The medical files were heartbreaking in their emptiness. There was medical evidence of anal rape, but all allegations made were dismissed as fantasy. They had been consistent in their account although naturally confused about places. Hospital, school and home were mixed up. All the police wanted were the details victims rarely find easy to say, and especially children. If there hadn't been incontrovertible proof of anal rape she would not have been offered anything.

The following week I realised I was speaking at a large conference on the same panel as Dr Liar. I felt petrified. It affected me bodily and I was running to the toilet in every interval.

Dr Liar was clearly a star in his element. He smiled benignly at me with no sign of anxiety.

DR LIAR: Hello Dr Sinason, we meet at last. I loved your last book and told a whole conference about it. You have clearly more on the boil since.

I would have been so happy at such a comment. For a moment a little spark of pleasure entered me. He was so charming and plausible. Was this because he was charming or was he a liar? What an impossible situation to be in at this conference now with the private contents of a therapy session going round in my head. This must be something that happened a lot to famous people. They must receive such projections all the time. I must stay clear and neutral. It was up to the police to provide an opinion.

However, something about Lara and Lana's personalities and authenticity was also involving me. I was seeing him with their eyes and not in a neutral way.

Feeling conflicted I struggled to listen to him talk.

He gave an excellent clinical and theoretical paper. I was slowly returning to therapeutic normality. Perhaps they had muddled up his presence with less clear early memories. But then, near the end he looked at me. He looked very intently and I found myself clenching my fists.

Dr Liar then said "I have started a charity to mentor suicidal young women. This is a time-bomb subject. But I am very pleased with the first results with a young woman called Lana".

He looked at me. And that was the moment. He knew that I knew that he was involved in something to do with her.

At the break I rushed into the toilet again to phone my husband and a police officer friend. I felt ill. That night I could not sleep and felt continuously nauseous. When the phone rang I felt scared it could be Dr Liar. I looked worriedly at letters that arrived. Would he write to me?

The professionals I went to could not do anything with my experience. It might make clinical sense but it did not make any evidential sense. Lara was in despair.

P2:   Now you know why I am still here and not all integrated.
MOTHER: I have had this for 15 years. It destroyed her father's health and you have to make sure it doesn't destroy yours.

Dr Liar was found out to be someone who had been very helpful to Jimmy Savile. I reported this to everyone. It made no difference. But to Lana, Lara and myself it did make a difference. A link had been made.

Dr Liar has since died. Eulogies were everywhere. Lara was accepted to study medicine. She wanted to become a psychiatrist to work with abuse and dissociative conditions.

Conclusion

When a VIP abuser is named the privacy of the treatment is intruded on. Whether you like or dislike the known person you have to work hard over internal bias. With some disclosures, police may get sound proof, but with many others there is clinical evidence but no resolution. In learning how to hold out for all possibilities we develop a strange strength – it is called bearing reality. We have to realise that the powerful are powerful. The people who form protective networks around powerful perpetrators do so very successfully. But every so often the truth comes out. We need to channel our frustration by aiding the training of police, speaking, writing and sharing. And it is through attachment-based work that slowly the truth comes through.

In my first published novel (Sinason, 2022) I examine the situation of VIP abuse further when a young woman with Down's syndrome discloses that she was abused on Halloween by the Deputy Prime Minister and an American rockstar. And no, there is no success with the case there either! I wanted it to be realistic. However, at the end of a painful conference where survivors speak up about VIP abuse, the tired female psychiatrist, Dr Kestle, is about to go when a shy young black woman approaches her with a bunch of primroses saying Dr Kestle won't remember her. But she does. Chalondra was a part of a patient called Tara.

> Chalondra says "We stayed with the therapist you got us and there are just two of us now, Tara and me. Tara agreed I could come to the conference because I have done counselling training but most of all, to give these flowers to you".
>
> "Yes", said Dr Kestle softly, taking them reverently. "Winter flowers to bring light and I told you that you brought light to Tara and the others like a primrose and not to look down on yourself".
>
> She opened her arms tentatively and Chalondra fell into them, primroses of light and colour enveloping them. "Thank you for coming today and bringing these", said Dr Kestle, "Today you have brought winter light to me at a time when I felt very dark".
>
> (Sinason, 2022. p. 360)

The precious relational therapeutic attachment in itself helps to cushion patient and therapist from the trauma of VIP abuse. We find good colleagues, supervisors, police officers, psychiatrists. We find a trustworthy group to aid growth in the face of corruption and cowardice. And a book, like this, from a good conference to participate in.

References

Bowlby, J. (1988). "On Knowing What You Are Not Supposed to Know and Feeling What You Are Not Supposed to Feel", in J. Bowlby (ed.), *A Secure Base*. London: Routledge, pp. 99–118.

Campbell, B. (2023). *Secrets and Silence: Uncovering the Legacy of the Cleveland Child Sexual Abuse Case*. Bristol: Policy Press.

de Mause, L. (ed.) (1976). *The History of Western Childhood*. London: Souvenir Press.

Ferenczi, S. (1988). "Confusion of Tongues between Adults and the Child – The Language of Tenderness and Passion", *Contemporary Psychoanalysis*, 254, pp. 196–206. German original in *Int.Z.f.Psa* (1933), 19, 5.

Freyd, J. (2023). "*What Do We Know About DARVO, Institutional DARVO, and Anti-DARVO?*". Plenary address at the 40th Annual Meeting of the International Society for the Study of Trauma and Dissociation, Louisville, Kentucky, 15–17 April.

Kempe, C.H. (1962). "The Battered Child Syndrome", *Journal of the American Medical Association*, 181, 1, pp. 17–24.

Milgram, S. (1974). *Obedience to Authority: An Experimental View*. New York: Harper & Row.

Sinason, V. (2022). *The Orpheus Project*. London: Sphinx Books.

Sinason, V., *et al.* (2019). "Problems Investigating Historical Child Sex Abuse", Letters to the Editor, *The Guardian*, 29 July. www.theguardian.com/uk-news/2019/jul/28/problems-investigating-historical-child-sex-abuse

Southgate, J. (2002). "A Theoretical Framework for Understanding Multiplicity and Dissociation", in Sinason, V. (ed.), *Attachment, Trauma and Multiplicity: Working with Dissociative Identity Disorder* (2nd edn). London: Routledge, pp. 86–106.

Tebbit, N. (2014). "Tebbit Hints at Sex Abuse Cover-Up as Pressure Over Missing Files Intensifies", UK News, *The Guardian*, 6 July. www.theguardian.com/uk-news/2014/jul/06/norman-tebbit-theresa-may-cover-up-child-abuse-dossier

van der Hart, O., and Nijenhuis, E.R.S. (1999). "Bearing Witness to Uncorroborated Trauma: The Clinician's Development of Reflective Belief", *Professional Psychology: Research and Practice*, 30, (1), pp. 37–44.

Chapter 6

The Parts, the Whole and the Real Person

An Attachment Perspective

Adah Sachs in Conversation with Emma Jack

This chapter looks at the hidden attachment relationship between the parts and the whole, viewing it as the foundation of the 'real person' and the basis for therapy. It is an edited version of a conversation which discussed the thinking of Adah Sachs on the question of *identity* in a person whose identity is dissociated, and the *Self* in a person who has many selves.

Introduction

The person with dissociative identities experiences themselves as a number of separate people. None of these 'people' or parts knows the full identity of the whole person because, as the term conveys, their identity is dissociated. Does this mean that the separate parts have no collective Self, or that beyond the individual parts there is no real person at all? Who, then, makes their main choices – or are we making the radical suggestion that a person with dissociative identities has no capacity for making a choice?

This chapter is the fruit of a conversation between Adah Sachs and Emma Jack on the question of identity, a person whose identity is dissociated, and the Self in a person who has many selves. Adah's thinking highlights the hidden attachment relationship between the parts and the whole, viewing it as the foundation of the 'real person' and the basis for therapy.

The Conversation

Emma Jack (EJ): Working with clients is probably always the way we discover anything. How did your clinical practice lead you to think that a shared Self exists, separate from a dissociated self?

Adah Sachs (AS): I'm not sure I'd say it is separate from the dissociated self or selves! I think The Self is the origin of the dissociative self or selves.

But let me start some steps back. I'm sure you will agree that we are all different, this is how we recognize each other in a crowd; and people who

DOI: 10.4324/9781032696720-7

share the same diagnosis are still just as different from each other. So, people who have dissociative identities all have things in common, which are part of their shared diagnosis: an extremely traumatic history, fractured memory, many parts that keep switching and a general air of high risk. But they are also all different from each other as people. They each have a different overall feel to them. You know, some are shy and some are assertive; some are poetic, some are practical by nature, some are artistic, or tearful, or argumentative or generally friendly. Just like with non-dissociative people, once you get to know someone with dissociative identities, their basic characteristics are simply there and you don't confuse them with another person, with or without dissociative identities. So, I began asking myself, are these differences that I notice an expression of their sharply changing parts, or is what I see an expression of them as a whole, the way they are just a different kind of person from the next person? Would they have been a different kind of person if they had not lived through the trauma that had fractured their identity and created the dissociative structure? And though there can't be a definitive answer to this question, the overall feel of each person is distinctly different. It appears to me that the sharp changes between parts, the intensified air of risk and the overall distress presentations are the trauma characteristics of all people with dissociative identities, superimposed on top of their individual ones. So instead of either self or selves, I started thinking of their Self: the substance from which the trauma had carved their parts.

EJ: I wonder if you are thinking of Self in terms of something we might call, essence?

AS: Yeah, like an essence, you could put it this way – which is not the sum of the different parts of personality, but the source of them. Parts come to life for trauma reasons, for the physical and mental survival of a person in impossible distress, and they carry the story of what, historically, has happened to the person. But they are also the story of the unique way in which this particular person with their own essence survived their horrors: the parts that this particular person created were not random, they never are; they are an expression of a unique Self or as you say essence, the specific narrative, personality and abilities which this person created for a part who, so to speak, had to get everyone out of a burning building alive.

It made me think that it would be wrong to say there is no reality to the person beyond the separate parts. I mean, such a line of thinking disrespects the fact that the person is still a person, an essence, beyond their trauma and their defending parts. That beyond what went so badly wrong, there was, and is, also a person that all that wrong had happened to, and that the parts are an expression rather than a replacement of that person. That in dissociative conditions the person's identity is dissociated, fractured, but not replaced or extinguished.

EJ: Is there a person that you can describe that really informed your thinking around this?

AS: Recently I spoke on the phone with a person I've worked with many years ago. Our conversation led to the question 'what do you think is the most defining thing about you as a person?' She thought about it and said, 'I'm good at a lot of things'. Which is very true, she's very capable and most things she lends her hand to she can do. She then said, 'even when I'm afraid I do things'. That's also true, she has courage and the will to try. I then said, 'which of these things mean the most to you?' and she said, 'There is something, it's a bit personal, I think kindness is a big part of who I am'. And I thought to myself, goodness, I've known her for so long and yet I had never actually put my finger on it so well, but it's absolutely true. And you can see it in the relationship between her parts, how they all relate to one another, with enormous, selfless kindness. I mean, they were trying to kill each other for years. But there was also a strong current of underlying care, a ruthless commitment that perhaps masked but didn't destroy the kindness shared between them.

EJ: What an amazing thing for her to be able to say that about herself! That's really lovely.

AS: Yes, these moments are very moving... The sense of intense underlying connection between parts can be very strong, but not in all systems. Sometimes the prevailing feeling around a person is of great coldness and loneliness, of parts with no connections, no names, no memories, no earth under their feet. And some feel like they are always on the warpath, or always about to die. Every person I've worked with had a 'feel' all of their own, and I imagine many therapists would have a similar experience. There are as many variations between people with dissociative identities as there are between people who are not dissociative. So, on the question 'do they have an underlying quality as a person?', my answer is of course they do, and why wouldn't they.

There is also an added, ethical concern here, which has always worried me in viewing dissociative identities as fully independent, which I say more about in another paper (Sachs, 2015). We can agree that different parts make their way to the surface or 'are up', whatever wording you prefer, at different times. We also know from observation that the switching of part is trigger-related. For example, parts can be triggered to appear in response to a certain word, sound or because they saw a man with a moustache. It can look like the appearance of parts depends entirely on unpredictable, external factors. But seeing it this way raises a serious question: do people with dissociative identities actually have *agency*, a capacity to make choices, as opposed to just acting in response to random, external triggers? If the answer is that they just react to random stimuli and have no capacity for a coherent choice, their liberties and basic human rights may be at stake. Because if a person doesn't have the capacity to make decisions, these rights may be taken away and someone else would have to decide for them, due to duty of care, which has huge and very problematic ethical implications. I think most therapists who know people with dissociative identities would say that they generally do have capacity. And I believe this also applies to the question of which part of the personality is up at any given moment, which I think is far from random. I call it 'the wisdom of the system': the system of the person knows what is needed now, and which part will be best to deal with the current situation to ensure survival. Even if we disagree with their choice, it is a choice, not a random action.

EJ: I agree that sometimes, I might make an intervention something like 'Can I ask the system, is the direction that we're moving in OK?' So, I don't know who that is that I'm talking to. Perhaps this is what you're attempting to define. Nearly always 'the system' will come back in some fashion and say something or do a thumbs up or down or something? I wonder what you think of the choices that you are aware have been made, and if they appear broadly to be in the service of the client.

AS: How do we know they made 'good' choices? There is more on this in another paper (Sachs, 2015). But briefly, I think my best answer to that is because they're still alive. Because their lives are frequently so full of danger, and so full of risks, and so full of physical attacks and pain, the fact that they're still alive is a bit of a miracle. I think there must be a guiding logic, a guiding wisdom in the system that makes choices on behalf of the person as a whole, even though many parts (or even the therapist) may strongly disagree with them. I think there are some things that the parts do agree on, and the choices are not random and not against the grain. We may not like their choices, like their going back [to abusers] to get hurt, or wanting to commit suicide, but it doesn't mean that they don't know what they're choosing. I certainly try to persuade them to act differently but it doesn't mean they are not aware of their choices and making them by the act of switching. Or by not switching. You know many people with dissociative identities have jobs, and some of them are high achievers with roles in medicine, the military, science, the care of children or other settings where safety is crucial. Therapists often worry, what if one of these people dissociated or switched? It could cause something terrible to happen. So, it makes sense to me that, there must be an overall entity that makes choices about switching, because baby parts are not found performing surgery or giving orders or forgetting to feed a child. There is clearly something, that 'wisdom of the system', that makes sure that this doesn't happen. A choice.

EJ: I've spoken to therapists who say they've been stuck with the client in the consulting room and can't get them out of a child state. What do you think's happening there?

AS: Yes, this is tricky, and not that rare... but I don't think that means the system has not made a choice. The system is making a choice, probably for reasons of attachment which is expressed by the presence of a young child.

Why would a three-year-old want to walk away from the attuned therapist? They wouldn't, because they have an attachment need, which at that moment is at a high level. This is a need of the whole system, because attachment needs never go away. And that need is what drives the sensible choice to not leave the attachment figure of the therapist. It may not be convenient for the therapist, but the choice is perfectly sensible. Resolving it is another matter, but this is a supervision question: how to address the attachment need, how to help the child part, and help the therapist.

EJ: What do you think are the differences between how the shared self is expressed in the different types of dissociative presentations, be they poly fragmented or installed mind control type presentations or the spontaneously created system? And would one's therapeutic stance need to be somewhat different for each of these?

AS: Let me start with a metaphor I often use: If I take a ceramic pot and throw it hard on the floor, it will probably break. The size or shape or the number of the fragments will not always be the same, depending on many factors – the type of ceramic, the intensity of the crush, whether the pot was already slightly cracked from a previous fall. Different factors make different people 'crush' differently under trauma, and the shape of the fragments, that is the specific clinical presentation, can be different, with varying degrees of difficulties to the healing process. But when I think about the Self, or essence of the person, I'm not sure if any of these makes a difference.

EJ: There is a lot more on trauma types and their impact in your paper 'Through the lens of attachment relationship: Stable DID, active DID and other trauma-based mental disorders' (Sachs, 2017). But for now, can you say a bit more about this?

AS: Maybe I can have a better answer if I go to attachment. So, if we think about the basics of attachment theory, the baby very quickly learns to behave in a way that will engage the attachment figure because this is a survival need. Now, if the baby is lucky, they don't have to do anything special. If they're distressed, the 'ordinary good enough mother' (Winnicott, 1960) attachment figure will instinctively respond in a helpful way. Apparently, this happens for more than half the population. Now, the less lucky half didn't have this kind of mothering, and I'm saying mother*ing*, because the attachment figure may be someone who isn't the mother. If the attachment figure was hard to engage and the baby had to jump through hoops to engage them, this can lead to less simple ways that the baby must act so as to engage the attachment figure, because attachment is a survival need, an instinct, like breathing, and a scared or distressed baby will do anything to engage the attachment figure. For some babies, the only way to engage the attachment figure is to mimic the parent – not just the behaviour, but also the affects, which might be quite disturbed. Or if a traumatized parent is very preoccupied with death, then the child may develop self-harming or high-risk behaviours, which are the only ones that deeply engage that parent. This is what Brett Kahr (2007) was talking about when he described infanticidal attachment. I call this a *symbolic* infanticidal attachment: the baby learns to symbolize for the parent the thing which the parent is most deeply engaged with, in this case, death. So when the baby grows older, they'll have a motorbike and ride it at night after having too much to drink and close their eyes in the process. But this is not because they want to die, it is because of the overwhelming need to engage the attachment figure. It's quite the opposite of wanting to die. It's the way to stay alive.

EJ: I think what you're saying is that 'engagement' means a real and intimate connection.

AS: Yes. Even when 'real' is pretty awful. Now to take another step into what I call *concrete* infanticidal attachment. This happens where the child can only fully engage the parent while the parent is in the process of abusing the child. It is important to remember that not every abusive parent will cause this type of attachment response. The parent who comes home drunk, shouts and hits everyone and the next day is sorry, is not going to cause this kind of attachment, because these episodes, while potentially traumatic, are not linked to engagement with the child – quite the opposite; when they occur the child is barely noticed. The 'real engagement' may happen when they go fishing together, or argue, or eat, any of which will be experienced by the child as feeling safe. But the child of the sadistic parent can only engage the parent while they are actually in the midst of an actual concrete abusive act. That's why I call it 'concrete infanticidal attachment'. Paradoxically, the child can only feel at peace and safe while suffering abuse, because they know that their attachment figure is fully engaged.

EJ: I wonder how you think this plays out between client and therapist?

AS: This is so important. It explains what sometimes prevents real therapeutic alliance to form, where the person seeks the sense of safety they only know while being hurt. Obviously, the therapist is not going to abuse the person in order create this engaged experience. But for some people, the ones who have this kind of attachment, it is impossible to feel really engaged without being in the throes of something horrendous. Very counter intuitively, the therapist who demonstrates the essence of secure attachment, you know, they're always there exactly as they said they would be, they're kind and thoughtful, they obviously never shout, scream or shake anyone, somehow misses the mark. This is because secure attachment is not created by calm, but by attunement; and for the person who only feels engaged during awful experiences this therapeutic experience can feel pleasant, but un-engaged, superficial, even alienating.

EJ: I had a supervisor who used to say 'the client needs to know who you really, really are'. I don't think we're talking here about personal disclosure or any details of your life, but rather I think it speaks to the client's need to be able to feel that the therapist is aware of and in touch with their 'shadow', to use a Jungian term. This is a hard thing to do. Not many therapists can or want to engage with clients in this way.

AS: Yes, I completely agree with you. I think this is a really vital point, and I think a lot of therapy with more traumatized people fails, not because the therapist isn't kind or caring enough, but because they fail to properly engage with the harsher experiences the person carries. That is not to suggest that we have to be abusive in our sessions. Of course not. But we need to be willing to follow them, undefended, when they speak about their experiences, and allow ourselves to be impacted by their accounts, to be horrified, shocked, upset, disgusted, scared – whatever it is we feel. We don't need to act in any special way, but when we are attuned with the feelings of another, that person can feel it. We all can. And these are the moments that allow the person to have a glimpse of secure attachment: knowing that the attachment figure is fully there.

EJ: It's making me think that what you're saying is that it's about the quality of the engagement. The feel of it. It's not about being the way that their abusive parents behaved, and not about being nice and calm. I think you're talking about an energetic engagement.

AS: Exactly. It's about when you're really there, especially in moments of distress, and the person can tell that they have engaged you and that attachment needs are, for a moment, fulfilled. For the severely traumatized person this is where therapy begins.

EJ: It sounds like it's important to really let them and their material 'land in you' properly. You can't just hear it and move on?

AS: Well, if you are genuinely 'letting it land in you', then of course you wouldn't just move on… and your staying with it is what makes the difference to their sense of being capable of engaging someone. They can make an attachment connection with a person who actually hears what they're saying and doesn't run away, doesn't hit them back, but stays with it. And when we feel that we just can't bear to attune at certain points, we can still keep the engagement by recognizing it, taking a breath and truthfully acknowledging it. I think this is a starting point, perhaps the key to everything in therapy, and not only with highly traumatized people.

EJ: I'm wondering, how might the therapist move from an attunement to horror and mirroring of distressed states to more ordinary states?

AS: I think of the good enough, the ordinary 'good enough' mother that Winnicott (1960) described. The ordinary good enough mother doesn't only respond to deep distress and mortal danger, but also to many small expressions that come from the baby. The problem is that when people keep throwing extremely boiling hot potatoes at you, you often find that you lose the sensitivity to very small and not very boiling potatoes. They look less important, and we stop paying attention to them. But it's very important to pay attention to all the potatoes, the big and the small, because they each are a window into the person's internal world, and each time we notice, we offer another moment of secure attachment – an experience of 'I am seen, therefore I am'. For example, a baby is in her cot and for the first time, she pulls her socks off. Mother might say 'oh look, you took your socks off!' And baby can feel the excitement. Of course she doesn't know the meaning of the words, but she can tell that something she did really engaged the mother, and this shapes the development of her future attachment language. In sessions, this means being really interested in all expressions, not only the harshest ones. A frequent problem of working with severely traumatized people is that the harshest often takes over the mind of the therapist and blunts our sensitivity to the importance and depth of the ordinary or the benign.

EJ: This reminds me of what Daniel Stern (2018) said about attunement being about a matching of the energy between mother and baby, not about specific activities. I wonder if that is part of what you are saying, something about fanning the flames or encouraging those little things or just noticing them?

AS: Exactly! You encourage them simply by noticing them. This is not to say that I ignore radical cries for help in danger and say 'Well, never mind, have you taken your socks off lately?' When we have direct cries for safety we must respond, they're essential to respond to. But if we only respond to those, nothing new will develop in the attachment language of the baby (or of the adult). What helps development is when small messages get picked up and engaged with, with real interest.

EJ: If I understand you correctly, you're talking about something coming from the client, that you pick up and elaborate together?

AS: Yes. I think that's why many dissociative people who have this very dangerous and problematic attachment pattern (concrete infanticidal attachment) hate things like breathing exercises, not just because maybe they've been abused through holding their breath, but because it could feel artificial, like the therapist came with an off-the-shelf bag of tricks, and is not paying real attention to them. So, if I see a person in a session, and they look distracted, or they answer me in monosyllabic way, or they're being rude to me, and tell me that I never understand anything, I am always thinking they may be trying to engage me through this behaviour. Because when someone upsets you, you're engaged. The quality of the engagement, pleasant or annoying or upsetting or scary, is less important than the fact that there is a real affective engagement. When you really pay attention, follow the other person, you will notice 'small things': a word that they have not used before, a change in their voice, in their movement, and you see something that may be small but is not unimportant. The point of mirroring is that when you see yourself in the eyes of another, it tells you that you exist, and that the other person is seeing you and thinking about you, and when you think of all that, you are thinking together.

EJ: So, in terms of therapeutic technique, do you think it's more about becoming a person who can see all the potatoes, not a person who can only see hot potatoes? I guess it needs the therapist to really tune into the grain of the session and be able to spot an embryonic little something whatever it is.

AS: Exactly, and be willing to be with whatever it is. When you're being with it the feeling that is created is 'we're sharing something', even when nothing major is discussed. While trauma work is essential to therapy with any traumatized person, I believe it's equally essential not to focus solely on trauma, because if you only focus on trauma, you may convey the message that only their suffering is of interest to you. No matter how much you speak to the contrary, if you become deeply engaged or affected by the person's accounts of trauma and only superficially interested in the person's music writing, you convey the same message as their abusers, who only really engaged when there was great suffering.

EJ: I wonder what's your experience of being impacted by this kind of work? I'm asking because I can hear that you are talking about engaging relationally in a very detailed and intense way.

AS: In thinking about the impact of the work on me, I'm thinking about a person I saw near the beginning of my work in this field, who told me a detailed, horrific story about the murder of a baby. I felt sick and heartbroken then, and I still do now, many such stories later. The impact of horror never leaves you; and if you stop feeling horrified, you're not engaging anymore. So, I'm afraid I'm not aware of any magic bullet that can spare you, the therapist, from the real engagement with the kind of trauma that causes people to dissociate. It is an essential aspect of this work.

EJ: I wonder if you can say something about the role of supervision. Particularly in regard to what you refer to as 'active DID' in your 2017 paper 'Through the lens of attachment', where the client is still being drawn back to an abusive group.

AS: The realization that in some cases, the awful abuse suffered by the person has never stopped and is still happening, in between the 'best' therapy sessions, is very hard to hold. We have to remember that therapists, as they should, are usually highly invested in reaching safety, processing trauma and holding hope. But when abuse is repeated and ongoing, despite all efforts, the therapist can easily become frustrated, angry with the patient, ashamed of being angry and ashamed of failing to make a difference, and altogether hopeless. The supervisor needs to genuinely engage with the therapist's feelings of defeat, anger, shame and hopelessness, feelings that the therapist may find really hard to share, or even acknowledge to themselves, and the therapy may suffer as much as the therapist. A supervisor who is experienced in this work is instrumental in spotting the state of the therapist and the subsequent cracks in their ability to be engaged and their various desperate, often unhelpful attempts to 'fix it'. Generally, the difficulties are the result of the impact of trauma and helplessness on the therapist, and the support of a supervisor in recognizing the impact can restore the therapist's ability to think, to feel, to hope and to consider ways to help. This is true in every therapy, but much more so in cases of what I term active DID.

When a person with active DID is harmed yet again, the person, their parts, the therapist and the supervisor are all affected; but not all of them as directly as each other. The supervisor is three steps removed from the actual event, while the therapist is only two steps removed from it, and some of the parts are one step removed while other parts were actually being hurt. This chain of impact makes the more distant participants able to help the ones most directly impacted. One really important role of the supervisor is to remind oneself, and to remind the therapist, who then reminds the person who then could remind the different parts, that none of them is alone in a repetitive, hopeless state of meaningless hurt, but that they are together with all the others who are affected and therefore linked. And these links are meaningful and important, no less than the hurt. The relationship between therapist and supervisor is one of these links, and these 'linked' moments can breathe life back into stuck and hopeless therapy states.

EJ: Can you give a clinical example of how you use this attention to small details in your work?

AS: Mmmmm… I'm thinking about a woman who had been sexually abused for decades in the most grotesque ways. Her view of herself was that she was just a piece of meat, a waste of space, that she was making me dirty by speaking to me and that she just shouldn't be at all. At some point in the most casual way, she said that she was being hurt so that someone else in the system didn't have to be hurt. This was a crucial moment in the therapy: she just saw herself as a person who made a choice. And it was not just any choice, but one that was brave and generous, as because of her choice, someone else was spared and didn't have to feel it. We have talked about it several times, and I could see how she was sitting taller in her chair, like the recognition of her power to choose as well as her bravery started to shift her 'waste of space' picture of herself. A few weeks later, another part of the same person who was frequently violent said they had decided to not beat someone up, and some teenage parts came and said they were also not beating 'so and so' up. And I said, 'This is so interesting, how exactly did you manage to do this?' I think they could tell that I really did want to know, and to hear all the details about how they didn't beat someone up. That made each one of them start having a grain of some sort of new out-look on themselves, their individual value and their relationships within the system. After a while, more people in the system started to mention that other parts were listening when they were speaking to me. They said it with a kind of pride. I replied by highlighting what an incredible discovery it was that other people in the system were interested, listening and best of all appreciating what these parts were like.

All these developments grew out of my one pointing out the generosity of the part who took on the abuse so that others wouldn't have to.

EJ: It looks like we are back to the subject of a Self. Can you say more about your thoughts on this?

AS: There is a very wide body of writing about the Self. Is it innate? Is it something we develop? At what age? Does it exist it in relation to others, or is it an internal experience? Is it the same as identity? Is it even real? To be very brief on this complex subject, I'm only going to speak here about Winnicott.

Winnicott said two things about the Self that can sound contradictory, but when you really think about them together, something fascinating comes up. We are all familiar with Winnicott (1960) explaining that the ordinary good enough mother is deeply identified with the newborn baby, which makes her able to recognize baby's needs, interests and uniqueness; and her accurate recognizing and responding to baby's needs and expressions is what facilitates the development of baby's Self. So from this we can conclude that in his view the deep engagement, the relationship, is what makes the baby feel real and discover their Self.

Not so commonly discussed is Winnicott's statement (1963, p. 187) that the deepest self, what he calls the True Self, *never engages with anyone*. It exists in complete solitude and it must stay that way. Anyone or anything that attempts to breach it causes traumatic damage: he calls this kind of intrusion 'a sin against the self'. This sounds like the opposite of the emphasis on engagement, like the Self can be destroyed rather than facilitated by a contact too close. Also, when writing on the True and False Self, he says that the False Self is there to protect the True Self from the intrusion of being seen, and that the True Self doesn't need much to be said about it because it is innate, it is there, it requires no action from us.

EJ: Might this Self be at all akin to something that one might call a soul?

AS: Good question. I don't know… Winnicott didn't call it that, but spoke about it as something so personal, so precious and so unique, that at its heart of hearts it can't be touched. Maybe this is akin to a soul, I haven't thought about it like that but I can see what you're saying.

Where the two seemingly contradictory statements of Winnicott, and then Bowlby's attachment theory, come together, is in the crucial role of the mother in standing between the baby and the world, because the baby is too young and fragile and isn't ready to protect themselves. And the role of the mother is to stand there between the world and the baby to protect the baby from any intrusion that can be devastating to the body, to baby's life, or to the psyche, or perhaps the soul, to the baby's *mental* life. The 'good enough mother', through her deep identification with and attention to baby, can mirror what she sees as well as protect it. It is when there is no protection or not enough protection that damage happens.

I think of dissociative identity like this: a person becomes dissociative when their Self has been breached, because no one stood between the world and the baby to protect the baby from the extreme intrusion of abuse. So, the various parts of the personality take the role of the absent protector: Like the proverbial mother, they each rush to stand between the Self and the impact of trauma too great to bear. Each part is therefore an attachment figure:

desperately needed and loved, even if they are also hated. We may speak about it later, but I think highlighting the attachment relationship between the parts and the whole is an important aspect of therapy with dissociative identities.

EJ: I frequently think with dissociative clients that, even though you appear to be working with one part, everything that you do feels like it is leaking through to all of them. A client, the one I wrote about in my chapter, drew me a beautiful picture of themselves and me sitting opposite one another and I've got a very long arm that's reaching out and touching their heart. The colour from my arm is travelling right through their heart and body and out of their feet. The word 'system' is underneath and that same colour from me is dripping into the system. I was very moved to see this picture.

AS: I don't know if it's true that all of them are listening all the time, but I always assume that some are. That seemed to be true about the group of parts who didn't beat someone up, like they heard something of the earlier conversation with the part who was able in that moment to find something good in herself. And those other parts appeared to want a bit of it, too.

EJ: I have always thought, I don't feel like a stranger, even when I meet a new part.

AS: I feel the same. It's hard to explain that in any other way. I think there is a link between all of them, which is an attachment relationship, a life-protecting relationship. Just think of how every time one part is at the end of their capacity to withstand whatever is going on, another part appears, rushing in to help.

EJ: What do you think are the implications of this, let's call it, a rudimentary self in terms of perpetrator parts?

AS: I think the perpetrating parts are the most distraught of them all and are often overlooked or rejected by therapists. I think perpetration can be soul destroying, because it is the most alien to the Self: this is how it was described to me by survivors. These parts carry the burden that most of the others couldn't face at all, and when the system begins to be aware of what they, with their own hands, have done to other people they often become severely suicidal. That's often the worst stage of the therapy, it causes immeasurable pain, because the hate that had been reserved for the abusers now goes against one's own hands. And we see that because perpetrating parts usually don't come to the sessions until very late in the work. And many times, in many therapies, they never come up at all, because therapists are not always welcoming to perpetrating parts, viewing them as 'the enemy' or heavily condemning all perpetrating, so these parts don't dare to join the therapy. We must always remember that the person you work with may also be 'one of them' in some of their parts, and that they probably didn't have a choice about it. So the dissociation of acts of perpetration is often much deeper than the dissociation of other traumatic events, as it is Self-protective. We really need to be very sensitive to the needs of these parts.

And let's not forget that the perpetrator parts have done the perpetrating so that other parts of the person wouldn't have to. So again, we're back to 'What is the connection between the Self and any one of the parts?' I think it's an act of protection of the very Self from any link, any connection, any impact of some events. All parts are protective. They're all protecting the Self from destruction. The understanding of the true and false self is often a bit superficial, like it's a matter of appearing as we think people would like us better. But the role of the false self is also to protect the true self from intrusion, like the role of the mother is to stand between the baby in the world so that no one touches the true self, no one, including the mother. This is basically what I'm saying about the parts and the self: that the parts are the attachment figures of the Self that they're protecting. When we can view them in this light, we can help the person learn a new attachment language, like a second language which is based on benign protection (Sachs, 2019). To go back to the beginning of our conversation. What made me think that there's also, you know, a whole Self to each person, I don't mean an amalgamation between parts, I mean a core of the person, and who they feel that they are inside.

EJ: What are your views on the scope for repair via attachment-based psychotherapy? I'm thinking also about what I thought I understood you to mean – that in cases where abuse is ongoing you think there's a need to start in the second phase of the ISSTD treatment model.

AS: No, I wouldn't say that. I think we should start by listening carefully, and responding to whatever it is that the person brings. Because stabilization is the result of secure attachment, and secure attachment, even a single moment of it, is created by attunement and not by any specific way of behaving. Starting at phase one, safety and stabilization is very sensible and I never encourage anyone to start therapy by talking about their trauma; but the person who chooses to start by telling me about a murdered baby may have done this because she needed to know more about me in order to feel safe. Maybe she wanted to know how I would react to horror, maybe she wanted to see how distant I will remain, and she couldn't reach any feeling of safety in my presence before 'testing the water'. For some people, there can't be safety before testing your realness, in their own way. So, it's not like I think we should start from talking about trauma, but that we should start from where the person starts. I suppose I try to do what mother would do, which is being there and paying attention, and respond to whatever happens.

EJ: As a final question, I wonder how have you found people with a dissociative presentation feel about an idea of a separate core to a dissociated self?

AS: I don't normally present theoretical ideas in my clinical work, so I don't know. Michele Jowett, one of the co-editors of this book and a presenter at the conference, wrote to me to say that she had always known that she had a core Self, and she could feel that it was an important conversation to be having.

EJ: Thank you so much for taking the time to talk to me about your work and your thinking around a core Self. It's been so interesting.

AS: Thank you, it was a pleasure to have this conversation with you!

References

Kahr, B. (2007). 'Infanticidal Attachment'. *Attachment: New Directions in Psychotherapy and Relational Psychoanalysis*, 1, 2, pp. 117–132.

Sachs, A. (2007). 'Infanticidal Attachment: Symbolic and Concrete'. *Attachment: New Directions in Psychotherapy and Relational Psychoanalysis*, 1, pp. 297–304.

Sachs, A. (2015). 'Who Done It, Actually? Dissociative Identity Disorder for the Criminologist'. *International Journal for Crime, Justice and Social Democracy*, 4, 2, pp. 65–76.

Sachs, A. (2017). 'Through the Lens of Attachment Relationship: Stable DID, Active DID and Other Trauma-Based Mental Disorders'. *Journal of Trauma and Dissociation*, 18, 3, pp. 319–339.

Sachs, A. (2019). 'Attachment as a Second Language: Treating Active Dissociative Identity Disorder'. *Frontiers in the Psychotherapy of Trauma and Dissociation, Journal of Trauma and Dissociation*, 3, 1, pp. 107–122.

Stern, D.N. (2018). *The Interpersonal World of the Infant*. London: Routledge.

Winnicott, D.W. (1960). 'Ego Distortion in Terms of True and False Self', in Winnicott, D.W., *The Maturational Process and the Facilitating Environment*. London: Karnac, pp. 140–152.

Winnicott, D.W. (1963). 'Communicating and Not Communicating Leading to a Study of Certain Opposites', in Winnicott, D.W., *The Maturational Process and the Facilitating Environment*. London: Karnac, pp. 179–192.

Chapter 7

The Perspective of an Expert by Experience

Learning to Thrive – So Many Cogs in the Wheel

Melanie Goodwin

Introduction

This chapter reflects how experts by experience have contributed to a wider understanding by enabling complex psychological presentations to be considered through the prism of their origins. The chapter is written on a solid foundation of the author's personal dissociative identity focused therapy and the many insights achieved throughout this experience.

The author draws on her considerable years of experience of helping to run First Person Plural (FPP), a charity for those with dissociative identities, their families, allies and the many professionals whose work is enhanced by a better understanding. FPP offered support through newsletters, emails, support groups and training materials. It offered a sense of a community, of belonging. Prior to its closure in 2023, FPP achieved international recognition for their contribution in raising awareness, teaching and resources.

This chapter demonstrates the transition from existing to thriving and the different components, cogs, that have been part of the author's personal process.

A Brief Introduction to My Background

I will use I, me, we and us at different times. I am writing this with my internal family very much on board so I respect there will be times when the pronouns are used interchangeably, authentically for us as a whole system, and ask you, the reader, to do likewise.

I live with dissociative identities. I would not be alive today if I had been unable to use dissociation to this level. I was completely amnesic about my situation until I was nearly 40. I was married and still am, possibly one of the lucky few with dissociative identities who have celebrated their golden wedding anniversary, had four wonderful children and was to all intent and purposes just getting on with life. With hindsight not so much living and thriving as existing, but happily existing.

Reflecting on and revisiting each presenter's work I have become increasingly aware not only of their expertise but their overall unified approach to

DOI: 10.4324/9781032696720-8

working with people like me. They were courteous, kind, compassionate and thoughtful when presenting at the conference and have captured their deep, core beliefs in their writing. Each chapter reads with these values coming through as the foundation of their work. To try and keep the feel of therapy alive I am giving you a brief outline of my pre dissociative identities focused therapy. Holding this in mind I hope will allow you to reflect therapeutically why I might react and feel so strongly on some points, points that might pass others by.

FPP was such an important part of my own personal journey and a lot of what I share is influenced by the enormous privilege in getting to know and spend time with many people who have dissociative identities. Although much is personal, I hope this chapter conveys the breadth of my understanding that is based on so much more than just my story. I use the word 'unique' slightly hesitantly as there are so many people out there helping others in so many ways. Being an integral part of running FPP for over a quarter of a century allowed me to meet and share in a way that would have otherwise been impossible. This has given me confidence in sharing my thoughts and at times opinions in the hope that it will resonate and help with common threads that allow others to feel less isolated and gain insights to be kindled.

When we tore our teddy to bits as a three-year-old we were told we obviously did not want one and labelled jealous of our new sister. It was to be over 40 years before this was rectified. Later I was told I was worried about my mock 'O' levels when I experienced what was described in the 1960s as a 'breakdown'. On both these childhood occasions I had experienced such extreme abuse just prior to this behaviour that the evolving dissociative system could not cope. I, as the outside part had no idea as to why this chaos was happening.

I can clearly remember thinking on both occasions that what I was told did not feel right. As a highly dissociative child I could not offer an alternative explanation. I was labelled sulky. It was therefore completely natural for me to accept others' explanations.

The initial weakening of my dissociative barriers was triggered by someone I was told as a child would not be abused if I never told about what was happening to me. She was tragically killed when we were in our 30s. With hindsight and a lot of therapy I came to understand that the parts who had been guardians of the secret no longer had to fill this role. The secret could be told. I was completely amnesic to my abusive childhood, so the explanation offered that I was struggling with bereavement sort of fitted but yet again did not feel it really addressed what I was experiencing.

I took my external family including my husband for bereavement counselling. We had suffered several significant losses in rapid succession, and I felt the children needed some help. Of course, I was fine, they had the problems! I had never had to sit still for an hour exploring emotions, what are they? After three sessions, my son's migraines had stopped and everyone except me felt they had been helped. I was seriously falling apart, and suicidal thoughts continuously haunted me day and night. They had always been a part of me in the background but now they frightened me. I began to understand they were like my safety net: if it became impossible, I could do something about it. I asked to continue to see this counsellor and she agreed.

It is many years ago and she kept me alive but the three phased stages of therapy and guidelines for treating dissociative conditions were not even a consideration then. Consequently, we did trauma work from the start. Using journaling between the parts we took the lid off Pandora's Box. At this stage I had no idea we were many and this had enabled us to survive a very challenging childhood, so what was being shared made no sense to me. We walked round in trauma land for seven years, I became very skinny, the anorexic part. I slept no more than three or four hours a night, the teenage part. I gave up many voluntary roles that previously had been important to me, the mother. At a deep level I knew I was barely surviving, treading on the thinnest of ice imaginable. I was determined to be there for my children, so I naturally contracted my life, to work and try to be a mother.

I wore black all the time; the thought of colours filled me with horror. I now think this was the first time we were all using 'auto-regulation' positively. We needed to take everything back to basics to help us regain some sense of control. I feel I have had glimpses of an autistic child's world. I felt overwhelmed by everything. Gradually, an automatic, often inappropriate response became a thoughtful action appropriate to self-regulation, a choice. I could not socialise, go on holiday or stay away overnight for over ten years.

I worked with this counsellor for seven years, I gradually began to realise we were many. I read *The Flock* (Casey and Wilson, 1992) and reread it and reread it. My story was very different, but the essence of the book really impacted me and suddenly my life began to make a sort of sense. I decided not to mention it to my counsellor for a few months. I needed to test out the possibility that we were many. I realised that the counsellor, this kind lady, had bypassed me, totally unintentionally, and connected with my three-year-old who for the first time in her life felt heard and wanted. The consequences for us all was that we used the word 'annihilation' a lot in our journaling, the risk of suicide was ever-present, and we as a whole walked around in so much emotional pain. We still do not have the words to convey how awful it was.

I now understand that as a whole our emotional development stopped at age three, so this child's pain was all our pain. It was hard for the adult parts to own and gradually accept that if our surface was scratched, we were incredibly immature. The shame, humiliation and pain associated with this were totally overwhelming.

We learnt that we had shut down our emotions at three and our dissociation had developed very literally. We had a vacuum around each part to ensure there was to be no bleeding of information. The outside parts were incredibly depleted as a person. We lived totally in the moment, there was no past or future. We became as independent as was possible for a three-year-old, we denied and deprived ourselves of having any needs and blocked all emotions. My main caregivers struggled with their own emotional immaturity.

The strength of dissociation enabled us to appear very stable and able, even though I had absolutely no idea of our reality. It also presented us with what felt for a long time like many insurmountable barriers when we entered dissociation focused therapy.

After seven years I broke us 'free' from the first therapy. That is how it felt as I had to drag the little ones away from the person they had become attached to. As a whole, we were becoming less and less functional and, shamefully, parts were bullying the counsellor. I knew I had to step up as the adult and take charge but had absolutely no idea what to do next.

The Conference Presentations: Their Short- and Longer-Term Personal Impact

I was extremely excited to be invited to use my expert by experience voice at this conference and not a little daunted. Sue Richardson supported and encouraged everyone concerned from the start and her contribution, for me, made the day very special. I want to relate how each speaker's presentation has influenced and allowed me to complete another part of my journey. Some offered a whole way of thinking while others caused those light bulb moments that are such a part of a person with a dissociative identity story. Others offered validation of my own story and journey and allowed us to create a sense of a timeline.

I have stuck with the notes I made on how I was reacting during the actual presentation. This feels important. I could read each chapter and make informed observations but to be truly authentic I have tried to re-capture the immediate impact. This parallels therapy where logic can get in the way. If maybe one part hears something in one way and reacts to how another part heard the same words and reacted. I have evidence of how often this happened for us, captured during therapy sessions that were taped. At times reading this you might feel it has little bearing on what you either heard or said, but for this monograph to have the impact I hope it will, part of my contribution is to be authentic rather than correct through academic reflections.

Reflections on Chapter One: Using an Attachment-Based Model to Understand and Work with People with Dissociative Identities

Mark's presentation got us all very excited. In the early days of getting to know my internal family my life became extremely chaotic, and we walked a continuous tight rope that we fell off on many occasions. This was when dissociative identity was known as multiple personality disorder and presentations at conferences were about trauma or dissociation or attachment or the body. There was little recognition of the other areas, each subject being addressed specifically with little or no overlaps. Even then it felt incredibly fragmented and unhelpful, as I instinctively felt they are all so interwoven.

The public use of the internet was in its infancy, there was very little written and the understanding by clinicians was minimal. I was terrified. I had gone overnight from being a very busy, highly functional if somewhat limited mum, working full time, to not knowing how I was going to get through a day or rather the next minute. Nobody was able to offer me any real answers and I was walking around in a complete state of terror, escalated by snippets of what I began to understand were memories. I experienced them as body memories.

Life savers were when I heard Bessel Van der Kolk and Ellert Nijenhuis speak at a conference and discovered Peter Levine's book *Waking the Tiger* (1997). These were totally revolutionary moments for us as a system. Ellert's talk about structural dissociation and his clear vision on the two systems, the apparently normal parts (ANP) and the emotional parts (EP) gave me, for the first time, a sense that what was happening to me had a shape, a structure and was not infinite. Through a growing understanding it allowed me to begin to bring some order to the chaos I was experiencing.

Van der Kolk talked about body memories. I had been struggling with strong, difficult to experience and in a sense witnessed dissociative body memories and he made it sound normal in these circumstances. Previously there had been no context in which to view these experiences.

Reading *The Flock* (Casey and Wilson, 1992) had started me down the path of what might be my/our reality but then I came up against the stigma of mental health, mostly within the NHS, learning very quickly to stay silent and hide as much as possible. Every contact I had with mental health services left me so distressed that I usually needed to take a day off work to recover, curled up under a duvet unable to speak. I now appreciate that we were regrouping having been scattered, so the part who ensured we went to work could take executive control again. The NHS depersonalised me with nearly every encounter.

The structural model of dissociation and the language used has been widely developed. The Haunted Self (van der Hart et al., 2006) remains one of the leading books on mentalising and dissociative identities within the context of the structural model. I was fortunate to be able to attend one of the first talks where the concept was still relatively basic, and I could grasp what was being conveyed. Very quickly we stopped using ANP and EP. Not only is it never as simple as that but it also felt disrespectful to all the different parts. I was coming to terms how far from normal I, the outside part, was.

I had found a language to begin to convey what was happening. When I found myself curled up in a ball in the cloakroom, I knew something had triggered my little one and at this time it was totally outside my control to have stopped this happening. Compassion began to creep in, insidiously. I still use the ANP and EP concept in teaching as it offers a starting point, an introduction, but I broaden it out very quickly.

Mark's presentation caused the same excitement as Ellert's had in the past. I feel the model of the seven systems involved in attachment in chapter one leads on so well from the structural model (van der Hart et al., 2006) and expands on the ANP and EP concept. I feel if this had been available in my earlier days of understanding it would certainly have enhanced our thinking. Me, as the outside part, at this time, needed to understand what was happening, how our brain worked, why and how it was rewiring, changing.

I think the best therapists working with complex dissociation will use their core modality while being able and confident enough to use many other resources, tweaking them along the way. I cannot stress enough though, whatever your approach, it must always be within very clear and firm boundaries; I consider this the keystone of therapy.

Considering the seven categories of caregiving, careseeking, self-defence, interest sharing, sexuality, external and internal environments I feel would help a client to reflect and learn about their internal family in a compassionate and inclusive way, both in context and language. It would also help to avoid defensive reactions. It highlights different areas gently, allowing each person to use the points in a way that works for them. I feel the words are offered as guidance.

Someone with dissociative identity is unlikely to have learnt about compassion for themselves, although they can show great compassion for others. Mark's explanation of this has resonated with us all. We have been very good at giving care to others, at times filling nearly every waking moment, a subconscious reaction, hard wired to a need of survival. It was definitely used to deflect from our reality. It would be disingenuous if I did not also acknowledge how this became an important part of who we are but as a conscious decision after some reflection on whether each presenting situation is appropriate. It is the first, rewired area that we moved to as a whole.

Only recently have I been able to internalise what compassion means. It is so much more than a series of actions. We thought we had cracked it when behaviours that we can now label as harmful had stopped. It is also not being fluffy as we tended to think. Being gentle with ourselves was a new way of being and felt quite frightening initially. These headings feel gentle. Models need to be regarded as a resource, not an evangelical cure, and Mark's use of language conveys this.

A cautionary word. Whenever we attended a workshop about a model, we quickly became distressed. It felt a contradiction as the model concerned had looked really useful. We learnt that those who develop models often present them as the only way or it felt like that to us. It tipped us back to feeling we were being programmed, having experienced programming from a very early age.

One of the downsides of having dissociative identities for me is I was not allowed to think, reflect as the outside part. This would have been much too dangerous as a child and was hard wired, so change was slow. I was a reaction without the luxury of reflection. These categories would have enabled me to start thinking about what it really means, I always needed a prompt and even as I am writing this, we feel excited at the potential of this resource used in the way Mark presented it.

Reflections on Chapter Two: An Exploration of the Relational Dialogue Between Client and Therapist

This presentation evoked the most joint reaction from all of us. I think Catherine's introduction to dissociative identity has enabled her to just know what it is really like. Living with someone can give you so much insight that is probably not possible through a therapeutic relationship alone. I think the first part of her chapter will really resonate for others in a similar position.

Her non-clinical approach to being with all the parts, recognising their differences, conveyed a deep sense of humanity. We connected with her emphasising that the therapist is a dependable human being and how their reaction and behaviour is absorbed as a role model, making the importance of owning mistakes and apologising essential within this relationship.

Sue Richardson talks on a training film made by FPP (2011) about how she knows when the client is making the transition from needy to trusting in themselves and becoming healthily independent when they say 'What would Sue say/do' in this situation?

Internalising and absorbing is such an integral part of the whole process. Be honest, human, when the client and therapist both feel stuck, acknowledge this and that it is healthy to feel frustrated. This conversation is held without criticism, blame or shame – is it is just how it is.

Respectful curiosity is used by all the authors and is so important. Through discussion we agreed with our therapist that he would check in to see what we wanted/needed during stuck times. If we were unable to speak, we agreed he would keep chatting about safe things to help us stay mentally in the room. At this stage of our journey, it was important that we were not left or abandoned as it felt as if we lost all connection, were disappearing out of the room. Abandonment may lead to feeling rejected and a downward spiral quickly evolves.

As therapy progressed, we liked silence as we gradually were able to think and reflect. Silence no longer felt dangerous, and we learnt how to stay, at times literally, in the room. Catherine identified that conversations about the process as well as the content are important.

Early on in my journey I realised I was too busy rescuing, making it alright and not really listening. I went on a course about listening skills, and it was quite a revelation. I also did the first year of a four-year counselling course, twice, to help me be able to be with others while not drowning myself. This has been invaluable and allowed me to respond, caring deeply but not to try and fix it. The best I could hope for was enabling the person to access their own grounding skills and offering a little hope.

These insights have also been so useful in how I initially connected with my internal family; I had no idea about relationship building and this gave me a starting place. It has also helped me to answer the hundreds of enquiries that I have managed for FPP. When I felt hopeless, I would acknowledge how hard, tough it was for them at this time. I would try and address any direct questions about practicalities, but this was often challenging with so few resources available. I would always try and find something that could offer the tiniest glimmer of light or hope but if there was none, I learnt honesty was vital. Many of these people had been lied to, labelled disrespectfully, or been fobbed off and I knew that was unhelpful.

These skills have flowed within and without, needing fine tuning many times. The ability to sit with the little ones while they struggled with their pain has been so important to us all. To allow them to approach me, sitting quietly in a safe space took years for some of the really young ones who held some of the hardest memories. I am a part of the whole. I did not hold the solution, but I could, as an adult learn how best to help.

Reflections on Chapter Three: What Are We Doing? Stabilisation Work with a Mind Control System of Altered Identities

This chapter supported and reiterated so many points that have been discussed. I welcome Emma's clarity on the importance of stabilisation and how the therapeutic journey is never linear. I believe that integrated living starts from the very first day of therapy. The impermeable barriers are no longer as effective, so the brain is slowly allowing tiny snippets of memory to become available to some and then all. Consolidating a new way of being may be addressed later but at every stage of knowing and change we were learning to live more together as a whole, often chaotically, and this needed our therapist's ongoing support.

I cannot overstate the importance of stabilisation; I do not call it stage one. It is definitely the starting place and needs a lot of time in helping the client to get to know their internal family, what each part likes and dislikes, psychoeducation about dissociative identities and how it may affect them as a whole. I think it is also important to help those managing daily living to function and hold onto who they are and their roles. In the early years the focus was on the parts who held the abuse stories and I have heard many outside parts say how their reality was not addressed, how alone they felt and yet they were expected to keep the show on the road. Stabilisation skills and a more integrated way of living are a thread that weaves throughout the whole of the journey, and I suspect will be needed for the rest of our life.

It is important to help the client to recognise the skills they already have and have used automatically throughout their life. Conscious identification allows them to become more easily accessible. This will help them to move from a habitual reaction to making a choice. This helped to empower us and was the beginning of managing flashbacks better.

I developed new grounding strategies and techniques that were revisited regularly, updated and tweaked as our journey progressed. I think one of the big breakthroughs for our system was when we realised that each part needed to develop their own stabilising techniques: what worked for the teen parts had no impact on the three-year-old. Until this moment I would come back towards the end of a session and try and do what was best for the part who had been doing the work. This would work inasmuch as I was grounded enough to drive home but the residue of that part's terror and pain continued to flow through our body.

Learning what each part wanted to do after a piece of difficult work meant not only was I able to come back after they had been grounded but their feelings had been calmed. For one little one it was a story read by the therapist while she was dominant, for another it was colouring. It could be a discussion around what ice cream they wanted on the way home. The important bit of this process was the part doing it for themselves. It had a transformative effect on the level of fear that flowed round our body; of course it did not make it disappear, but it became less intrusive for us all.

Visual experiences have been important in my learning. I watched the dramatisation of *The Curious Incident of the Dog in the Night-Time* (Haddon, 2003). During the play they captured the overwhelming feeling of an autistic child so powerfully. It was very triggering in the moment but allowed me to later reflect on how situations I beat myself up over were so hard because we were overwhelmed. This gave me permission to be much kinder to us all. Knowledge and then understanding has played a vital part for me. Initially I had to be in the midst of a situation to know too late that it was unhelpful. Gradually I have been able to assess a situation ahead and through internal collaboration decide what is possible. As a system it has been so important to be totally honest at all times. We have never used our situation as an excuse, but it may be a reason.

A beautiful short film, *Petals of a Rose* (Crumpler, 2022), is currently considered one of the best educational films to help educate a wide audience. It captures some of the challenges we face daily. I use it as a teaching resource, and it powerfully supports what we try to convey verbally.

Reflections on Chapter Four: On Being With: Working Creatively with Clients with Dissociative Identity

Orit's presentation again offered many 'Oh yes' moments. I appreciated the clarification between choice and habit. This highlighted for me the importance of the use of language and how this differs from person to person and for each part. Choice immediately puts me on the defensive as though I could have prevented something. I think it is so important that a therapist always stresses that it is a working towards change.

For someone with dissociative identity it takes time because it is not about just knowing, it is about brain rewiring. When my heart knows, the rewiring in the brain is complete.

We hear therapists talking about the conflicts and contradictions and how hard it can be to sit with them. It is equally hard for the client, possibly more so as it is present for 24/7, not just the length of a therapy session. I really wanted to have help but for some of us it held very different meanings. For some it was giving in, it would only make things worse, some parts were threatened with extreme punishments if we ever told. Telling has led to many terror-filled days and nights, but gradually, with patience, kindness and growing trust this has changed.

Gradually the therapist will help their client to hold both realities as true and allow time to bring about change. This process happens as the attachment strengthens, built on solid foundations of trust. Change can be forced but if so, is usually unsustainable. For our system the anorexic part was eventually able to find an internal peace. Me trying to get us to eat and be sensible never worked. It caused internal conflict, fear and pain as she was not able to fulfil her essential childhood role. Through understanding and our therapist holding us as a whole throughout she resolved her issues and gave up her defined and limited role, but she remains very much part of us all.

I was brought up as a well-behaved child within a respected family. This has added layers of complication for us all because both the abuse and a good family are true. I have spent many hours arguing that the abuse should not have caused so much distress: after all I had a pony! Orit captured this conflict and gave me permission to think about and explore it again. It is not a self-indulgence, it is my truth.

Many of my friends and colleagues with dissociative identities lose time; they have the evidence because they end up away from home or similar, while others, myself included, do not experience it in this way. It so often made me feel I was faking the whole thing because I could not identify with this 'proper' experience of losing time. For us it is so much more subtle.

The only way I can describe it is I am on a train happily travelling to a destination of choice, a danger is perceived so the man in the signal box pulls the lever and off we go down another track, destination unknown. I learnt and understand that I have spent my life trying to make sense of what was happening and preventing external others realising I often had no idea. I narrowed my existence down to a very basic way of predictability, so I/we could then manage any unforeseen situations. I stayed in the same job and building for nearly 40 years. It makes sense but also makes me sad that I existed in this way.

Reflections on Chapter Five: When the Alleged Abuser Is Famous: Some of the Problems in Dealing with Alleged VIP Abuse

Valerie's presentation touched on so many aspects expanding in particular for me on the culture within the criminal justice system. I have total admiration for those who have the courage to come forward and report their abuse. I chose not to, for many reasons, but mainly because I knew the whole process would eat me up and I had lost enough of my life to those who do not believe me or tell me black is white.

I know I acted a bit as judge and jury to my whole system in the early days of therapy. I had absolutely no memories and yet I was expected to believe and own what all the different parts were sharing. Cognitively not a problem but the ability to really relate and connect to what I was hearing was impossible.

None of what I termed evidence could be verified, so how can I know we are not really mad but very good at appearing boringly normal, a double bind. This is not really surprising as to stay alive so many developmental stages had either been curtailed or culled. My brain was not going to allow the flood gates to open and swamp us, I often felt very frustrated at the seemingly slow pace.

Valerie captures the power imbalance held by the police and judicial system; we surrender ourselves to their interrogation in the hope we will be treated with respect at the very least. This is not dissimilar to walking into the therapy room. Of course, there are things that the therapist needs to put in place with no space for negotiation, but I cannot stress how important it is to work in partnership, sharing the decision making wherever and whenever possible. This will not only help to redress the power imbalance but may, for the very first time in that client's life, make them feel they have some say over their life.

This has to remain a constant throughout therapy, not a whim that is done with. If this is a genuine way of working the therapist's voice and body language will support their words. People with dissociative identities have sixth, seventh and eighth senses. We pick up very quickly on anything that is not 100% real. This means at times it might cause conflict, but the therapist and client being true, open and honest is a fundamental requirement within the therapeutic relationship. Although at times it might cause conflict and lead to ruptures and then hopefully repair, providing a forum for growth is so important.

I had one counsellor who entered the room going into her counselling mode. Another was real, warts and all. One built my trust, the other did not. She was not abusive in any way but too reminiscent of childhood, you never quite knew if what you were seeing was real. I think the therapist's authenticity helps the client to start to trust themselves.

I began to learn, as indeed did the individual parts, how much more enjoyable life could be, chugging along within the window of tolerance (Siegel, 1999). As we learnt to co-habit this space, we realised that the anxiety levels decreased, and we had communal access to many more skills. We also were able to tolerate and benefit from a maintenance dose of anti-depressants that remains important to us all, a success not a failure. Previous attempts to take an anti-depressant had caused a sense of being even more fragmented and made our head feel like it was going to explode.

It was important during the trauma work that the different parts initially were accepted in a space that would later become way outside the shared window of tolerance. If this was not respected, trying to ground us induced a switch so the memory was no longer accessible. I appreciate how hard this must be at times for the therapist to trust what appears to be an out-of-control part, but I think it is essential. Allowing us to access the memory that is causing this extreme state can often see an immediate lowering of the hyper- or upping of the hypo-arousal.

We have learnt to appreciate that the ability to trust within a stable therapeutic relationship needs to be well established before some of the most difficult work can begin. Ruptures in the early days felt life threatening before we learnt we could talk about it and the world did not end. I remember thinking I can now go to impossible places because I trust my therapist to get me back. Another very important moment.

Reflections on Chapter Six: The Parts, the Whole and the Real Person: An Attachment Perspective

Early in Adah's chapter the first pertinent challenge for me to think about is dissociating rather than dissociative. I feel an awareness of this enables the therapist to be real, a human being who is attuned to what is actually happening rather than what feels like a clinical observation and labelling someone as being dissociative.

Of course, dissociating in the moment may not be happening but being clear about the differences feels so important. For me it started a process of reflecting, leading to an understanding of being fully there in the moment with the ability to differentiate between a before and after. My old default position was often not fully dissociating away but not being quite there, observing rather than engaged. This is something I have struggled with all my life and it is only recently that I can feel this rather than know it with my head and often diary! Putting words to this in the therapy session would have been very helpful, so much is about challenging old habits but you first of all have to identify them.

For me the core and essence of this chapter is giving credence to the parts having an individual sense of self. I feel this has only more recently begun to be understood. I always struggled to connect with a single sense of self with different aspects like everyone has. I felt like I was failing in being unable to do this. We all felt much more than an aspect, much more whole and rounded. By aspect I mean what I witness in friends and colleagues, where they remain one person but are different when in mum mode or daughter mode.

For us as a system, many parts had very different personalities, likes, dislikes, approach to situations and life as a whole as well as the usual confusion for people with many identities around different allergies, physical reactions and gender. Much was influenced by trauma but it always felt disingenuous to say they were like that because of what happened to them; they always felt so much more.

In the early days while they were getting the courage to start therapy, as an individual they perceived themselves as incredibly limited but as each part grew in confidence, built on a bed of growing trust, they blossomed. Not dissimilar to any child being heard, respected and metaphorically safely held. Of course, there were limitations as they all shared one body with the time constraints this automatically brings. The different parts developed within their own age, gender and so on but never grew older, and when they had reached a place that felt right for each of them they went back more deeply inside. I experience it as they nestle calmly within what is now a safe body. They experience it as being able to connect with living through the outside part, a wonderful place to be. The biggest change is they are not consequently being triggered by external things, as each part has been able to process their own traumas to a point where they no longer impact every moment of every day. It might not have caused a full switch but the responses to different situations were, with hindsight, influenced by other parts, sometimes one, often many. This meant that me as the outside part was often confused in how we had responded and spent a lot of time back tracking but without awareness while feeling the need to be constantly apologising.

Naturally, internally they began to communicate with others of a similar age and not dissimilar adverse childhood experiences. A lot of healing took place within these groups but only after a considerable amount of individual work had been undertaken. Over the years groups nominated a spokesperson to let me know if things were difficult and their needs required addressing separately. This happened less and less as the overall needs were being met by the whole. It felt on reflection like a long and often painful period of transition until we all feel we have reached a balance that works for us.

Now separating out is usually in times of stress and new challenges. Medical appointments still often depersonalise us as well as medical procedures remaining complex. Sometimes little ones separate because they are very excited about something and their joy is felt more strongly by them standing alone. They all still hold a very definite sense of their own individual self while allowing the external parts to sort of represent the whole.

As I sit writing this, I know who I am. I feel I am grounded in who I am. My sense of self remains constant. I also know at any moment I might not be fully there and someone, equally as grounded, makes their needs known to me. We have an overall solidness that is new while knowing we are still many.

A very important point Adah raises for us is the sharing of the common threads of our sense of self. Towards the end of therapy we reflected on traits that were shared by many but witnessed and experienced slightly differently as a response to their own individual situation. Kindness runs through us all as a genuine aspect we believe in collectively. We hold a very strong sense of justice and fairness. We still experience unfairness as one of our most painful experiences.

So much of us was not destroyed but put on hold, held in a deep freeze to allow us to survive all the unfairness of our childhood. For me, experiencing the pain this causes us in adulthood often feels intolerable and we think if we had been able to tap into this emotion during childhood it would have destroyed us. I never cease to marvel at the human drive to survive against impossible situations.

I do not have a faith but the only word that I feel does justice is they never got our soul. Within this are held the many things shared by so many with each amended to be part of their individual history. It is held deep in the centre of our body and layer upon protective layer was being added continuously throughout our childhood. Slowly and safely they have been peeled away until we are connected.

We have one little one who wanted to write a book for others who were being abused to give them tips on how to survive and get the least hurt as possible. It was a real wake up moment about how as a whole we have always wanted to help others through understanding. There are so many times in my life this shared characteristic has been used. We have had a habit of fighting unfairness for others all our lives and are learning this is an important strength, but there are times now that we can use it more wisely and therefore productively.

I would like to finish with something we all did together. We trained for a triathlon. It was not about age, although that is what most people see, and think it pretty good as it was our first (and last) and we are in our 70s. Yet again we were being told our reality but now, with understanding, we can let it go while firmly holding onto our truth through knowing, again possible through our strength in our individual selves.

For us it was so much more. For the first time in our lives, we were all able to join in. Nobody wanted to stop or sabotage it so we followed a training programme and stuck to it. We were seen out running and people asked what we were training for. Being seen is an enormous leap for all of us. We also had moments of humour when I suggested my teens took over the running but unfortunately this is no longer possible.

The night before we had a briefing, and again on the morning, and we all stayed fully grounded, heard and remembered what we were being told and then we completed the whole thing together, but in so many different ways.

We were not pleasing anyone else, it was just for us. If that is what sense of self means I feel we have reached a very good place thanks to extraordinary dissociation focused therapy and so much hard work from us all.

Learning to Thrive: Transformation Through a Transformative Therapeutic Relationship

> Through just one relationship with an understanding other, trauma can be transformed and its effects neutralised or counteracted.
>
> (Fosha, 2009, p. 10)

This quote felt like I had been offered a lifeline as we started on our dissociative identity focused journey. Reading a lot about attachment usually left me feeling demoralised and overwhelmed. How was I, a 40-plus-year-old woman with a family of her own going to manage to achieve a 'good enough attachment'. I also knew through reading and rereading Carl Rogers' *On Becoming a Person* (1990) that the clue to my future lay in this book. I spent the early hours of the morning on a bean bag, playing Simon and Garfunkel's 'I Am a Rock', on loop and reading Roger's book from cover to cover, and as I finished it starting again immediately. I have never been able to retain information but had gleaned this book's essence.

Gradually, I logically began to identify that I was living life as a robot: an effective and efficient robot. I had a good group of friends; my marriage only became extraordinary with hindsight and my children's physical needs were being well met. I had been fortunate in choosing safe, healthy pathways and had learnt a lot by watching and copying. To the world I was just a very ordinary woman getting on with a busy life. If you had asked me to talk about my childhood or feelings very quickly this thin veneer would have been shattered.

Learning About Stabilisation

I was able to re-enter therapy with someone who was experienced in working with dissociative identities. It took four years for us to become stable enough to do dissociative identity focused therapy. This therapist knew intuitively not to come near me psychologically or physically. He never left his chair at any time including when we arrived and when the session was over. Remy Aquarone talks about slowing therapy down on FPP's archived resource 'A Logical Way of Being' (www.mairsinn.org.uk/publications.html). This was so important, at one level nothing was happening, I spoke very little, but this therapist's unwavering solidness and continuity allowed us to find an equilibrium, the start of a secure base.

Our very strong dissociative barriers prevented us from being able to talk or reflect on our childhood: we had memories that came from photos or family stories being told. We had no idea that our memories were two dimensional, no feelings or links to emotions or other events, just the bare facts. During these four years we began to trust our therapist; of course we had no words for this, it was a happening.

Our big breakthrough came one day when the part who made the transition from the abuse on the floor by our bed at night to getting us back into bed and ensuring that the two worlds were kept far apart was able to come and lay flat on her front during therapy. She could not talk; her tongue was too big in her mouth. I felt humiliated and mortified but my therapist stayed totally grounded, just very welcoming. His non-judgemental approach enabled me to begin to connect, very slowly, to what was really happening. This part gradually found words and began to talk. She was the go-between and was amazing.

When the abuse starts pre-verbally the body often tells the story. Gradually in therapy as the whole begins to assimilate what is being shown a narrative develops. The attachment journey had begun but I called it the magic in the room. The sense of attunement and attachment were being established on the slowly forming secure base that was built on trust.

I found the term 'attachment' much too powerful, and I really did not understand it. I think I had so little experience of this as a child it remained a mystery. I found it much easier to consider the process as learning about healthy relationships with the main caregivers. I still struggle with the word 'attachment'.

On reflection the instant 'attaching' to my first counsellor activated the very powerful feelings of being annihilated as a child with the direct link to suicidal thoughts being dominant. I made my first attempt at trying to end our life as a three-year-old. I knew cats went away to die so I took myself off to the grain loft and hid under a sack, so this was all too familiar. Me as the outside part was fighting these feelings daily, we lived on a precipice. Learning about stabilisation with therapist number two gradually gave us the skills, in turn enabling us to begin to feel empowered and that we could manage and do something about these overwhelming feelings and not act on them.

We began by reclaiming me as a mother before we moved onto new, completely unfamiliar territory. We made an internal agreement that we had to write a goodbye note to my husband and four children before we were allowed to end it. This worked well. By the third letter some of us were bored and the immediate threat of suicide had passed for now. As someone who had never learnt about and how to manage feelings this was an enormous task. This was one of the first grounding techniques we developed. In context a very positive development.

I think it is important to consider the whole picture with each client. I grew up at a time when Truby King, whose methods specifically emphasised regularity of feeding, sleeping and bowel movements, was for many mothers their bible. I was exposed to a form of programming as a baby being fed four hourly regardless of whether I was hungry earlier. The anorexic part who evolved at 16 was influenced by this very early experience. She was incredibly disciplined and blinkered, allowing no sense of ambiguity.

My therapist and I struggled to develop a therapeutic connection. There were magical moments based on his intuition. We often would draw during a session. This particular time we had drawn the therapy room and called it the safe secrets room. At the end of the session the part whose role was to keep us tough and away from feelings tore it into several pieces and threw them down as she stalked out. The rest of us were sad at an all too familiar situation. When we arrived the next time on our chair was the picture very carefully stuck together. I can still feel the wonder in the moment and this part started therapy. There were no words, one very kind and caring action. This allowed her to begin to trust not only the therapist but all of us.

We struggled so hard to hold onto any sense of connection outside the therapy room. We talked about it and discussed ways that would help but my therapist's suggestion that he should text a very brief message morning and evening for a while was met with a resounding refusal. Gradually, after many ongoing discussions, I gave in and said OK. For over a year he never once let us down. It worked on the brain like brain gym but with so many more layers. We knew when the time was right to stop but it still has a powerful effect on me that someone cared enough to do this.

The therapist holding our doll/baby during our sessions for weeks was another important link in learning to trust and build up a healthy attachment. This felt so dangerous at the start but gradually we began to relax and eventually took the baby back, unharmed in any way. I am not suggesting that any of these things would work for someone else but my therapist's ability to know what was needed and when to offer it in a very pragmatic way enabled our journey to be greatly enriched and for us to reach places I would never have imagined possible.

So much of the work revolved around a steady plod of rupture and repair and a willingness from all my system eventually to engage with therapy and to work extremely hard for many years. However hard we worked we could not have done it without this relationship. We all know how lucky we are and never a day goes by without us being thankful.

A Reflection on the Work of First Person Plural

I am going to close by sharing a little about FPP, that sadly closed in 2023 after 26 extraordinary years.

Early on in the life of FPP, Sue Richardson accepted an invitation to run a workshop for people with dissociative identities to look at attachment and what it meant to them. This was extraordinary in several ways. Firstly Sue, an attachment-based therapist, was willing to talk to a group of potential clients outside the therapy room. Not something that happened in the 1990s and still a concept many therapists struggle with.

  Secondly this was at a time it was thought to be unwise to have two people with dissociative identity, then known as multiple personality disorder, together in one room. I have never been able to get to the bottom of this myth, but FPP loved breaking down barriers.

  Sue started by asking the 12 people attending what the word 'attachment' meant to them. I think many thoughts on this list are very sad:

- Contaminated
- A bad thing
- Unnecessary/necessary
- Unwanted dependency on others
- A missing, unidentifiable ingredient
- Bonding
- Parent–child relationship
- Beneficial (mutual)
- Clinging
- Scary
- Complicated
- A mystery
- Intertwined
- Life threatening

Sue then spoke about what attachment is and we came up with a list of words that we thought would relate to a child experiencing a good enough attachment to their main caregivers. It felt so hard to imagine how it would feel to be safely close to your main caregivers; the words came from a place of logic rather than a place of knowing. Not one person in this particular situation had any meaningful experience of being attached to share.

  Over many years people talked about wanting to meet with others who really knew what it is like to live with dissociative identities. FPP started holding Open Days. These days were for people who were in a relatively stable place and had a lot of internal communication, so little ones stayed safely inside. We also asked members to build in a safety net for afterwards if they needed it. We wrote clear and very boundaried ground rules that we visited every time and amended over the years as our experience and understanding grew. It was a place for the adult parts to talk and share about their everyday challenges.

  We did jigsaws, colouring and some FPP members shared their skills in card making, decorating buns and other crafts. And we talked. We had a lady bring a collection of harps, magical. My rendition of 'Old MacDonald Had a Farm on a Harp' is still one of my highlights. We hosted two workshops led by a community choir.

  These days worked well apart from on the few occasions when someone was perhaps not quite as well as they thought. The Open Days gave us the confidence to start regional groups: some worked well, others did not. We also started online groups during Covid. I do not think that without the early Open Days we would have had the confidence to even consider this.

One of FPP's core beliefs is we were all working towards self-responsibility; it was an important element in everything we did.

In 2011 FPP produced their first training film, 'A Logical Way of Being' (www.firstpersonplural.org.uk/training/learning-resource-films). It featured three people with the lived experience and three highly experienced clinicians. Gill Sandell the producer worked her magic. It remains the most influential resource we produced. It was groundbreaking then and remains an aid that is still being used worldwide in 2024.

Conclusion

I would like to take this opportunity to thank the many, probably hundreds of people who I have met, some I have got to know well, others in passing and some it was just an email. Every single one of you have made a difference to me and are a part of my journey. I could not have asked for anything more. If I had not had dissociative identities I would not have had this opportunity to share and receive caring, friendliness, respect and love. I hope I can offer a tiny glimmer of light that it is possible to thrive.

Accepting the invitation to be part of this groundbreaking conference offered me a chance to make some strides in my journey, it helped me to establish a sense of a timeline and continuity, a pulling together of my own story. This allows me to reflect on the years of therapy, connected to emotions and an understanding of how they fit into the overall shape of what is my life.

I carefully do not use the word 'heal' as it does not sit comfortably: I thrive and walk in my own life.

In addition to the references below, I have included books, articles and films that have made a profound impact on me over the years.

Bibliography

Alderman, T., and Marshall, K. (1998). *Amongst Ourselves*. New York: New Harbinger Publications.

Bass, E., and Davis, L. (1988). *The Courage to Heal*. New York: Harper and Row.

Boon, S., Steele, K., and van Der Hart, O. (2011). *Coping with Trauma-Related Dissociation: Skills Training for Patients and Therapists*. London: Norton.

Bray, M. (1991). *Sexual Abuse: The Child's Voice*. Edinburgh: Canongate Press.

Bryant, D., Kessler, J., and Shirar, L. (1974). *The Family Inside: Working with the Multiple*. London: Norton.

Casey, J.F., and Wilson, L. (1992). *The Flock: The Autobiography of a Multiple Personality*. New York: Ballantine Books.

Crumpler, D. (producer) (2022). *Petals of a Rose*. www.dylancrumpler.com

First Person Plural (2011). *A Logical Way of Being*. www.mairsinn.org.uk/publications.html

First Person Plural (2014). *No Two Paths the Same.* www.maisinn.org.uk/publications. html

Fosha, D. (2009). 'Dyadic Regulation and Experiential Work with Emotion and Relatedness in Trauma and Disorganised Attachment', in Solomon, M.F., and Seigel, D.J. (eds), *Healing Trauma: Attachment, Mind, Body and Brain,* London: Norton, pp. 221–281.

Gerhardt, S. (2004). *Why Love Matters: How Affection Shapes a Baby's Brain.* London: Routledge.

Haddon, M. (2003). *The Curious Incident of the Dog in the Night-Time.* London: Jonathan Cape.

Heard, D., Lake, B., and McCluskey, U. (2009). *Attachment Therapy with Adolescents and Adults: Theory and Practice Post Bowlby.* London: Karnac.

Herman, J.L. (1992). *Trauma and Recovery.* New York: Basic Books.

Hocking, S.J. (1994). *Someone I Know Has Multiple Personalities.* New York: Launch Pr.

Holmes, J. (2001). *The Search for the Secure Base: Attachment Theory and Psychotherapy.* London: Brunner-Routledge.

Hughes, D.A. (2009). *Attachment-Focused Parenting.* London: Norton.

Hunter, M.E. (2004). *Understanding Dissociative Disorders: A Guide for Family Physicians and Health Care Professionals.* Carmarthen: Crown House Publishing.

Levine, P.A. (1997). *Waking the Tiger.* New York: North Atlantic Books.

Matthew, L. (2002). *Where Angels Fear.* Dundee: Young Women's Centre.

Miller, A. (2012). *Healing the Unimaginable: Treating Ritual Abuse and Mind Control.* London: Karnac.

Mollon, P. (1996). *Multiple Selves, Multiple Voices: Working with Trauma, Violation and Dissociation.* Chichester: Wiley.

Napier, N.J. (1993). *Getting Through the Day.* London: Norton.

Rogers, C. (1990). *On Becoming a Person: A Therapist's View of Psychotherapy.* London: Constable and Company Limited.

Siegel, D. (1999). *The Developing Mind.* New York: Guilford Press.

Sinason, V. (ed.) (2002). *Attachment, Trauma and Multiplicity.* London: Routledge.

Solomon, M.F. and Seigel, D.J. (eds) (2009). *Healing Trauma: Attachment, Mind, Body and Brain.* London: Norton.

Steinberg, M., and Schnall, M. (2001). *The Stranger in the Mirror: Dissociation: The Hidden Epidemic.* New York: Quill/ HarperCollins.

van der Hart, O., Nijenhuis, E., and Steele, K. (2006). *The Haunted Self: Structural Dissociation and Chronic Traumatization.* London: Norton.

van der Kolk, B. (2014). *The Body Keeps the Score: Brain, Mind and Body in the Healing of Trauma.* London: Penguin.

Walker, M. (1992). *Surviving Secrets.* Buckingham: Open University Press.

Chapter 8

The Perspective of an Expert by Experience

Clinical Theory and Practice

Michele Jowett

Introduction

This chapter shares reflections around the clinical and theoretical work presented at the conference, and how it resonates with my lived experience. Drawing on my experience of pitfalls encountered in different therapies, it highlights some important issues that therapists need to be aware of when working with someone with a dissociative identity.

My use of pronouns to refer to parts of my personality is interchangeable as I have dissociative identity and this is how I would ordinarily use them.

Reflections on Chapter One: Using an Attachment-Based Model to Understand and Work with People with Dissociative Identities

Mark Linington refers to 'survival' as not just a means to preserve one's physical and psychological well-being but attachment to relationships. I think this is of prime importance where sexual abuse occurs in childhood and the survivor is reliant on attachment to the perpetrator to survive. It is integral to the concept of dissociation as a defence against annihilation of the attachment figure and how dissociation between identities enables and preserves that attachment. The perpetrator manipulates this need for attachment, fuelling their drive for power and control which is at the heart of all abuse. Mark mentions the Structured Clinical Interview for Dissociative Disorders (SCID-D), authored by Marlene Steinberg (1994, 2023) which assesses and diagnoses dissociative disorders by exploring each of the five domains along the dissociative continuum. It's important to note that the SCID-D is not only a valid and reliable diagnostic interview for assessing dissociative symptoms and disorders, but when administered by an empathic clinician, can enhance the therapeutic alliance, and facilitate attachment-oriented therapy. Given the qualitative nature of the assessment and the subjective exploration, the therapist's understanding is broadened as information is volunteered that might ordinarily be delayed, and their empathy enriched, thereby helping to build a therapeutic alliance upon which successful attachment-oriented therapy is based.

DOI: 10.4324/9781032696720-9

Caregiving

As a person who exudes caring personally and professionally, I relate very much to the caregiving system. In my personal relationships, there is more of a leaning to Type 1 caregiving whereas in my professional relationships, a Type 2 caregiving system is identifiable. However, both types are interchangeable. Internally, both types are visible. I have parts who will step forward to provide immediate comfort to a part in distress and those who will honour a part's autonomy and engage in ways that step out of the rescuer position, as denoted by Karpman's (2014) drama triangle, and into a caring role. I, too, hover between Type 1 and 2 in my co-consciousness, dependent on the part's developmental progress, with Type 1 being adopted more with little ones, and Type 2 with older parts. It's important to note that parts will demonstrate Type 1 and Type 2 caregiving systems in their engagement with me, honouring their protective roles.

Careseeking

The careseeking patterns that Mark denotes as avoidant, anxious and disorganised are resonant within my system due to the habitual scaregiving responses they received. These patterns impede the goal of careseeking as they compromise relational boundaries thereby perpetuating the need to careseek in a distressed way. The fear system which is part of the self-defence system resonates with my own system as collectively their role is to defend and protect me. However, the way they defend is not always conducive to a healthy outcome given the emotions they hold such as anger and rage. Their defensive response will be at odds with that of the attachment parts who will offer conciliatory gestures in their careseeking drive. The hypervigilant parts are integral to the fear system, scanning for threat and danger and ensuring the protectors are ready to step in and defend. Each part is created and primed to protect me, and part of their healing journey is recognising the threat of the past is over and to learn adaptive ways to defend.

Interest Sharing

The interest sharing system offers safety as opposed to the threat that accompanies the careseeking and caregiving system. Safety emanates from engaging with an interest which is a benign object unlike the threat that comes from engagement with a person and the risk of loss. In interest sharing with a peer, should loss occur, which is the universal inherent fear shared by the system, the interest remains, and the loss is diminished. On reflection, I engage with an interest alone for the most part but am open to interest sharing where the loss is less impactful. Where trauma is relational, trust is given sparingly and is hard earned but easily lost. An interest can build a bridge for a survivor and soften the fear that accompanies trust. It is the act of being alongside that is foundational to trust and interest sharing can facilitate this. Importantly, interest sharing can enhance cohesiveness and communication amongst parts as they share in common interests and practice being alongside another.

Interest sharing has been instrumental in helping me to cement a relationship with my own parts and I am often struck how an interest I have that seems at odds with my character is channelled via a part. For example, I have an unlikely want to box but recognise it is being driven by a 17-year-old male part. I can interest share through my love of horses with certain parts and in our mutual joy of horse riding, reading, walking in nature etc. Each interest is not exclusively my own and provides a bridge between our internal and external worlds. The careseeking system that Mark worked on in his relationship with She-Wolf and that gradually she was able to build internally has been harder to establish in our own therapeutic relationship due to the risk that trusting in that care poses. It is a lengthy process and not linear but understandable where abuse has been relational. However, it is a vital prerequisite to establishing the secure relationship necessitated for trauma processing.

Sexuality

Sexual intimacy is a complex and multilayered conundrum for people who have experienced sexual abuse, and that complexity is exacerbated when a person has dissociated identities. My terror of sexual relations and the disgust that accompanies it is offset by a part who is outrageously flirtatious. Her flirtatiousness is a means to attach to and receive male attention. Created from the image that was communicated to her as a 'slut' and behaving accordingly, she careseeks through her coquettish wiles. However, when interest is reciprocated, parts who carry the terror of sex, together with the vigilance of the observer part who is primed for danger, assume control of the body. Where sexual relations were consensual, another part would take executive control. Her role was created to endure sex, but a dance would ensue between her and the hovering parts who are afraid of sex. A self-harming part would also surface during and after sex, biting his hand during the act and furiously cutting afterwards to extricate the internal 'badness' whilst vigorously cleansing his soiled and repulsive body in the shower.

External and Internal Environments

The system responsible for the external environment is held by me and a part who holds the obsessive-compulsive disorder. My external environment symbolises the inverse of my internal environment. Where there is chaos, noise, clutter and disorder internally, my external environment is structured, quiet, sparse and orderly. The part who holds the OCD ensures the environment is clinically clean, fastidiously tidy and minimalist thereby offering us safety and a feeling of control. Mark refers to the segregation of the internal environment and the different attachment-based systems which is a key feature of dissociated identities and relatable to my own system. This segregation and attachment diversity impacts real life relationships adding to the chaos of both the internal and external environments. The harsh, yet protective, persecutory parts in my internal system have enabled me to internalise the badness of my primary attachment relationships thereby preserving the perceived good in them and fuelling the badness in me projected by the perpetrators.

Keystone System

In exploring my own keystone system as the outside part, the caregiving self is pertinent, emanating from an absence of care from my primary caregivers. Reflecting on my parts and their own keystone systems, it is evident that each is protective and often complementary whilst conducive to establishing the co-operation that is integral to working harmoniously. Dissociative identities are uniformly protective. They were created to protect the outside part from harrowing pain. However, when I reflect on the protective common denominator further, I recognise how parts are protective of each other, although this might not always be apparent, but protection weaves an intrinsic, indelible thread.

The Restorative Process

As I reflect on the restorative process, it chimes with the exploration of the core treatment of therapy which is to facilitate co-operation, communication, and collaboration amongst the different identities. Mark refers to the 'locus of connection' between the therapist and the identity but just as pertinent is the locus of connection to the outside part. In recognising the purpose of each identity's system and how it was protective, the outside part is enabled to empathise, most notably with the persecutory parts. The keystone system is a facilitative means to explore the systems and their role as well as to help identify how different identities and their systems can collaborate better. It mirrors the essential work of the first stage of the triphasic model and provides an effective tool to facilitate this. However, each person with dissociative identities will have habitually referred to their systems according to their own interpretation, having developed a robust understanding of their roles. They may resent this being compromised with the keystone systems, perceiving them as a threat to their autonomy and control.

The Clinical Example

In the clinical example, I relate to the three features that Mark refers to Bridget and her identities displaying throughout his treatment of her: her expectation of punishment, the significance of empathy, most notably, for fearful feelings and the responsiveness of the therapist. All are indicative of an early attachment deficit and continue to be palpable in my own treatment and recovery.

It is interesting to see how She-Wolf develops a secure attachment to Mark across time and is reflective of how the therapist can model the secure attachment that was absent in childhood through conveying the core conditions, consistency and commitment. She-Wolf is empowered in that secure attachment to gradually explore healthier attachments in her external relationships but reverts to 'fight' when feeling threatened. I have watched this transition occur with an angry part in my own system who despite inevitable fiery ruptures in her relationship with our therapist, reverts to repair and the homeostasis of a secure attachment.

Mark comments on his discomfort surrounding Bride, and her flirtation towards him reflects the imperativeness of a therapist's commitment to exploring their countertransference. In Mark's case, his feelings of fear and dread reflected his concern that he was being placed in a perpetrator position and, stepping outside of the drama triangle, assumed an assertive one. Significantly, once Bride recognised her flirtation was not reciprocal, she felt relief. I believe this relief reflects the discomfort a part might hold surrounding their protective purpose yet, deigned to honour it from their creation, they do so unwaveringly. My angry parts will often bemoan their angry role due to the exhaustion it demands and can find relief when their anger can be exchanged for humour with the therapist. Bride alternates her relief with a reversion to type as flirtation was the cast in which she was created and what feels familiarly safe.

On reflecting on Mark's work with Bride, although my own flirtatious part shares Bride's propensity for making relational connections with men through the sexual system, additionally, her behaviour is a conditioned response, that is, to elicit male attention, a sexual transaction must be exchanged. For Bride as for other survivors, learning how her careseeking needs and want for affection are enmeshed with her experiences of sexual abuse is the first step in helping her flirtatious part to develop healthier attachment systems and ensure her well-being. Similarly, an angry part who is gradually building a secure relationship with our therapist is striving to reflect before reacting impulsively, a response emanating from the working model expectation that the therapist will hurt, betray or abandon her. Learning new attachment systems is not an easy process for any parts. Part of that difficulty emanates from their identity being ingrained in their protective behaviour hence their reluctance to renounce it. Adopting a new way of being is a threat not just to their identity but their very existence, and so it is important that adapting to new attachment systems is done with sensitivity and at a pace that is respectful to that transitional process.

Just as interest sharing enabled the cubs to play and model that interaction with all identities, so, too, is that reflected in my child parts who play together. The care that is modelled by older parts to the younger ones enhances the development of care amongst other attachment systems with interest sharing being integral to this process. Mark refers to the process of establishing an internal intersubjectivity, enabling identities to be seen as subjects with their own current or historical lived experience and sharing the same physical body rather than representations of dissociated traumatic experience. This has always been not just recognisable for me as the outside part but palpable. However, in my need to refute my abuse, there is a disparity between the cognitive awareness and the experiential. To accept the latter is to accept my abuse as those identities are synonymous to it. As Mark identifies and illustrates through his work with She-Wolf, it is the development of attachment systems that honour wellbeing and connection that are integral to the work and foster a secure attachment not just with the therapist but with other identities.

Overview

Although I welcome Mark's approach using the keystone systems that he describes, I do not think they are remarkably different to the work of the first stage of the triphasic model where the five Cs (Richardson, 2020), namely, Compassion, Communication, Connection, Co-operation and Co-consciousness, are built in direct opposition to the survival strategies of dissociation and disconnect. What Mark's chapter clearly illustrates is the attachment wound that lies at the core of dissociated identities and how the secure attachment the therapist provides is the vehicle upon which healthier internal attachment systems can be fostered and enjoyed.

Reflections on Chapter Two: An Exploration of the Relational Dialogue Between Client and Therapist

Catherine Holland refers to the fear that therapists can experience when confronted by dissociated self-states. This is often a reciprocal fear when one considers that dissociative identities emanate from relational trauma and the impact of that on the client towards the therapist. I can empathise with the fears of both therapist and client given the anticipation of unknown parts, the protective role that each fiercely holds and how that can manifest in chaotic and unexpected fashion. However, each part has one overriding need from the therapist that is universal to the system: they need to be heard just as a client without dissociated self-states does. If this is held in mind, and a part's voice can be given expression irrespective of the content, in my opinion fear can be eradicated.

Incongruity and Shame

The incongruity between the person that presents to the outside world, which in my system is the person authoring this chapter, and the people she adeptly masks can be stark. Catherine was confronted by this disparity in Jen, her university flatmate, thereby compromising the friendship and making it challenging to navigate. As I reflect on this, I recognise that in my system of altered identities a highly functioning façade (me) helps to disguise our shame at having a condition that courts perplexing controversy, intrigue, myth and refutation. For us there are also other psychological motivations that drive the need for me to operate as a type of disguise, emanating from deeply entrenched historic wounds that cause me to seek approval, likeability, respect and belonging (as a way of feeling safe). When that disguise (me) cracks due to daily stresses that prompt other parts to surface in their role as protectors or in their immediate response to triggers, the shame that I fiercely and fastidiously guard against is palpable. When I am confronted unexpectedly by shocked and quizzical expressions, I realise a switch in identity has occurred and begin a very familiar (to me) process.

I seek to ground myself and when I am fully present again, I am compelled to apologise with an elaborate and well-rehearsed excuse. Shame is also symptomatic of the trauma from which dissociated identities are conceived, a trauma I have struggled to give credence to for over 30 years in tandem with society's rampant dissociation. It is a parasite that eats away at our core, blinding us to qualities that capture others' and our true identity. In my drive for survival, I had internalised my perpetrators' badness so that I could attach, and in the process ignited the suffocating flame of shame that plagues me within.

Protector Parts and Challenges

As Catherine identifies, dissociated identities comprise a mosaic of protector parts. Protection is what drives the system's functionality providing sentry to the outside part so that she might be shielded from the horrors that hold her mind hostage. Although laudable, dissociation becomes problematic when those horrors become conscious to the outside part, and she is forced to reconcile the devastating narrative of her past. For me, this has been my hardest journey to date and the biggest obstacle to my healing. One of my perpetrators had a very dual persona. By day, he was loving and kind, by night a prowling, sadistic monster. To guard against the latter, I dissociated, my brain fragmenting into different identities to courageously assume the degradation and horrors performed repeatedly against them. Once those amnesic walls began to crumble in my early 20s in response to an unanticipated trigger, I began to associate to what I had dissociated, and my world imploded. How could I reconcile the man who was loving and kind with the man responsible for the atrocities in my mind? It is a psychological battle that continues to be fought and that has created distance from my parts.

I think Catherine identifies very well the challenges that dissociated identities pose for loved ones and the imperativeness of having support for those challenges which, like treatment for dissociation itself, is not always readily available. However, as Catherine attests, people living with dissociated identities are so much more than their dissociation. They have qualities that, perhaps, make the shame that underscores their dissociated identities more palpable in tandem with how those qualities serve to disguise them as they did for Jan in her early relationship with Catherine. Certainly, I identify with that shame and recognise that the qualities that people admire in me are a shield against the dissociated identities I am at pains to mask. Ironically, I would not choose to be integrated, preferring to live together harmoniously, yet I am unwavering in my commitment to hiding their existence. This shame is a manifestation of the controversy, intrigue and myth that dissociated identities court, coupled with their aetiology, and I am aware, to my additional shame, of how that might be received by the parts within.

Masking

The concept of masking that Catherine refers to is not something that I identify with in relation to my parts which reflects the uniqueness that is so integral to each system. However, as the outside part, I am very mindful that I do mask but in a sense of becoming blended with a part. Although present in a situation where it demands it, I am aware that I am adopting a part's personality to manage the situation which is different to a full switch where a part has executive control. Where a situation has triggered anger, it can be useful as the anger I might express can be somewhat tempered in comparison to an angry part having executive control and communicating a tsunami of expletives. I think masking is a concept that people without dissociative identities can also relate to as I think everyone can become adaptive where there is a demand for conformity.

Processing and Timing

Catherine refers to the need for the therapist to be always in the moment, an imperative to recognise when there is a shift in identity so that the therapist can equally shift her focus. For a person with dissociated identities, hypervigilance is part of their armoury as they are conditioned to be receptive to the merest nuance of fluctuation in mood as this would indicate threat. It strikes me that the therapist treating a person with dissociative identities shares a similar level of hypervigilance to shifts in mood albeit for very different reasons. Several of the authors have referred to how important it is to make *all* parts feel welcome including the introjects and angry parts. It is often these parts who are integral to moving the therapy forward due to their willingness to speak blatantly unlike the appeasing, conciliatory parts who are seeking attachment. Their anger is also indicative of an element of self-worth that is absent in the latter. Timing is an essential consideration when working with a person with dissociated identities although too much focus on the timing can communicate to the client that what she has to share is not important. It is a hard balance to strike whereby space is given for the client's voice to be heard, yet at a pace that guards against decompensation. For my system, the need to be heard is their most pressing and the therapist's repeated caution against moving too fast before safety and stabilisation are established is irritating to them. Some will rebel through withdrawal or manipulation of her attention whilst others will concede to the therapist's thinking but reluctantly. Over time, as our trust has grown in the therapist, we have come to believe that what is held *will* be heard and to have an appreciation of the need for safety and stabilisation. However, before that trust has been gained, any attempt by the therapist to thwart what needs to be shared has been met negatively and interpreted as rejection and unimportant. As my 14-year-old male part, Sad, will unfailingly and repeatedly assert in defeat, 'it's no big deal'.

The Concept of the 'Host'

Catherine refers to a part like me, the outside part, as the 'host'. I think this can be a misnomer. Although I understand that the outside part is perceived to be 'hosting' those parts inside, both external and internal parts are all constituents of the whole. In my experience, dissociated identities, experientially, *feel* separate, authentic, and distinct from each other, denoting realness and individuality as opposed to Jan's system where 'she' has a cognitive recognition that they are fragmented parts of her and not separate. The outside world shares her cognitive recognition thereby compromising the outside part's felt sense of realness. I think the word 'host' can fuel this conception of parts being separate to the outside part hence my decision not to employ it.

Psychoeducation

Catherine refers to resources such as psychoeducation which can provide agency where there has been none. This has been tremendously instrumental in my own recovery, enabling me to navigate and understand better my somatic responses, my behavioural patterns and to provide relief and reassurance that I am not crazy. It has afforded me order amongst disorder and control over what has felt uncontrollable. In my research, I have also acquired a fascination for dissociated identities and their ingenuity, a passion to inform the uninformed and an indefatigable respect for those who live with them and journey beside them professionally and otherwise. Catherine depicts how the treatment of dissociated identities necessitates an eclectic mix of models although at its core is the triphasic model, i.e., safety and stabilisation, trauma processing and integration. Anything else, in my opinion, is adjunctive. What is paramount is a robust foundation of training and good supervision with someone skilled and experienced in dissociated identities. They emanate from a creative survival mechanism and, invariably, creativity will be integral to how parts express their pain underscoring once more the importance of adjunctive therapies.

Relational Challenges

Catherine depicts how the diversity of Sky's system compromises and brings challenges to her relationships given their differing needs, and, perhaps most importantly, their differing attachment styles. This is a difficulty I can relate to within my own system and that will often cause relationships to flounder. Until those attachment styles are explored, and a more harmonious balance and interplay can be reached amongst parts, discord and disruption within relationships will continue. Harmonious resolution demands time, an abundance of patience and the hard and often confronting work of therapy. It is through the therapist's attunement, continuity of care and the containment that she provides that a secure attachment can develop reversing those historical dysfunctional attachments. I think Catherine's work with Star depicts this beautifully whereby space is given to be heard and held, coupled with safe exploration of a client's processes and behaviours without judgement. Catherine's portrayal of the harmonious collaboration that can be achieved internally and the marrying of the outside part's own strengths with those of the parts whilst remaining out front is, perhaps, the essence of successful treatment with dissociated identities.

Finding a Language

Catherine identifies what is pertinent to the treatment of dissociated identities. She refers to the imperativeness of developing a language for the various processes, conflicts and behaviours that are inherent in a system. So often, parts will express themselves behaviourally similarly to children and adolescents where understanding and language are absent, whether due to developmental arrestment, trauma or being preverbal. Finding that language can be empowering and liberating whilst guarding against behavioural patterns of old that are dysfunctional and destructive. Certainly, in my system, I have parts who have used self-harm to express the inexpressible, and our therapist helping us to develop a language has diminished such injurious behaviours. Orit refers evocatively to 'tongue suicide' which describes vividly how language is cruelly stolen from survivors of childhood sexual abuse whether through threat, shock or overwhelm, and the therapeutic space provides opportunity to reclaim it. I have two young parts who were struck mute in response to their traumas, and we are still hopeful that their own 'tongue suicide' can be reversed in the process of therapeutic attunement.

Distinguishing Between Past and Present

Catherine refers to the need to differentiate between both past and present as well as the parts and the whole. In my system, the younger and adolescent parts remain stuck in trauma time, meaning past and present become blurred;

when there is a trigger there is the need for grounding and orienting to the present day. When my perpetrator died, I recall my own shock at the younger part's stubborn disbelief that it was their perpetrator and their expressions of angry indignation when I tried to inform them otherwise. Trapped in trauma time, they were unable to recognise that years had elapsed and the elderly man they were observing was the same younger man who had abused them.

Blending

It is important that the therapist remains vigilant to the phenomenon of blending and, indeed, the outside part (like me). Given the surfacing part does not have executive control of the body, I am adept at noticing when I am blended. It is a disorienting space to inhabit as I hover between myself and another identity, remaining me yet not me. Given how blending can change the course of a session in respect of the part's motivation for surfacing, it is imperative that the therapist remains attuned to this more subtle of switches.

Boundaries

Boundaries are an imperative of therapy although one that is replete with challenges for the person living with dissociated identities. We often jest it is our most reviled word in the English language largely because we have been adept at breaching them! I now have a deeper appreciation of why they are conducive to good and ethical practice but, as a client, they are often misconceived as indicative of a therapist's lack of care for us. Breaking them was a means to test the genuineness of that care which, in turn, perpetuated that misconception as the therapist was ethically bound to hold them. Where a therapist's boundaries have been wide open, the therapy has spiralled into chaos and created an unsafe space, culminating in either an abrupt and dramatic tightening of those boundaries that has left us bewildered, angry and distrusting, or, indeed, the treatment being terminated due to the therapist feeling deskilled. This, in turn, has fed the historic maternal rejection wound and our ingrained belief that we are unworthy of help, too complex and too damaged.

When I reflect on why boundaries have posed such a challenge within the treatment frame, I believe it is the attachment the parts develop to the therapist, and, indeed, don't develop, that is a significant cause in them being compromised. In the absence of a secure attachment, transitioning out of session, for example, can feel very threatening to a part as they experience historic feelings of abandonment and loss just as they might when confronted by therapist leave. For many years, therapist leave, or an unexpected cancellation, left us in such a distraught place that our only way to manage it in the absence of a secure attachment was to blunt the pain of her desertion through cutting and burning our obliging limbs. Our conviction that a therapist would not return fed our distress and, sadly, was reinforced on occasion when the therapist informed us of her impending departure on her return for which we would assume blame. Integral to treatment is the development of a secure attachment to the therapist and it is when that has been established that boundaries can be better adhered to as I have observed in my own therapy. Just as some parts will immediately attach to feed their starving emotional needs, so too will parts remain distant and test the boundaries to determine if the therapist's care is genuine. I have shamefully learned the degree of manipulation my own parts are capable of in their misguided attempts to determine that genuineness and in the process have become caught in a self-fulfilling prophecy where their testing behaviour has manifested in the treatment being terminated. It is imperative that a therapist holds her boundaries, is attuned to her countertransference and is able to explore this reflectively and in her own therapy or supervision. Catherine identifies this counter transferential response when she refers to the need to develop empathy not just for the client but also for parts of herself that might get triggered. Our boundary breaches were an unconscious protective means to prove that the therapist could not be trusted and to test the genuineness of her care. With each unanticipated termination of treatment, those distrusting parts who had tested the therapist's genuineness of care took smug satisfaction in their beliefs being validated whilst those who had attached were plunged into the familiar abyss of grief.

Uniqueness

A very valid point that Catherine refers to is the uniqueness of each system. In my search for verification of my dissociated identities and, indeed, abuse, I have often asked my therapist if something I am experiencing is usual. Her response has been to assert the individuality of each system thereby relegating what is normative solely to the criteria highlighted in the DSM-V and ICD-11. Each system carries a unique history and army of parts to manage and defend against early trauma. I have learned to trust in how my dissociative identities manifest rather than to evaluate comparatively which I have had a propensity to do in my unconscious desire to invalidate my memories and defend against the harrowing truth. The therapist and client are walking a journey of discovery together and each journey the therapist undertakes alongside their client will be unique.

Integration

Catherine's reference to Odette and her desire for integration highlights that where integration is not possible or sought, a system that is collaborative, demonstrates respect for one another and is able to compromise perpetuates harmony, equilibrium and high functionality. This is conducive to sustained recovery. Personally, we choose not to be integrated as every part forms a piece of the mosaic that defines who I am. The parts came into being to offer protection and enable survival and although that is no longer needed in the way it was historically, it is needed in more diluted ways in the present day. I believe that some parts might become blended, but it is an organic process that I cannot determine at this point in my recovery and one that, ultimately, will be determined collectively.

Impact of Traumatic Memories

I relate to Catherine's caution pertaining to the impact on the outside part of parts surfacing and their respective traumas. Having been amnesic of the trauma and unaware of my parts, it has been incredibly confronting to learn of both. This is an ongoing process for me both where awareness of the trauma and parts are concerned but, equally, in the sporadic manner in which both have surfaced across time and continue to do so. Readiness to engage with both is an imperative alongside gentle support and empathy from the therapist whilst ensuring exploration is at a manageable pace. Psychoeducation has been instrumental in facilitating this process for myself, creating waves of normality in a tumultuous sea of abnormality.

Reflections on Chapter Three: What Are We Doing? Stabilisation Work with a Mind Control System of Altered Identities

In chapter three, Emma Jack refers to the fact that as a therapist, she never stays in her chair indicating that treatment of dissociated identities is not conventional in the traditional sense with client and therapist seated opposite each other and reflecting the creativity that is inherent to the condition. It is noteworthy that, although the client's system is familiar to Emma, new parts are continuing to surface after seven years of treatment. I have experienced this in and outside of therapy and continue to be surprised by their rude arrival, followed by discomfort and mental interrogation of the part's authenticity in my quest to determine the verification of my diagnosis.

Tri-Phasic Model of Treatment

Emma refers to pertinent considerations during the assessment that are foundational to the work, thereby ensuring it is tailored to the client's unique presentation whilst ensuring the tri-phasic model of treatment is upheld and a secure base is formed from which to work. Although the tri-phasic phase is prescriptive, each system is unique and will need to be worked with accordingly. Emma underscores the imperativeness of the first phase of treatment – establishing safety, stabilisation and symptom reduction – and alludes to the important fact that although phase one precedes phases two and three, it is not a linear process and will need to be returned to when there is destabilisation. Another consideration that has been integral to my therapy within phase one work has been the need for affect to be worked on so that feelings might be associated to and felt during the trauma processing phase whilst managed through the grounding skills accumulated in the first phase.

Dissociation was an effective means to protect me from the pain of the deepest betrayal and to maintain attachment to my perpetrators for my survival. Consequently, it is a conditioning that I do unthinkingly in response to discomforting feelings and that with the support of my therapist I am learning to recognise and interrupt. Associating to feelings and being able to ground is vital before trauma processing to protect against traumatisation. I think there can be a propensity for people with dissociated identities to want to rush to traumatic memories in their mistaken belief it will exorcise their trauma. This was certainly true for me. However, what I have learned through therapies where this has been sanctioned is that it culminates in further traumatisation, and rather than exorcising the trauma it makes its revisitation more devastatingly felt and without anchorage to shield against overwhelm and decompensation.

The propensity to accelerate treatment to trauma processing is also driven by parts who are impatient and eager for their voices to be heard in a world that has silenced them. Despite psychoeducation around this, it remains a struggle and a sad reflection of society's dissociation to their pain. Additionally, in the maternal transference, there has been an unconscious drive to seek protection from the therapist in the reenacted trauma in tandem with a need to punish her as she is forced to witness the sexual depravity inflicted upon the parts.

Therapeutic Relationship

I think that Emma raises a very good point that the use of Rogers' (1957) three core conditions – empathy, non-judgement and unconditional positive regard – is not enough to foster a therapeutic alliance when working with a person with dissociated identities. Although foundational to the relationship, such conditions can be viewed with suspicion and for diverse reasons. We have questioned the authenticity of such core conditions, believing that they are offered not because they are genuine and indicative of authentic caring, but because the therapist is paid to offer them. This belief is reinforced each time that therapy has abruptly ended and in a manner where the core conditions have, regrettably, been absent. Some parts, most notably angry ones, will view such conditions as patronising, believing that they are reflective of the hierarchical position and power differential that is analogous with therapy and don't bear witness to the strength and resilience that are integral to survival. Similarly, books on the treatment of dissociated identities and research that offers a similar tone will be perceived through a patronising lens, and usually aborted.

I think Emma's citation of Ocean Vuong (2019), 'Sometimes being offered tenderness feels like the very proof that you've been ruined', beautifully captures the shame that makes receiving the core conditions so difficult to bear, reminding the client of her victimhood and her inherent badness. Her perceived badness and her perpetrator's goodness facilitates attachment to the latter and her survival. Attachment to my own perpetrator was made easier by his Dr Jekyll and Mr Hyde disposition, presenting as Dr Jekyll by day and Mr Hyde by night. I dissociated the bad and attached to the good whilst most of the parts were only conscious of the bad. As is customary in those who perpetrate, his charm duped those who knew him into believing he was a good person thereby reinforcing my own perception born from the unconscious need to attach and survive. As Emma shares, therapy is a space for the client to reclaim her goodness from the perpetrator and return the badness to them, a process that will require the therapist to become the bad object in the dizzying transferential dance. This requires a commitment by the therapist to be mindful of her own countertransference and, indeed, the client of her transference to avoid a reenactment of the past. Emma refers to the importance of demonstrating to the client who the therapist really is rather than to present opaquely. In our experience of such a presentation, it has compromised trust significantly and created frustration in my system as their efforts to scrutinise the therapist's face and body language to ensure safety are thwarted. Relational trauma demands relational reparation and that can't be achieved where only one person in the relational dynamic is present.

I agree that the first task of therapy is to get the client to engage with therapy. I recall sitting on the very edge of my chair in the first session ready to take flight and ensuring the therapist knew that the box of tissues sat waiting expectantly on the table beside me were redundant. Engagement began when I could relax back into my chair and wipe the tears that coursed silently from my eyes, although the latter took many years. I eventually gained an understanding of both therapy and the therapeutic relationship that drives it. I had no concept of the different models and approached it through the lens that, like a physician, the therapist would make me better. I now understand that no therapist no matter how skilled can fix me. Rather, they can help facilitate change but the only person who can fix me is myself. Certainly, there has been conflict surrounding attending therapy in my system and that remains so. An oft-cited phrase we will use is 'we begin therapy for therapy'. Each therapy that has culminated with the therapist leaving us and been replete with relational challenges dents the system's trust dramatically and their motivation to start anew. Some refuse to attend, and adhere to that stubborn refusal, their trust seemingly broken indefinitely despite attempts by the therapist to earn and restore it. I have noticed that due to the numerous ruptures within therapy relationships across time, and that have not been followed by repair, even attachment parts, ordinarily ravenous for love regardless of any harm, struggle to trust again, preferring to take shelter in the safety of dissociation. It is a reminder of the need to identify and explore both transference and countertransference to mitigate against these ruptures and for repair to be facilitated. Ultimately, it is safer for attachment needs to be met and fulfilled internally rather than externally.

I agree with Emma that although the therapist might be with a part who professes not to know her, the system as a whole does know the therapist, as information will have been channelled vicariously through the part who has executive control at any given time. I have many parts who have never surfaced in therapy and would be unknown to the therapist except in name, but not one who does not know her. As Emma highlights in the case example, when she responds to one person in the system, she will be speaking to all the parts whose response to what she is sharing will be received from multiple perspectives, creating potentiality for a switch to occur where there is division, disagreement or disharmony. I think the ability to be alongside the client is crucial to building safety and trust which is evidenced in Emma's encouragement of Nevar to join her so that she can help to settle the little ones. She responds to his suspicion with fact and neutrality, speaking to his cerebral self and side stepping the emotional. Such emotional pacing is fundamental to treatment as although content is dissociated, it is the feelings that the system abhor, and to engage with these too quickly is likely to cause decompensation and rapid switching.

Therapeutic Process

Emma refers to how identities can be frightened of the therapist and believe that they will be harmed as she experienced in Nevar's system. I think fear of harm from therapists is universal to all systems given that early abuse has been relational, and it is something of a brutal paradox that reparation is also relational via the therapeutic relationship. Parts will be hypervigilant to threat within the therapy session and where harm has been occasioned as it has been in my own therapies, the cycle of fear is perpetuated with every subsequent therapy. Any sudden movement by the therapist can be triggering even behind a laptop screen, as was the *de rigueur* mode of working during the Covid-19 pandemic. Due to the degree of harm people living with dissociated identities have suffered, and from primary carers whose trust should have been implicit, an expectation of harm from the therapist is anticipated. It is prudent for the therapist to have no expectation of trust and to recognise it will be hard earned. However, it is only in committing to the therapy that beneficence can be experienced and trust established. I am often struck by the dichotomy between parts steadfastly determining not to trust and how that resoluteness is challenged in the face of perceived love and care. Such is its power, it can break down defences and release our most haunting primal cry of attachment. However, when that perceived love and care is recognised as boundaried and conditional, trust is swiftly withdrawn, and dissociation becomes its obliging and effective successor. It is a difficult dance the therapist must execute, creating an environment that is containing and provides the conditions that promote a secure attachment yet shielding against attachment needs that are all encompassing and run deep. Ultimately, the work of therapy is for the external love that the system hungers for to be found internally where collaboration, co-operation and communication provide the nourishing ingredients to satiate attachment hunger. This is an ongoing and challenging objective in my own healing as my intellectual recognition of this is at odds with the experiential, creating a painful pattern of seeking external love and inevitable loss.

Emma refers to the importance of the therapist being mindful of her own dissociation given the sadistic and harrowing content she is being confronted with. Attuning to the client's discourse is of paramount importance given it might be the first time she is being heard or, indeed, due to a deficit in being heard previously. The client's collective hypervigilance will render her sensitive to any indication of dissociation in the therapist which might be challenged by a part. We have been very sensitive to information that has not been retained by the therapist and have brought it to her attention with an indignant, 'I told you that'. Any recognition that it is not possible to assimilate and remember every detail is overlooked until she brings it to our attention followed by an apology from an attachment part or myself. A stifled yawn can be a potent trigger, suggesting the therapist is bored with our discourse, its stifled disguise exacerbating our upset instead of it being brought into the room. Transparency is very important to us, and we welcome a therapist sharing that she is tired or feeling unwell rather than observe her attempts to hide it and feel irritated, or worse, internalise it and feel culpable.

I think the 'tipping point' Emma refers to is unique for each client but, generally, it indicates a freeing of something that has created impasse and immobility in the therapy. There is clarity of vision and a stripping away of old thinking and defences, perpetuating engagement in the therapy whilst propelling it forward and reactivating attachment needs. I agree with Emma that to reach a part the use of materials, games, activities, etc. is paramount as it is when working with non-multiple children, and is an organic, non-confrontational process that is tailored to the needs of a particular part. Taking a part's lead regarding how space within the room is occupied is also important. I have a part who refuses to sit on a chair, so low is his self-worth he feels he belongs on the floor and, conversely, parts who refuse to sit on the floor as it is representative of danger, threat or dirt. A nine-year-old female part cannot allow her feet to touch the floor, a trait fashioned from trauma and one I remain amnesic of. A 14-year-old female part will only remain at the perimeter of a room and will touch the wall for safety, behaviour emulated by Little, a young and essential core part, in earlier therapies that she was able to eventually relinquish as her trust grew and a secure attachment to the therapist developed. Every part will have determined a safe space within the room at the outset of therapy and any triggering aspect will be brought to the therapist's immediate attention directly or indirectly.

Emma quotes Daniel Stern: 'How can you get inside of other people's subjective experience and let them know you have arrived there without using words?' In my experience, that knowledge is felt by the client, an interpsychic bridge stretching between therapist and client that facilitates the 'pervasive and germane sharing of affective states' that Stern refers to. I think 'companiable relating' and the being alongside as coined by Heard and Lake (see chapter three, p. 55) is key to the establishment of trust and the perpetuation of exploration and rescindment of defences so that attachment reactivation can occur. Observing this in my own therapy between a part and the therapist is very gratifying and beautiful to witness whether in playful activity on the floor or sat together. Companiable relating does not have to be with discourse in our experience, occurring in silence with a meeting of minds. Play facilitates companiable relating whilst potentiating the 'relaxed self-realisation' that Emma quotes from Holmes and Slade (2018, p. 47).

Internal Collaboration

As Emma highlights, achieving internal collaboration is key to a successful therapeutic outcome. Where caring and kindness has not been modelled in a client's life, the parts have no template on which to develop it but can learn it via the therapist. I have watched this develop in my own system across time but in a manner that is less directive and more organic as healing evolves. I like to think that my own capacity for kindness, hence the part's name for me, 'Nice', is influential, for despite not knowing kindness as a child it is important that I bestow it on others so that they might know its joy. My kindness, however, does have a narcissistic edge in that the warmth it generates in others is reciprocated in me. Like Nevar and the boy parts that surfaced, choice presents challenges for us from the most banal to the most difficult. Although not a conscious process, its difficulty emanates from the need for approval, fear of doing wrong and having had no choice as a child. Having a sense of self that is coloured by fragmentation makes choice complex and confusing as I struggle to identify the 'I' in what is wanted or needed instead of the 'we'. Choices are rudderless when my self-concept is nebulous due to conflicting variables in its constituent parts: self-esteem, image, and ideal self. Choice is equally hard for my parts as it was for Emma's client's parts and in learning autonomy and self-agency via the relationship with the therapist, choice is recognised as safe and viable within the context of a relationship. Activities done conjunctively with the therapist, where choice is integral to the activity being carried out, facilitate this process and, as Emma states, promote Winnicott's relaxed self-realisation.

Reflections on Chapter Four: On Being With: Working Creatively with Clients with Dissociative Identity

In chapter four, Orit Badouk Epstein refers to 'the fear of the infant who knows the world mostly through fear where there is nowhere to hide except

within themselves' and where scaregiving is defining to the attachment relationship. I resonate with this statement, perceiving dissociation to be that
hiding place. Whether that presents as shutting down, trance or switching to a
different identity, it is an effective and reliable means to escape and hide in the
face of 'scaregiving'. Without this ability to hide via the armoury of dissociation, I doubt survival would have been viable. Little will often share that
she has gone to her 'safe place' and that she is 'hiding', which is the language
she will use to indicate she has dissociated. At such times, I lose all sense of
her, yet she is essentially present by the very fact she returns. I agree that fear
can consolidate the attachment bond between the child and the parent in the
absence of solution, and that dissociation is a means to survive the horror a
child is being subjected to. For my parts, fear became familiar and in familiarity there is, ironically, a paradoxical feeling of safety. This, in turn, fuels the
attachment bond given the child's need for safety in an environment that is to
the contrary. Such familiarity has created an illusion of safety in adult relationships where we have not been safe including within therapy, and where a
trauma bond has instinctively and, to our detriment, evolved.

The Role of Language

Language is, as Orit asserts, a 'form of relationship making'. It provides a
bridge between two people and enables relationships to grow and develop.
Where language is absent as a consequence of fear, and where relational
growth and development is aborted, there is a propensity to develop an
internal dialogue with parts of self thereby offsetting the loneliness that
enforced silence by a caregiver can create. Certainly, where my own voice was
silenced, I found company internally but, also, externally via imaginary and
dissociative play with dolls, reading stories and using my imagination to
adopt parents both known and unknown to me that I did not have in reality.
  Orit refers to the language of love being enmeshed with terror, coercion,
guilt and shame for the mind-controlled child. Although not a victim of mind
control in the wider sense, I resonate with that complex enmeshment that
renders the victim confused and needing to internalise those narratives via
introjects to survive. I have a maternal and paternal introject who wield
similar power to those they emulate and whose purpose is to ensure the perpetrator's secrets remain unspoken. Each has adopted the language of the
perpetrators and just as young parts attached to the latter for the purposes of
survival, so, too, have they attached to the introjects. This has created challenges in the therapy room where fear has heralded 'tongue suicide' with
respect to the parts sharing their trauma. However, older parts, most notably
angry ones, will match the introjects with their own vitriol in their determination to disempower them in the way they could not disempower the perpetrators. I have wrestled with abject shame knowing that I carry the residue
of the perpetrator's malevolence internally as the introjects are a part of me.

However, psychoeducation has helped me to develop understanding and, although cognitive and not yet experiential, compassion for them in the difficult role they were created to play. With the support of the therapist, they can be helped to understand that in 2024 their role is no longer needed and that their help can be channelled in healthier, adaptive ways.

It is important for me to assert as I continue to navigate my shame that introjects do not sexually abuse despite the image that they were created in. In my system, there is also an older sibling introject who was a witness to the abuse and whose knowledge of it was used to manipulate and wield power over my perpetrators. Having developed a pathological jealousy towards me for the 'attention' fostered on me, she determined to add another layer of disruption and terror to my already ravaged life. Her introjects, the Crazies, are subhuman, located at the very back of my mind, black, shadowy and disengaging yet are menacing by their very presence.

As a person with dissociated identities, I am hypersensitive to language. A common refrain we hear is 'she is DID' which implies the person *is* their condition, but she is, of course, so much more. It is important not to define people by a label which although helpful in guiding treatment and providing clarity and understanding to the individual, is not helpful in its diminution of identity, already compromised by its fragmentation into parts. The reference to our narrative as a 'story' is also a trigger for angry parts to surface. It implies the trauma is fictitious and chimes with the false memory propaganda of the 90s which was devastatingly injurious to survivors and the therapists that supported them. Each system will adopt a linguistic preference for how their dissociated identities are referred to. I hover between 'parts' in my astute recognition that they are constituent parts of my whole self and 'warriors', a noun my therapist coined after sharing the song 'This is Me' with her from the musical 'The Greatest Showman'. In my experience, what I know cognitively, i.e., my parts are a part of me, conflicts with what I feel experientially, which is that they are separate people living inside of me. Colin Ross (2018, p. 19) refers to this as 'the central paradox' reflecting the conflict between what is known intellectually and what is felt.

Quite often, dissociated identities will use creativity to communicate their trauma in the absence of words. When one considers that dissociated identities are a creative response to trauma, it is not surprising that creativity is channelled artistically to express pain. Certainly, this is true in my system where writing, drawing, poetry and music are used interchangeably and to good effect. My parts are also creative in their thinking where trigger words are too threatening to convey. Little habitually draws a picture of herself and marks with a black pencil where she was repeatedly and ritually hurt. On one occasion, she labelled each black mark with a number from one to five denoting the ritualistic order in which acts of sexual degradation occurred. A seven-year-old male part, Tom, then surfaced to explain what sexual act each number indicated and employed the phonetic alphabet to describe the sexual act. This beautiful dance between the two little parts gave words to the unspeakable. Tom evidenced these acts given his role was to float to the ceiling whilst Little was being subjected to the abuse and distract her, a rather ingenious and effective survival strategy. Whilst writing my autobiography, I developed a creative means to communicate the abuse, spelling out the words according to each letter's location in the alphabet and protecting me from flashbacks. Although I have no aptitude or affinity for mathematics, numbers have been a creative shield against the impact of trigger words and a means to communicate them for both me and my parts. It is no coincidence that many of my parts have numbers as their name although not always indicative of their age. A nine-year-old female part, Nine, uses storytelling to protect her from the pain of her memories, cleverly weaving symbolism and metaphor to good effect. I marvel at these creative strategies my parts have developed and commend their ingenuity.

On a more sombre note, self-injury and anorexia have been used to communicate our pain where words have been inaccessible. Although the psychological drivers to cut, burn and starve are multilayered, they are an effective visual means to convey to an unhearing, unseeing world our very deep pain. Regrettably, although scarred skin and jutting bones provide effective communication, the discomfort they generate forces people to turn the other way, dismissing our pain once more and fuelling the shame that such survival strategies promote.

Orit refers to Winnicott's perception of the subjectively conceived and objectively perceived self as interacting components within human perception and how when these are fused mental life can be 'alive and creatively usable'. Reflecting on this, I was struck by how in a dissociated, depersonalised state when I have left the body and am observing my fragmented self, I am objectively perceiving my associated, subjective self. This is always an enriching mental experience that makes me feel energised and creative despite the dissociation. It is something of an irony that a survivor's most pressing need is to be heard and yet the language with which to communicate has been violated by the perpetrator's tyranny and threat. How does one express the wordless? Although the narrative is important, it is the attunement of the therapist and the act of 'being with' that enables words to form verbally and artistically. Attunement fosters trust, and without trust, language remains elusive.

Tonality that is soothing and calming from a caregiver is crucial to attachment and is something that we seek in a therapist. Our deep-seated need for gentleness of voice is often expressed to elicit safety and attachment. Regrettably, it has not always been communicated by the therapist. This leaves us frustrated given the frequency with which it is asked for and knowing the difference to a session it can make. Of course, therapy is relational and the interplay between transference and countertransference will impact expression, but where tonality feels triggering, attachment and safety are unfailingly compromised. Orit describes the 'moment of meeting' which is a pivotal and deeply spiritual experience for us. It is an intoxicating alchemy that transcends time and space. It is divination and grace. It is a psychic fusion and one, as client, we have fervently sought. The 'moment of meeting' is not anticipated and, therefore, provokes an element of surprise when it is experienced, leaving a thirst for more in its wake that is rarely satisfied promptly but when it is, its spontaneity makes its presence more appreciated. The 'moment of meeting' transcends a good therapeutic alliance and renders it sacrosanct. It is, as Orit defines, a moment of 'I know you and you know me'.

Polyphonic Dialogism

As Orit illustrates, the therapeutic relationship provides opportunity for the developmental pathways that were arrested in childhood to be established, something I am watching emerge in my own young parts. 'Polyphonic dialogism' beautifully depicts the chorus of voices that compete for space. Each voice contributes to the expression of the whole, communicating the imprint of society's most heinous crime, and reaching a crescendo as they plead to be heard. However, 'polyphonic dialogism' can be intrusive to the outside part and the cacophony of voices is at times destabilising. It can also be distracting whilst in conversation with people, trying to focus on a mental task or falling asleep. Noise can present in other ways. I have a part called DJ, for example, who will play songs on a loop consistently throughout the day and night which is not only intolerable for me but the system as well, whose own intolerance is vehemently communicated adding to the overwhelm of noise. Regrettably, I am unable to listen to music as DJ will subsequently play what I am listening to mercilessly. His role is, of course, protective, the music a distractive defence against emotional pain, but with no concept of the pain he is causing cerebrally. A journey by car can be raucous as a 54-year-old observer part will alert me to any dangers on the road and trigger frustration in a 21-year-old angry part given his meticulousness to the most benign potentiality. Ironically, as invasive as the parts 'polyphonic dialogism' can be, when there is silence inside, I feel unsettled, disoriented and anxious, a solitary warrior fighting for her survival without an army to support and protect her.

Orit colourfully illustrates how parts will surface in response to another part's conversation with the therapist. This occurs often in my system when a part has expressed anger. Anger will swiftly be followed by shame and the part that holds that emotion will emerge contrite and acquiescing. These are often parts with an anxious, preoccupied attachment style surfacing to placate after the emergence of their avoidant, insecure allies. Shame can be offset by parts who are dissociated, unable to converse due to the overwhelm of pain that ravages them. Often, it is me as the outside part who holds the shame and whose need for apology will be communicated via an email to the therapist following the session.

The Trauma Bond

Orit attests that 'we can't survive and love at the same time'. Reflecting on this, I disagree as the ability to love my perpetrators was crucial to my survival and, indeed, my ability to attach. Oblivious to the abuse due to dissociative amnesia, I was able to love the good and dissociate the bad as, indeed, were some parts. Conversely, most of my parts experienced only the bad, thereby developing a trauma bond disguised as love and attaching to their perpetrator for their survival. Orit refers to 'disabled moments', whereby the client experiences overwhelm at the therapist's gestures of nurturing kindness reflecting what is needed but not wanted, and the latter experiences fear, helplessness and panic as she recognises the enormity of her client's crime against her. The overwhelm that we experience in response to such gestures emanates from feeling unworthy and the shock that such gestures prompt makes us question their motive. Familiarity breeds safety and where nurture has been absent, its presence poses threat. The lure of kindness can be considered a trap and viewed with abject caution.

Work with Introjects

Orit depicts very well the complexity of working with introject parts. Honouring that every part deserves a voice and to be heard in the therapy room, it can be challenging to hear the caustic words of the introjected parts as they vie for control of those in their charge. These parts will assume the characteristics of the perpetrators and command the loyalty of their subordinates to good effect. Orit reminds us through Lilly that often introjects project the historic wounds of the perpetrators they emulate just as the latter did to the core self, creating a splintering into fragmented parts of self. Perhaps, it is only when we turn towards their own pain and allow it to be seen and heard that their need to project can be annihilated.

Overview

It is, as Orit attests, the 'security of the relationship' that binds client and therapist, offering a secure attachment for the very first time. Language between therapist and client facilitates empowerment, allowing the layered skin of patriarchy to be shed and for the freedoms of connectivity and collaboration, love and thinking to be fostered instead. When my eyes can meet those of the therapist, that moment of meeting is a moment of implicit and unequivocal trust.

Reflections on Chapter Five: When the Alleged Abuser Is Famous: Some of the Problems in Dealing with Alleged VIP Abuse

It is interesting to reflect on Valerie Sinason's sentiments in chapter five surrounding the therapist's fear when working with a person who has suffered childhood sexual abuse. I think the need to be heard is so often pressing in the client that the impact of their devastating narrative on the therapist can be overlooked. Of course, this is not something a client should have to consider as it feeds her pervasive shame and challenges the sharing of her narrative further. Although I have grappled with how our own traumatic narrative might impact the therapist, my parts are blinded by their overwhelming need to be heard and any reticence is focused on their fear of being disbelieved. For some, this need is entrenched in the maternal transference where they are seeking the protection and nurturing that was inexcusably absent whilst others are driven by a need to punish the mother in the transference, forcing her to witness what she dissociated. This is not conscious, of course, but has become clear to me in my reflections across time and something that has been explored in therapy. Valerie refers to how we all contain aspects from each age inside us and, interestingly, many of my parts depict those age-related aspects, which are steeped in trauma, in having numbers as names. Another parallel Valerie refers to that impacts therapist and client is fear and shame. For the therapist, there is the fear of what the client has been through and the shame she bears of not being able to stop it. For the client, there is the fear of what she is going through or has been through and the shame that she allows it or allowed it to happen. I have parts who carry both these emotions and whose behaviour is a ramification of both.

Dissociation and the Wider Context

I strongly agree that most mental health conditions emanate from the wounds that were experienced in childhood. Dissociated identities not only emanate from extreme trauma in childhood but are a unique, creative and ingenious means to survive it. As a society, we must stop asking what is wrong with you and, instead, ask what happened to you? However, societal dissociation of trauma and its clinical medicalisation renders a reductive approach to its devastating impact and ubiquity. It is the fact that trauma does not discriminate and afflicts all classes that society struggles to digest and is a struggle that has not dissipated since the repression of Freud's seduction theory which Ross (1997) proposes contributed significantly to the refutation of dissociation. When I reflect on my own perpetrators and their middle-class status, I question how much that might have influenced society's blindness to my distress. Had I been born into a working-class family, I question whether our cries to be heard would have been taken more seriously and my abuser's perpetration been more plausible? The higher up the class system that sexual abuse infiltrates, the greater the conspiracy of silence and repudiation of its ubiquity. Likewise, when perpetration is synonymous with celebrity, dissociation steps in to protect us from the recognition that our reverence was built on a toxic lie. Where there is a resistance clinically to associating to the pervasiveness and toxicity of sexual abuse, it manifests in deepening the client's desperate cry to be heard. The imperativeness of self-awareness, countertransference phenomena, self-care, personal therapy and supervision is fundamental for the therapist to guard against her own defences and risk a rupture in the relationship.

Justice Denied

Valerie points to the hints of improvement in the criminal justice system but rightly emphasises the enduring inadequacies that deter victims from pursuing justice and render it a criminal misjustice system (Herman 2024). I think this is particularly pertinent to people reporting with dissociative identities. The criminal justice system is ill equipped to support a survivor whose abuse exists behind amnesic barriers and held by her respective parts. There is a dramatic lack of understanding surrounding dissociated identities within the police force and a dearth of intermediaries available to work with young parts. Unless a survivor's trauma is processed and her dissociated identities integrated, the risk of re-traumatisation and decompensation within that challenging legal process is significantly high. Where a crime occurred in a location contrary to a survivor's current residency, two forces collaborate with the latter responsible for collating evidence from the victim and the former facilitating the investigative process post the victim providing evidence. Without a police force that is uniformly educated in supporting people living with dissociated identities, that collaboration and investigative process is significantly compromised by gaps in knowledge from one force or another. Training in dissociation and its formal diagnosis of dissociative identity disorder is sorely needed if people living with dissociated identities are to be given a fair hearing and fully supported.

Valerie refers to deceased celebrities' sexual crimes that were executed in plain sight being exposed after their deaths and investigated. I am struck by the unfairness of a system that pours resources into investigating sexual crimes committed by a celebrity posthumously and a dismissal of sexual crimes committed by perpetrators who are deceased and exempted by obscurity.

I think the therapist is in a very difficult position where validation of a crime is sought from a client by her therapist. Given that believing my abuse has been the most challenging part of my journey to date, and complicated by the parts who deny its reality, I have needed the therapist to hold that belief for me. Although I understand cognitively the need for a neutral stance, emotionally it imbues me with fear that the therapist has doubt. In turn, this not only reinforces my own uncertainty but makes trust that much more tenuous. Stating belief that something has happened to the client, but that all the evidence might never be made available, validates the abuse whilst preserving neutrality.

I support Valerie's assertion that the truth will come out if we educate the police and use our collective voice to facilitate systemic change. For as long as

I draw breath on this earth, I will make this my life's mission as there is no stronger, compelling voice than that of the survivor.

I will not be silenced.

Reflections on Chapter Six: The Parts, the Whole and the Real Person: An Attachment Perspective

When I read Adah's chapter on the self, I was aware of a very palpable frisson of energy and excitement that emanated from feeling seen, heard and validated in my thinking for the very first time by an eminent professional in the field. There was an alignment of thinking that has escaped me in my reading, research and therapies until now. This innervated response was shared collectively inside as we all celebrated feeling a euphoric and relieved sense of *she gets it*. Although something of an oxymoron, my experience of dissociated identities dictates that they are associated dissociated and the glue that binds them together is the self. By this I mean that there is awareness and unawareness between parts, but it is the self that is the common denominator and the cohesive link between them.

My thinking aligns with Adah's that those dominant qualities that define each identity and that are all protective in essence would exist without their creation and are the self's gestalt. During the abuse, these qualities had to be dissociated from the self and transferred to the identities for the purposes of safety and survival. As Adah suggests, no person is defined by their trauma alone in the same way that they should not be defined by the condition that enabled their survival. A personal irritation we wrestle with is when we hear the oft-cited phrase that a person 'is DID'. A person lives with dissociated identities but is not their condition. They are so very much more. The identities may hold aspects of the self's personality that she is unable to hold herself for the purposes of survival, but she is also a separate self with her own strengths and weaknesses.

I think the question that Adah asked her former patient is revelatory in that she was able to identify an aspect of herself that resonated with all her parts including the more hostile parts. Interestingly, kindness was not one she could easily attest to but one undefiled by her perpetrators. I considered this question myself and two adjectives came immediately to mind and, perhaps, unsuspectingly so when considering some of the more apparent qualities I could have chosen. Being funny and determined are very strong traits and when I question if these qualities are synonymous with my parts collectively, I recognise that they are. Although I have funny parts created for the purposes of protection and survival, there is humour in all categories of parts as, indeed, there is stubborn determination.

I agree that each person living with dissociated identities is unique just as non-multiple people are. Who holds executive functioning at any given time is determined by whatever motivates that identity to come forward. This might be a trigger or a role they are created to assume for the purposes of daily functioning. People living with dissociated identities do have the capacity to make choices. It is not random as might be perceived. Choice is preceded by a reason and a motivator which is driven by the part that comes forward but is acceded to by the rest of the system. As Adah eloquently articulates, it is the 'wisdom of the system'.

I think that wisdom is apparent in how choices are made and executed even if they might appear irrational or incorrect to the eye of the beholder. Choice emanates from a need to protect and survive and although any one part might be making that decision, the collective wisdom of the system will be instrumental in its execution. With respect to a trigger and ensuring parts do not surface in places where it is not viable such as the workplace, this will be governed by the whole system. I, as the outside part, will be using all the strength I have to prevent a switch from happening in conjunction with the triggered part using his or her own resources to stay inside. For me, that resistance is a very physical process as a switch has always been a very somatic experience. I will be physically fighting my body's conditioned response to a switch to stop the part from exiting who, simultaneously, will be resourceful in trying to stay inside. Little, for example, will say her safe numbers to ground herself. It is a collaborative process and an instinctive one. I work as a volunteer for a charity that supports survivors of rape and sexual abuse where I am exposed to many triggers. My parts know that they are not permitted to surface and, unfailingly, rely on their resources to respect that boundary. Instead, they can surface in a break after a call and go back inside when I resume. Without this robust control, I could not do my job.

I agree that a part who won't allow the outside part to come back is making a choice and, in my experience, it is *always* for the purposes of attachment. That need is insatiable and shared by the system making that choice a collective and wise one as they are starving for love. It is their drug of choice, and, like all drugs, it is never enough. I have left therapy on many occasions with a little part roaming my home city despite the valiant attempts of the therapist to bring me back before the end of the session. The part will be trying to find the car which the wisdom of the system has guided her to, and I have sat for a good couple of hours waiting to come back into my body and be grounded sufficiently to drive. It is a high price to pay for an hour's attachment but in the eyes of the system, a worthwhile one. I agree with the proponents of dissociated identities that it is an attachment disorder and what better example to demonstrate that ideology.

I am unable to comment on whether the different presentations of dissociative identity pertaining to poly fragmentation and installed mind control alter the personality of a survivor that was inherent prior to the trauma as they are not my experience. It is my belief that for those survivors whose presentation is more organic such as my own, the lens through which the world is viewed and how it is responded to might alter, and dramatically, but the essence of the personality remains impenetrable and unbreakable. I believe that essence is the self. I would also agree with Adah's observations around attachment and the need for the baby to engage with the mother through behavioural and affective mimicry to survive. This I relate to profoundly on a personal level in my efforts to attach with my own mother. Even as an older child, I would emulate her in an unconscious effort to attach. I also relate to the safety and attachment that is enabled by the sadistic abuse coined by Adah as 'infanticidal attachment', and as I pause and reflect, question whether a survivor can experience attachment through both mimicry and infanticidal attachment. Experience dictates that they can.

My experiences of therapy also underscore Adah's observation that an infanticidal attachment compromises the therapeutic dyad. My parts and I struggle to engage with a therapist who demonstrates secure attachment not just because we don't trust it, as such kindness and engagement has always been contractual, but because it is unfamiliar and the familiar, i.e., infanticidal attachment, symbolises safety and engagement. As Adah articulates, 'it never touches the depths'. Parts will also state that a secure attachment is given in return for a fee, thereby dubious of its authenticity and resentful of its perceived superficiality. Emma refers to therapists being willing to exhibit their 'shadow side' and I think this is vital as not only does it enable us to know who they really are but to enable realness instead of superficiality. This has been evident in unrecognised countertransference responses which have created rupture but also familiarity, engagement and safety in both its anticipated occurrence and where it has been followed by repair.

Survivors of sexual abuse are hypervigilant, a protective conditioning that guards against further abuse, and will recognise a therapist's inattentiveness immediately. This is a very powerful trigger for us that will often create a dissociative response. Without focus there can be no engagement and without engagement that is not real there can be no therapeutic relationship. It is the bedrock of good therapy. As Adah comments, it is the ability of the therapist to truly hear what she is being told, be with it in all its ugliness and hold it firmly in her grasp without letting it go. It is this alchemy that heals.

I think Adah's comments around engaging with the 'small potatoes' is a vitally important one and one we felt seen and heard in for the first time without the prompting we have had to exercise in therapy. I have continually harboured frustration and resentment around the therapist's focus on the things that we are not doing (the boiling hot potatoes) in comparison to those we are achieving (the small potatoes). Those small gains that to us are large victories pass unnoticed unless indicated but whose subsequent recognition is marred by the fact it had to be pointed out. Our failings as we perceive them are paraded in full sight, but our successes fall under the radar, creating a disengagement and detachment. My current therapy is the first where this has been heard and remedied, thereby feeding our reciprocal engagement and, indeed, attachment. We are learning to tame the need to engage the therapist through the sadistic historic content, self-destructive behaviour and dissociation that we are conditioned to depend on, satiated as we are from her engagement to the gains and positive qualities. The injurious but ubiquitous label to describe self-destructive behaviour as 'attention seeking' is an appalling mis-interpretation of what is better defined as 'attachment seeking', and a sad indictment of society that attachment can only be achieved through the engagement of others via self-injurious means. As Adah says, we must change the first attachment language and develop a second one by recognising that the client is not just her trauma. She is a person with positive qualities that were nascent before her trauma and whose successes and achievements beg for recognition in tandem with her difficulties. I think Adah raises a very pertinent point when she discussed the relationship between engagement and existence. To engage with another is to validate their existence, and so many survivors feel unseen and annihilated. For so many, they seek engagement through shocking narrative, anger or self-destructive behaviour as the second language of attach-ment has not been communicated to them. It is the 'embryonic little something' that Emma beautifully articulates that can diminish the first attachment lan-guage and, in the process, let them know that they are seen.

I agree with Adah that for the recipients hearing survivors' trauma, and who are truly attuned and engaged, the horror does not dissipate. It reinforces the imperativeness of supervision so that the therapist has a safe space to share the impact of those horrors and process it. I think Adah's example of the little part who was responsible for making other parts of the system laugh is a beautiful example of how that quality created engagement not just between her and her parts but her and Adah. As a person with funny parts who were created for the same reason – to survive the trauma – I relate to this very strongly and have been witness to humour facilitating engagement with our therapist and, most notably, for angry parts. Humour is an effective leveller and diffuser. Developing the second language of attachment is healing for the client and cushioning for the therapist.

I agree that the supervisor can hold hope for the therapist in the face of ongoing abuse for the client and her own sense of hopelessness. It is impera-tive that the supervisor is skilled and experienced in this kind of abuse so that she can relate to the therapist's processes and support them. Her own experi-ences can enhance engagement with the supervisee because the horror she is listening to will have familiarity and shield against defensive disengagement. Adah is correct to point out that the supervisor, therapist and some of the identities are one step removed from the enduring trauma which makes for tolerable listening and to enable the content to be held for the client. How-ever, as empathy dictates, they are also one step involved in the client's world requiring a consistent commitment to supervision and self-care.

Adah's example of the client who was able to see herself as kind and brave having reflected on her selflessness in assuming some of the abuse so that other parts didn't have to is indicative of a second attachment language between client and therapist but, equally, between the client and self. In recognising that she is more than her trauma, she is enabled to feel seen in not only the eyes of the therapist but through her own and that shift is wholly transformative. I recall my current therapist alluding to the protective role that anger has played in keeping us safe and how exhausting this must be which created a shift in my angry part, 21. Instead of it being derided, it was recognised as protective, kind and exhausting which fed 21's low self-esteem. In turn, this ameliorated her dynamic with me as I saw her anger and vitriol towards me through a different lens that in time shifted to respect. We now share a happier relationship and an often comical one. In our experience, learning a second attachment language has created behavioural and relational shifts that have made day-to-day functioning calmer and offered a depth of healing that speaking the first attachment language failed to.

Adah speaks to the division between the 'I' and the 'me' of the self, the former being the one who experiences things and the 'me' who is in the eye of the beholder. I agree that there is an overlap between them rather than a broad disparity. It is this overlap that needs to be married in the therapy so that the first and second language of attachment can sit side by side and be attuned to. The therapist needs to see and hear the trauma and its impact on the client's sense of fragmented self yet, simultaneously, introduce her to a second language of attachment where her true and shining essence can be excavated from beneath the rubble of the deleterious abuse and paraded in front of her so that she may know that she is so much more than her trauma. I agree that the road into the 'me' cannot be created. The merger between the 'I' and the 'me' is organic and when it occurs in the therapy room it can be a beautiful meeting of minds between therapist and client. I agree that the 'I' starts via engagement with another and, ordinarily, the mother in whose eyes the baby is reflected but evolves into a self as the baby discovers her own identity that isn't symbiotic to the mother. I find Winnicott's 'true self' very resonant where the self exists in complete solitude and is not penetrable or accessible to the outside world. This is very palpable to me, and it occurs to me as I write this that it is the unnameable safe place I go to when I dissociate: I go to the depths and sanctity of self. I agree with Winnicott that it is the mother's duty to stand between the baby and the world and guard her from its harms. Where the mother fails in her duty to protect, the abused infant attaches and internalises the world's badness for the purpose of survival. I agree with Adah that a person who endures the degree of abuse that is synonymous with the aetiology of dissociative identity has had their self compromised by the absence of protection and seeks to find it via creative and symbolic means. It occurs to me that this might be why so many dissociative identities are creative.

I have it on good authority as a person living with dissociated identities that they are always present. How do I know this? I simply do! There is a palpable energy within. Some parts I will know to be present because they are speaking to me but there is an indubitable recognition and knowing that they are all present. This is evidenced in their universal knowledge of what might have been shared between one part and the therapist, for example. So often, a session will end, and a part will surface unannounced with something to say about it despite having no awareness of that part's presence in the session.

Adah refers to the perpetration as 'soul destroying'. I do not believe soul or, indeed, self are destroyed due to the fierce protection of the parts and the attachment that they provide. I believe the mind and the body can be broken albeit not irreversibly, but the soul and self remain impenetrable, fiercely safeguarded as they are by the parts. I agree that perpetrating parts are the most distraught which is understandable given the shame and guilt they wrestle with. In manipulating their perpetration, it is an attempt by the perpetrator to slaughter the self but an unrecognised failed one due to the part's protection and attachment. One of my own perpetrator parts is only five and is mute. Such is his shame, he has tongue suicide. He has never attended therapy and I have been in and out of therapy over the course of 30 years. Interestingly, this little part, Little Sad, resides within Sad, a 14-year-old part who also holds a lot of shame and self-disgust and whose unraised eyes, like Little Sad's, hold so much sadness and shame. I think Adah raises an important point that their shame has been perpetuated by the therapist's overt condemnation of perpetrators and impeded their ability to attend sessions. These are choppy waters that must be navigated sensitively. To engage with the perpetrator parts whose wounds run unimaginably deep, it is essential to adopt the second language of attachment so they might recognise that their shame is misplaced, and that any perpetration was the manipulation of the master and monstrous puppeteer and not the puppet he orchestrated. As Adah states, all the dissociated identities are protective. It is their collective raison d'être and, most certainly, I would not be penning this chapter without their protection. They stood between me and the world where maternal feet should have stood, and they saved my self from annihilation of body, mind and soul. It took me many years to recognise this and to celebrate them for their incalculable courage and to sift through the sands of guilt that have choked me since. As Winnicott wisely articulates, the identities have bent themselves to the self, I, the outside part, and, indeed, each other so that the self is not intruded upon in the mother's abandonment of protection and care. The core remains intact, pure and sacrosanct. Adah comments that some of the core is intruded upon by the trauma but the remainder is untarnished. It is my belief that the core, the self, remains whole and complete because the identities have shielded it from the onslaught of the perpetrator's depraved intrusion but the concept of wholeness and completeness is clouded by the wreckage that the identities hold. I liken it to a translucent quartz crystal I was kindly gifted that is beautifully whole on the outside (self) but replete with fragmented pieces within (dissociated identities).

The notion that the identities are the attachment figure of the self that they are protecting and that their role is to preserve the life of that self is a pertinent one. In this regard, they symbolise the mother but the attachment they provide is not of the disorganised type synonymous with unprotecting and abusive mothers but a secure one, and in so being, the self remains whole and cohesive. I agree that there is an intelligent and alive core to every individual that remains impenetrable to the horrors of abuse, and the identities have formed a ring of protection around it.

I think Adah sums it up beautifully when she defines why she believes that therapy should start wherever the client wants it to start rather than to wait for safety to be established. This, of course, is at odds with the tri-phasic model that promotes safety and stabilisation before exploring the trauma. However, as Adah says, rather it is about establishing ground rules and for the therapist to model predictability and, I might add, continuity. Listening to the client, attuning to her so that engagement and attachment can be facilitated is key to creating the shifts that foster growth and healing. I agree that if a therapist waits for safety to be attained, the therapy will never start and know this from my lived experience of therapy. Safety follows engagement and attachment. A survivor does not need to feel safe to attach as is evidenced in her attachment to the perpetrator. Rather she needs to feel seen, heard and engaged within the first language of attachment so that she might learn and know the healing beauty of the second. Just as Adah says, like the mother who pays attention to her child at any given moment, so too the therapist to her client.

I am so very grateful to Adah for sharing her thoughts surrounding the self and applaud her thinking that, perhaps, challenges so much of the thinking in the literature on dissociated identities. Her words are brave but, equally, wise and built on years of experience working with survivors living with dissociated identities. For so long, I have been too afraid to echo her thinking believing that I was erroneous in my thoughts and quick to allow my dubiety surrounding my abuse and dissociated identities to fester in that quagmire of mistaken thinking. Reading Adah's chapter filled me with relief and, most notably, because my thoughts were being echoed by one of the most eminent clinicians in the field who I have long respected. I believe that I, Michele, am the core self and my parts echo that belief. I am the person who was horrifically and sadistically abused and the person who the parts fiercely protected each in their individual, courageous, selfless way. My self remains unannihilated or intruded upon because they stood between me and the world where my mother's feet should have firmly stood, and they fiercely protected me so that I might live in the absence of my mother's protection. I am self and they are my attachment figures to whom I owe the sanctity of my self and, indeed, my very life. Thank you, Adah, for giving me a voice to share my truth with the world. I hope it listens.

References

Herman, J. (2024). *Truth and Repair: How Trauma Survivors Envision Justice*. New York: Basic Books.
Holmes, J., and Slade, A. (2018). *Attachment in Therapeutic Practice*. London: Sage.
Karpman, S. (2014). *A Game Free Life*. San Francisco, CA: Drama Triangle Publications.
Richardson, S. (2020). 'Internal Attachment Relationships: The Five Cs Versus the Two Ds', *Attachment: New Directions in Psychotherapy and Relational Psychoanalysis*, 14, 1, pp. 99–106.
Rogers, C. (1957). 'The Necessary and Sufficient Conditions of Therapeutic Personality Change', *Journal of Consulting Psychology*, 21, 95–103.
Ross, C.A. (1997). *Dissociative Identity Disorder Diagnosis, Clinical Features and Treatment of Multiple Personality*. New York: John Wiley and Sons.
Ross, C.A. (2018). *Treatment of Dissociative Identity Disorder*. Richardson, TX: Manitou Communications.
Steinberg, M. (1994, 2023). *The SCID-D Interview: Dissociation Assessment in Therapy, Forensics and Research*. Washington, DC: APA Publishing.
Vuong, O. (2019). *On Earth We Are Briefly Gorgeous*. London: Penguin Press.

Index

abandonment, threats 42

Absence of Attachment Representations (AAR), impact 4

absent/neglectful parental state of mind, internalisation 8

abuse: communication 150; corroboration, absence (acceptance/rejection) 85; distinctions 49; endemic nature 10–11; mother complicity 32; parental denial 72–73; reporting, courage (requirement) 120; social recognition, increase 83; uncorroborated abuse, client report 85

abuse-based attachment, continuation 18

abuser, brutality (meeting) 68

abuser, famous status: climate, change 82–84; fear, inducing 84–86; historical context 81–82; impact 80; interaction, problems 80, 120–121, 152–155; police investigations 87–89; real-life example 90–93

abusive trauma 27

activated energy, deceleration 36–37

active DID 100, 104; harm 105

activities, creation 55

addiction (comorbid factor) 49

additive behaviour patterns 43–44

Adult Attachment Interview: administering 5; coding, design (limitations) 4

affect, modulation 49–50

affiliation (explanation), trauma-coerced attachment model (usage) 7

agency, feeling 56

aggression, forms 7

alienation, increase 65, 66

altered identities: client meeting 50; clinical example 51–58; clinical experience 53; communication 52; contact 55; final intervention 58–59;

mind control child altered identity 57; mind control system, usage 48, 117–118, 142–147; stabilisation work 48, 117–118; suspicion 54

ambivalent attachment pattern 64

amnesia 72–73, 110; level, identification 49; states, enormity (realisation) 38

anger, shame (relationship) 151

anorexia 150

anxiety: comorbid factor 49; discharge 56

apparently normal personality (ANP) 72–73, 76; concept, usage 115; usage, cessation 114

approach-avoidance conflict 2, 44

approval, seeking 136

assessment: abuse, types 55; dissociative identity 51–52; dissociation, specific considerations 55; impact 48–51; initial assessment, example **27**; usage (attachment-based systems) 25–27

attachment: absence 140–141; behaviour, reactivation 5; biological system, manipulation 8; bond, consolidation 148; dissociation, relationship 3–6; experience 157; experiences, quality 9; figures, annihilation (defence) 130; figures, engagement 100–101; figures, fright (induction) 19; human need, manipulation/attack 17–18; insecure attachment situations, disconfirmation/invalidation 3; journey, initiation 125; language, development 103; language, learning 108; lens 104; loss, phobia 5; multiple attachment patterns 5–6; needs, ignoring 69; needs, reactivation 55; perspective 96, 121–124, 155–156; phobia 5; pseudo-attachment 7; reactivation, occurrence 147;

For Product Safety Concerns and Information please contact our EU
representative GPSR@taylorandfrancis.com
Taylor & Francis Verlag GmbH, Kaufingerstraße 24, 80331 München, Germany

www.ingramcontent.com/pod-product-compliance
Ingram Content Group UK Ltd.
Pitfield, Milton Keynes, MK11 3LW, UK
UKHW031437120325
456146UK00005B/103